When the last red man shall have perished, and the memory of my tribe shall have become a myth among the white men, these shores will swarm with the invisible dead of my tribe....

At night when the streets of your cities and villages are silent and you think them deserted, they will throng with the returning hosts that once filled and still love this beautiful land. The white man will never be alone.

Let him be just and deal kindly with my people, for the dead are not powerless. Dead, did I say? There is no death, only a change of worlds.

> —SEATTLE (Seathl), Dwamish chief,
> speaking to Isaac Stevens, Governor
> of Washington Territory in 1854

I HAVE SPOKEN:
American History Through the Voices of the Indians
was originally published by
The Swallow Press, Inc.

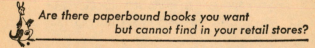

I HAVE SPOKEN

*American History Through the
Voices of the Indians*

compiled by
VIRGINIA IRVING ARMSTRONG

introduction by
FREDERICK W. TURNER III

PUBLISHED BY POCKET BOOKS NEW YORK

I HAVE SPOKEN: American History Through the Voices of the Indians

Swallow Press edition published June, 1971

POCKET BOOK edition published August, 1972

Standard Book Number: 671-78555-9.
Library of Congress Catalog Card Number: 74-150755.
Copyright, ©, 1971, by Virginia Irving Armstrong. Introduction
copyright, ©, 1971, by Frederick W. Turner III. All rights reserved.
This POCKET BOOK edition is published by arrangement with
The Swallow Press, from whom permission must be obtained
for reproduction in any form.

Printer in the U.S.A.   Cover art by Alan Magee.

The nation's hoop is broken and scattered.
There is no center any longer, and the sacred tree is dead.
Black Elk

CONTENTS

Photographs appear between pages 108-109.

INTRODUCTION

History, history! We fools, what do we know or care? History begins for us with murder and enslavement, not with discovery. No, we are not Indians but we are men of their world. The blood means nothing; the spirit, the ghost of the land moves in the blood, moves the blood. It is we who ran to the shore naked, we who cried, "Heavenly Man!" These are the inhabitants

The knowledge of history is always sheerly potential.

Johan Huizinga

of our souls, our murdered souls that lie. . . . agh.

William Carlos Williams

This is so unusual a book that we have to find keys to it wherever we can. Thus two inscriptions here, one from a Dutch historian, the other from a white American physician and poet. Doubtless there are others, and if I were an Indian, I should probably find my keys among the sayings of the grandfathers. But I am white, and this book, though it can with considerable profit be read by anybody, should be of greatest interest to white Americans who conquered the Indian and settled on his lands.

In the first inscription, Huizinga refers to the fundamental difference between the conditions of knowledge in the physical sciences and mathematics on the one hand, and history on the other. In the first areas, knowledge is actual, given, and (to students of these areas) known. Yet the knowledge of history is always in a state of becoming and is entirely dependent upon the uncovering and interpretation of the materials that make it up. There is no History waiting for us like some giant and architecturally perfect edifice that we will at long last discover in the tangled growth of an intellectual forest. History does not exist for us until and unless we dig it up, interpret it, and put it together. Then the past comes alive, or, more accurately, it is revealed for what it has always been—a part of the present. The materials of *I Have Spoken,* recondite surely for most of us, constitute an important piece of our common history, unearthed and made actual.

The second inscription sounds one of Williams' major themes: the anti-historical bias of American culture and white Americans' ignorance of how much we actually share with those whom in our arrogance and fear we dispossessed. No, we are not Indians, but we are men of the same continent. We are humans, moving upon the same landscape, and in that large perspective differences of blood and customs seem dwarfed. In that same perspective we can see through Williams' words that it is true that it was the Europeans who ran naked to these shores—naked of any knowledge of the land or of its inhabitants; that naked as were those who hailed Columbus, we too brought so little to the settling of this New World. And it is true also that if the Indian was at first disposed to see us as gods (though later as demons), we in our way saw the red men as children of paradise (though later merely as children of a Great White Father). In *I Have Spoken* we can begin to see ourselves through the eyes of another race of men, and this should be an important part of the process of understanding the history which man has made upon this continent.

It becomes clearer with each passing year that this is precisely the greatest need of all Americans: a continental history. By this I mean a whole, fully integrated history of this continent from the granite base of the land mass itself, up through the layers of soil to the grasses and plants, the trees, the huge geological configurations; the animals who lived and died out and those that still live; the first men who, following those animals, crossed the widening and narrowing land strait; the rise of cultures here and their myths which describe for us how it felt to stand defenseless in a gigantic landscape and then how the people of those cultures learned to propitiate their world; and finally, the coming of the European and what he has done since he settled in with his imported implements of ideas, his slaves, his dreams. An enormous undertaking, this five billion year history, but one that must be seriously begun if we are to understand who we are and where we ought to be headed.

In the past few years, indeed, such a project has been begun on many fronts. Think here of writers such as Frank Waters and Peter Farb whose books have sketched for us some of the major features of that ur-history; of the explorations of the natural world and man's place in it in the works of Joseph Wood Krutch, Loren Eisley, and Peter Matthiessen; of Charles Nichols' rescue of the slaves' narratives; and of the new poetry of the earth of Gary Snyder. These are hopeful signs, threads stretching back to earlier writers who began on this task years ago—Whitman, Daniel Brinton, George Bird Grinnell—but whom we seem to have forgotten. I remember being intrigued some years ago by a line in Edmund O'Gorman's book, *The Invention of America,* where he writes an entry in the imaginary diary of the North American continent: "At long last, someone has arrived to discover me!" We need to construct such a diary, using both recoverable materials and the powers of our imaginations.

It is in this connection that Indian history—*their* history, not our version of it—becomes so important. In it we see the potential for the recovery of that primal past which will, if we but surrender ourselves to its lessons, explain much about ourselves and our world that now seems almost desperately unknowable. Wherever Indian history survives and wherever we encounter the remnants of it, we move closer to the rhythms of our land, rhythms which we are divorced from, as the Sioux Luther Standing Bear pointed out years ago:

> The white man . . . does not understand America. He is too far removed from its formative processes. The roots of the tree of his life have not yet grasped the rock and the soil. The white man is still troubled by primitive fears; he still has in his consciousness the perils of this frontier continent, some of its fastnesses not yet having yielded to his questing footsteps and inquiring eyes. He shudders still with the memory of the loss of his forefathers upon its scorching deserts and forbidding mountaintops. The man from Europe is still a foreigner and an alien. And he still hates the man who questioned his path across the continent.
>
> But in the Indian the spirit of the land is still vested; it will be until other men are able to divine and meet its rhythm. Men must be born and reborn to belong. Their bodies must be formed of the dust of their forefathers' bones.

This is no accident, nor is the scarcity of Indian history which makes clear this condition. Without invoking the spectre of conspiracy, I say that there has been among whites a planned destruction of the past—or at any rate, all of it that did not illustrate the national mythology. This fact became clear to some in the 1920s when certain folklorists set about in earnest to collect Afro-American traditions. The collections of those traditions bear the unmistakable marks of mutilation, suppression, and attempted obliteration. In short, their condition reflects back upon a people careless of its past and so unaware of its present. In recent years the attempt to recover America's black past has been renewed with an urgency born of desperation, for it has only been through riots, bombings, and murders that we have come to see that an understanding of the past is vital to a sense of the present.

Much the same is true of that part of the past that concerns the Indian. Here, too, the destruction of tribal traditions was a planned, concerted effort carried out over long years by such diverse agents as missionaries, army officers and soldiers, school teachers and bureaucrats. Collections of Indian history until the late years of the last century were random ones, usually interspersed in documents written for other purposes, and many of the best of these, interestingly enough, were written by Europeans whose sense of history was more developed than that of a people busily engaged in making over a New World in its own image.

This attempted destruction of the African and Indian pasts can also be understood as a consequence of our physical subjugation of these peoples: the victors write the histories; the vanquished are rendered historyless. It was this and something more. In the white man's opinion, oral history was non-history, a bundle of foolish superstitions without authority or value. Worse, such traditions seemed to be the very things which stood most in the way of the psychological subjugation of blacks and red men. Thus the history of the New World was to be begun again, this time from the top down: written history from the white point of view, fixing its attention on economic trends, trade agreements, election processes, military engagements, and diplomatic entanglements.

When this rewriting was completed to, say, World War II, white Americans could look back upon a past that seemed by this arrangement neat, orderly, glorious, and —yes—perhaps divinely necessary. The structure was entirely coherent and self-explanatory. School children learned it with the same ease and nonchalance that they learned to spell "Mississippi." It has become the fate of these school children to guess that there must have been yet another kind of history, a deep, dark, subterranean stream of history running all this time under the bright ribbon of that version of the continental past they were given in their formative years. The events of the past decade in particular have shown them in violent and oblique ways that their knowledge of themselves and of the land they live on is terribly incomplete. The long-silenced voices of the blacks and of the Indian have risen to challenge the words of the textbooks. And to these has been added the wordless voice of the land itself, crying out against the continued despoilment of it, threatening to turn finally upon the despoilers and swallow them whole like the *vagina dentata* of Indian legend.

But by this time these school children (that is, we ourselves) were all but incapable of reading the emerging record of the substratum of New World history. Our minds and ears were closed; oral history still seemed less than authentic; and the histories of the Afro-Americans and Indian less important on the world stage than the Plymouth Rock-Washington litany. The result has been that while we have been coerced into surmising that our view of ourselves was not the only one possible, we have not yet been able to really look through other angles of vision. So apparitional is our sense of history that it is only with the greatest difficulty, if at all, that we can imagine, for example, the Sioux leader Red Cloud standing before a packed house at the Cooper Union—that same Cooper Union where Lincoln had spoken in 1860—and making the kind of tough, forceful, and eloquent speech that is reproduced here (Speech #168). This is not only a failure of our imaginations (disastrous enough in itself), it is crucial ignorance. It is a divorce from the whole reality of our land. In its final stage it expresses itself in a propensity to see ourselves as agents and principal actors in world history and all others as props in our production. Elevated to the level of foreign and domestic policy, as this view in fact has been, such a sense of history results in tyranny and genocide.

II

The words of the Indian, then, are a potential source of cultural health for us. They are a way into another and necessary view of our world, and we need to take them seriously, not merely as "folklore." Let us look briefly at the Indian documents assembled in *I Have Spoken.*

The arrangement is chronological, which is the simplest and most direct. It has another virtue, however, that is far more important and this is that it illustrates the development of themes and rhetoric to meet the inevitable onslaught of the hairy men from the east. From Henry Hudson to O. O. Howard, the major theme of these documents is land: who owned it, what title meant, and how much of it could be sacrificed without destroying the sources of life itself. But notice how in responding to the advancing whites the Indian was compelled to move from strong assertions of his natural rights to appeals to what he could only hope was common humanity. Notice, too, how the arrogance of the whites grows as they move ever westward (much of this arrogance may be deduced from the responses of the retreating red men) until we come to the very end of the long trail there on the westward-most rim of the land where General Howard confronted Toohulhulsote, Chief Joseph, and the Nez Perce. Here the Indian speakers made a kind of last stand, challenging for one of the last times in that century the notions, the actions, and the terminology of the whites. It is instructive in this instance to compare General Howard's version of this confrontation with those of Chief Joseph and Yellow Wolf. In his own words Howard condemns himself and those whose agent he was, but the deep differences in world view and relationship to the earth are even more striking in the Indian versions of this episode. To Toohulhulsote's talk about the "chieftainship of the earth" and the "law of the earth" the exasperated officer is said to have retorted, "Shut up! I don't want to hear any more of such talk." The general here was lamentably in keeping with the current state of red-white relations. In a larger sense this retort reflects that great divorce from the land and its whole history of which I have written above.

The other theme that Mrs. Armstrong's arrangement allows us to follow is that of the history and future of the

Indian race. In the earlier documents there is considerable mention of the proud pasts of the Indian nations, their deeds, their strengths, and their generous treatment of the strangers in their lands. But then there enters, nation by nation, voice by voice, a vision of the future, or, worse, a vision of no future. This theme of the extinction of the red men spreads like a dark cloud shadow over these documents until at the end what was a fearful possibility has become a fearsome fact and the Oglala Sioux Many Horses voices the final "strategy" of the Indian survivors: pretended cultural assimilation (#216). This is another view of manifest destiny, and it should be a sobering antidote after all these years of jejune confidence.

While we can see these themes develop here, we can also isolate certain constant elements in these documents. There appears a pattern in many of the Indian speeches delivered to whites. It looks to me something like this:

1. expressions that the Indian is a man of peace—this apparently with reference to the particular nation's dealings with whites;
2. a backward glance toward earlier charities extended to whites;
3. recitation of the Indian's landed heritage;
4. recital of more recent history—Indian land concessions to the ever-advancing whites;
5. hopes voiced that such a process may here and now be permanently arrested;
6. concluding expressions of peace and amity.

As a rhetorical strategy this should have been effective: it was balanced and rounded, it seemed to deal from a position of equality and strength when actually this was almost never the case, and it made its appeals to the better instincts of man. But the rhetorical strategy failed like its military counterpart, and the Indian orator became but another subhuman caricature in the national mythology. Here in these pages he is rescued from this fate, and his skill, his sense of history and the earth's realities, above all his profound seriousness of purpose, are exposed for us to marvel at and pay tribute to. These qualities should also cause us to ask some serious questions about ourselves and how it was that such a race of men could be seen as dirty, ruthless savages whose utter annihilation was necessary for the triumph of a democratic republic.

There are, of course, a good many documents here that do not conform to this pattern. Indeed, some of the very finest examples of Indian oratory do not. As is so often the case, great works break patterns and establish ones of their own. I am particularly drawn to the singular qualities of the speeches of the Cherokee, Dragging Canoe (#49), the Pawnee, Sharitarish (#104), the Creek, Speckled Snake (#111), and the Flathead, Charlot (#180). Each of these has its own kind of excellence, ranging from the defiant valor of Dragging Canoe to the sage grandeur of Sharitarish to the bitter irony and invective of Speckled Snake and Charlot. This latter speech is surely one of the toughest and most comprehensive critiques of white culture ever framed by anyone, for it directly confronts the white man's opposing mythology on just that ground—that of an opposing mythology. To see ourselves as merely subscribers to a competing system of belief with its own pantheon of incredible creatures (snakes, messiahs, virgins) is to let go forever the notion of a chosen people, a dominant race, or any inherently inferior ones. Through these furiously bitter words of a doomed leader we can see what we should long since have taken to heart and what the Indian, living side by side with tribes of differing customs and languages, already knew: that as men faced with differing problems of survival, we were bound to develop differing survival strategies. To call these strategies mythologies is in no way to denigrate their effective truths, and it should be, if we think about it carefully, a way of understanding the common basis of humanity.

And if we can make this breakthrough, then perhaps we can also regard men like Charlot not as savage opponents of The American Way, but as patriots of their nations, equal in their devotion to traditional ways to our own Washington, Hale, and Lincoln who upheld the white American way. As one reads these speeches, one sees the force and vision of the great leaders of Indian resistance —Pontiac, Tecumseh, Black Hawk, Manuelito, Sitting Bull, Chief Joseph. These men are not the villains our childish textbooks portrayed them as; rather they are the flowers of an older system which withered in the face of another, stronger, more ruthless, less comprehending. In these pages the patriot leaders are liberated from our old stereotype by the power of their words. We have only to read them aright to begin to liberate ourselves from some disastrous fictions of our own making.

It would be improper to end here on a note of the doom and destruction of the Indian cultures. In the long view of this continent's history, that more comprehensive and genuine view I have been trying to define, it may well be that the white man and his rule are but a phase in an archaic existence which will see many other phases before another polar ice sheet sweeps down upon the land and grinds our pride into glacial debris—or until some other new unimaginable natural phenomenon demonstrates that man is not the final fact of nature. Nor is it wholly inconceivable that before such a stage in geologic time is reached some other combination of events will restore the Indian to his original status as the ruler of this land. Perhaps he is already on his way, and perhaps this is what the Dwamish chief Seattle had in mind when he spoke these words:

> When the last red man shall have perished, and the memory of my tribe shall have become a myth among the white men, these shores will swarm with the invisible dead of my tribe. . . .
>
> At night when the streets of your cities and villages are silent and you think them deserted, they will throng with the returning hosts that once filled and still love this beautiful land. The white man will never be alone.
>
> Let him be just and deal kindly with my people,

for the dead are not powerless. Dead, did I say? There is no death, only a change of worlds. (#147)

It has been just this possibility that has haunted the white imagination for the past two centuries—the dauntless suspicion that for all his claims of superiority, his victories, his monuments to industry, there is a view of history in which all this is but momentary, and to the extent that it is proud, vain. It was this suspicion that inspired the closing lines of F. Scott Fitzgerald's *The Great Gatsby* where the shining palaces of the Long Island rich seem for a moment evanescent beside the beauty of the land itself:

. . . . as the moon rose higher the inessential houses began to melt away until gradually I became aware of the old island here that flowered once for Dutch sailors' eyes—a fresh, green breast of the new world. Its vanished trees, the trees that had made way for Gatsby's house, had once pandered in whispers to the last and greatest of all human dreams; for a transitory enchanted moment man must have held his breath in the presence of this continent, compelled into an aesthetic contemplation he neither understood nor desired, face to face for the last time in history with something commensurate to his capacity for wonder.

If we can write the continental history, construct the diary of our land, and if we can then read what has been written, we will enter for the first time the life of our land and so free ourselves from this fear that we and our works do not after all count. The words contained in the pages of *I Have Spoken* are potential parts of the process of liberation, and we should be grateful for them as one is grateful for a great and unexpected gift. These are the words of our continent, of our ancestors, of our past; they are the sounds of the land we should be seeking to live with. As William Carlos Williams writes:

The land! don't you feel it? Doesn't it make you want to go out and lift dead Indians tenderly from their graves, to steal from them——as if it must be clinging even to their corpses——some authenticity, that which——

That authenticity is here and it is ours if we will but reach out for it.

FREDERICK W. TURNER III
Amherst, Massachusetts

PREFACE

Of the reams written about the American Indian, nothing can speak more surely than the words of his own mouth, of which he himself left almost no written record. It was the white man—the Spaniard, the Frenchman, the Englishman, other sojourners on the continent, and later the native white Americans—who, in council, by campfire, in lodge or hogan, in forest and plain, or riding with the Indian on the warpath, were the principal recorders and interpreters of those utterances which have come down to us.

The rich repertoire of Indian oratory roots in a wide spectrum of occasions, ranging from war to entertainment, from sanctions to announcements. From childhood an Indian learned the art of public speaking. This art was employed and developed in tribal council speeches, in peace negotiations with other tribes, in coup-counting speeches, in public ridicules, in religious ceremonies, in story tellings, in war preparations and actions, in tribal clubs, and in treaty-making with the white man.

The Indians' was a thoroughly oral culture, elaborated only by pictorial material, such as winter counts. With the coming of the white man—explorers, trappers, soldiers, government agents—a written record began to emerge of the extraordinary gift of speech which the Indian had long possessed. Primarily in minutes of treaty negotiations, in diaries, in memoirs, in anthropologists' notebooks, the Indians' words were preserved—and often soon forgotten. A few individual speeches had significant exposure and public history in the white community—on declamation days (e.g., Speech #52), as advertisements for Christianity (#116, #210), in anthologies of great oratory (#105). Biographers, dramatists, historians, and statesmen continually singled out the oratorical skill of the Indian. However, little was done to collect Indian speeches and writings in any concentrated format.

The entire pathos of the fate of the Indian in North America is contained in the following pages; in them his voice rises and returns as a living thing, tortured, scarred, plaintive, yet always eloquent. In essence, his words, plain or poetic, can never be completely lost; once read they are bound to remain hauntingly in the mind, as vividly beautiful as the remembered sight of a pheasant left bleeding to death in the snow.

VIRGINIA IRVING ARMSTRONG
Barrington, Illinois

That the civilization of the Indians would be an operation of complicated difficulty; that it would require the highest knowledge of the human character, and a steady perseverance in a wise system for a series of years, cannot be doubted. . . .

Were it possible to introduce among the Indian tribes a love for exclusive property, it would be a happy commencement of the business.

Secretary of War Henry Knox
to President George Washington
July 1789

It has been a great many years since our white brothers came across the big waters and a great many of them has not got civilized yet; therefore we wish to be indulged in our savage state of life until we can have the same time to get civilized. . . . There is some of our white brothers as much savage as the Indian; for that reason we think we might as well enjoy our right as well as our white brothers.

Chickasaw chief Shullushoma
to Secretary of War John C. Calhoun
December 1824

NOTE ON FORMAT

The organization of this collection is simple: chronological. I arranged the speeches not in terms of geography or tribes or types of occasions, but as events happened in time, from the 17th century to the present day. The book can be read fruitfully by opening at random, but there is, though I did not fashion it so, a definite continuity and development to be seen if read from beginning to end.

Availability was certainly not my criterion for selection of speeches, for while many must be dug painstakingly from dusty archives, there are literally thousands of recorded Indian speeches to choose among. I chose on the basis of interest and significance. That is, did I find the speech interesting to read? And did it reflect some significant aspect of Indian life or important theme of Indian history?

We must accept a kind of second- or third-handedness about the speeches, since most of them are available to us only in translation, the quality of which surely varied considerably. Furthermore, speeches have not always been recorded or retained in their entirety. For instance, formula phrases and ritual gift-giving references, common to so much of Indian oratory, have often not been preserved in the versions which have come down to us—e.g., opening remarks of proffered friendship, the "Father" or "Brothers" used to begin each paragraph, the "I have spoken" ending, "We confirm what we have said with a belt of wampum," etc. In addition, I have introduced my own excerpting, because the fuller speech was repetitious or less significant. I have used a few complete or long speeches, however, to illustrate patterns and developments (#168, #202, and others).

In most cases I have used early sources for the speeches, as close in time to their delivery as I could find. With very few exceptions, the speeches are printed here as taken from the sources, with original spellings, punctuations, capitalizations. I introduce each speech with an explanation of time and place and occasion, as brief as possible, in order to let the Indians speak for themselves. For the larger context, and often for more speeches, the reader can pursue the sources cited in the Notes section.

Scattered throughout the book, there are, as a muted counterpoint, a few speeches by white men. These are printed in italics, simply to distinguish them readily from the Indian voices.

V.I.A.

I HAVE SPOKEN

1 Henry Hudson in 1609 sailed up the river that later would bear his name. The Indians he found living in circular bark lodges were friendly and hospitable.

On our coming near the house, two mats were spread to sit upon and immediately some food was served in well-made bowls; two men were also dispatched at once with bows and arrows in quest of game, who soon after brought a pair of pigeons which they had shot. . . . The natives were good people, for when they saw I would not remain, they supposed I was afraid of their bows and arrows, and taking the arrows they broke them into pieces and threw them into the fire.

2 POWHATAN's Algonquin Confederacy covered tidewater Virginia from the Potomac south to Albemarle Sound. John Smith reported his 1609 speech at Werowocomico (Gloucester County).

Why will you take by force what you may obtain by love? Why will you destroy us who supply you with food? What can you get by war? . . . We are unarmed, and willing to give you what you ask, if you come in a friendly manner. . . .

I am not so simple as not to know it is better to eat

good meat, sleep comfortably, live quietly with my women and children, laugh and be merry with the English, and being their friend, trade for their copper and hatchets, than to run away from them. . . .

Take away your guns and swords, the cause of all our jealousy, or you may die in the same manner.

> 3 TESSOUAT, Ottawa chief, spoke to Samuel Champlain at Muskrat Lake in the spring of 1613. Nicolas de Vignau had, by letter, misinformed Champlain about his travels and his discovering a new northern land of great promise, which glowing reports led Champlain to set sail again to explore the new land, only to endure severe hardships.

[Tessouat to de Vignau] You are a liar. You know very well you slept here among my children every night, and got up again every morning; and if you ever went to the Nipissings, it must have been when you were asleep. How can you be so imprudent as to lie to your chief, and so wicked as to risk his life among so many dangers? He ought to kill you with tortures worse than those with which we kill our enemies. You are a liar. Which way did you go? By what rivers? By what lakes? Who went with you?

[To Champlain] Give him to us and we promise you he shall never lie again.

> 4 WALKS-IN-THE-RAIN, a minor Winnebago chief, reported a victory to his elders before the village campfire, 1634, at the time Jean Nicollet visited the spot, now known as Neenah, in northern Wisconsin.

Hanho-o! Grandfather! . . . of ourselves we could never have succeeded. . . . I sent out scouts to explore the land. . . . They came back with the news that the enemy was not far off. . . . They were unaware of our presence on the far side of the hill.

2

Then we offered tobacco to the spirits and prayed for help. I opened the war bundles. . . . I took out the sacred objects and practiced the powers bestowed upon men. I rubbed my body with the paint from the bones of the Water-Spirit, which has made my body invulnerable and invisible.

I knew the moment I blew on the flute the enemy would become numbed. . . . My eagle-pouch gave me power to swoop down upon the enemy and tear him to pieces, just as the eagle does his prey. The Thunderbird and the Sun had bestowed upon me and my companions the lives of four men; the Spirits had promised I would return safely, without losses. . . .

When the last of the Night-Spirits had departed, we crept stealthily along the ridge of the hill . . . where the small party of our enemy was encamped. . . . We surrounded them. We gave the war whoop and fell upon them. . . . Come-With-A-Mighty-Tread killed the first man. It was I who struck my enemy's body to gain the greatest of all war honors. Then Lone-Tree and Big-White-Wings killed two others, one apiece. The rest, cowards that they were, fled.

5   MIANTUNNOMOH, a Narragansett, because of the treachery of the Mohegan chief Uncas, was under suspicion by the Connecticut fathers, who urged Massachusetts to attack him. In 1642 Miantunnomoh sought out his old enemy Waindance at Meaticut, on the east end of Long Island.

Brothers, we must be one as the English are, or we shall all be destroyed. You know our fathers had plenty of deer and skins and our plains were full of game and turkeys, and our coves and rivers were full of fish.

But, brothers, since these Englishmen have seized our country, they have cut down the grass with scythes, and the trees with axes. Their cows and horses eat up the grass, and their hogs spoil our bed of clams; and finally

3

we shall starve to death; therefore, stand not in your own light, I ask you, but resolve to act like men. All the sachems both to the east and the west have joined with us, we are resolved to fall upon them, at a day appointed, and therefore I come secretly to you, because you can persuade your Indians to do what you will.

6 Unintended irony can perhaps be extracted from Roger Williams' 1643 translation of the Biblical story of creation into language for the New England red man.

Wuttàke wuckè wuckeesittin pausuck Enìn. Wuche mishquòck. Ka wesuonckgonnakaûnes Adam, túppautea mishquock.

Last of all he made one Man. Of red Earth. And call'd him Adam, or red Earth.

7 OPECANOUGH, the ninety-year-old brother of the deceased Powhatan, masterminded an attack on colonials between the York and Pamunky Rivers in Virginia. In 1644, seized and dragged before the governor, Sir William Berkeley, he was shot by a guard. Dying, he rebuked the governor for allowing gaping whites to surround him.

Had it been my fortune to capture the governor of the English, I would not have meanly exposed him as a show for my people.

8 KIOSATON, Iroquois chief, came before the French Governor Montmagny in September 1645, to plead for the return of two prisoners, taken when a party of Iroquois accompanying Jesuit priests were ambushed.

Give ear. I am the mouth of my nation. When you listen to me, you listen to all the Iroquois. There is no evil in my heart. My song is the song of peace. We have had many war songs in my country but we have thrown them all away. . . .

I passed the place where Piskaret and the Algonquins slew our warriors in the spring. I saw the scene of the fight where the two prisoners here were taken. I passed quickly; I would not look upon the blood of my people. . . . I turned my eyes away so I would not be angry.

I heard the voices of my ancestors crying to me in a voice of love, "My grandson, my grandson, restrain your anger; think of the living; rescue them from the fire and the knife." When I heard their voices I journeyed hither.

9 An Iroquois hunter, in 1650, returning home with a canoe of moose skins, was murdered at Pointe Claire in Lac St. Louis by five French officers, who sold the skins. Indian identifying marks proved ownership. A military council and the French commandant heard the men's confessions, then sentenced them to die.

They were led out, and all five were bound each to a post. The Iroquois were astonished at the ample justice that was rendered to them, and entreated mercy for four of them; because, as they said, they had lost only one man, it was not just to kill five for him, but one [only ought] to die. They were given to understand the five were equally criminal and, without exception, merited death. The Iroquois . . . redoubled their entreaties to obtain mercy for four, and for this purpose made presents of porcelain collars, but all five men were shot to death.

10 NIKINAPI, aged Illinois chief, was one of four Indians bearing calumets to welcome the Marquette-Joliet party in 1673 at a camp of the Peorias.

I thank you, Black-Gown, and you, Frenchman, for taking so much pains to come and visit us. Never has the earth been so lovely nor the sun so bright, as today; never has our river been so calm, or so free from rocks, for your canoes have removed them as they passed; never has our tobacco had so fine a flavor, nor our corn appeared so beautiful as we behold it today.

11 CANNONCHET, the Narragansett, in 1675 offered to Philip (Metacom, son of Massasoit, the Wampanoag chief) the refuge of his swampy meadow during King Philip's War. In retaliation that fall, Captain Benjamin Church burned Cannonchet's village with the women and children, and captured many warriors. Cannonchet was taken near Providence and sentenced to die.

I was born a prince; if princes speak to me I will answer. Since none are present I am honor bound to keep silent. Oneko, the noble son of Uncas, shall be my executioner. I like it well; for I shall die before my heart is soft, or I have spoken anything unworthy of myself.

12 OKANICON, a chief of the Delawares in New Jersey, 1677, was chided in council with the English for the drunken behavior of some of the chiefs. He replied:

The strong liquor was first sold us by the Dutch, and they were blind, they had no eyes, they could not see it was for our hurt; the next people that came were the Swedes, who continued the sale of strong liquor to us, we love it so we cannot refuse it, it makes us wild; we do not know what we are doing; we abuse one another; we throw one another into the fire. . . . Through drinking, seven score of our people have been killed.

The cask must be sealed, it must be made fast, it must not leak by day nor night, in the light, nor in the dark.

13 A Chippewa chief told how it was in the 17th century when the French laid claim to the two great waterways of the continent and the vast central valley and built a fort at Niagara in 1678.

When the Frenchmen arrived at these falls, they came and kissed us. They called us children and we called them father. We lived like brothers in the same lodge, and we always had wherewithal to clothe us. They never mocked at our ceremonies, and they never molested the places of our dead. Seven generations of men have passed away, and we have not forgotten it.

14 TAMMANY, a Delaware chief, spoke in English at a 1682 treaty signing with William Penn, near present-day Philadelphia.

We shall live as brothers as long as sun and moon shine in the sky. We have a broad path to walk. If the Indian sleep and the Yengeesman come, he pass and do no harm to the Indian. If Yengeesman sleep in path, the Indian pass and do him no harm. Indian say, "He's Yengees; he loves sleep."

15 William Penn, June 23, 1683, signed the famous, final peace treaty under a tree by the Delaware River; this kept peace with the Indians for over half a century. Penn stipulated that for every five acres cleared, one acre must remain forested.

Having consulted and resolved this business, the king [chief] ordered one of them to speak to me. He stood up, came to me and took me by the hand. They do speak but little, but fervently, and with elegance. I have never seen more natural sagacity, considering them without the help (I was going to say spoil) of tradition; and he will deserve the name wise who outwits them in any treaty about a

*thing they understand. . . . We have agreed that in all dif-
ferences between us, six of each side shall end the matter.
Do not abuse them but let them have justice and you will
win them.*

16   BIG MOUTH, Onondaga chief, met in present-
day upstate New York, September 1684, with
Le Febre de la Barre, Governor of Canada.
Earlier agreements reached by the French
with the Iroquois Confederation were being
strained. Big Mouth had acquired from the
French his name, *La Grande Gueule,* for his
skill as orator.

DE LA BARRE: *The Senecas, Cayugas, Onondagas, Oneidas, and Mohawks, have robbed and abused all the traders
that were passing to the Illinois and Miamies, and other
Indian nations, the children of my kind. . . . I am ordered,
therefore, to demand satisfaction; and to tell them, that in
case of refusal, or their plundering us any more, that I
have express orders to declare war. . . . [Further,] the warriors of the Five Nations have conducted the English into
the lakes, which belong to the king, my master, and
brought the English among the nations that are his children to destroy the trade of his subjects. . . . Your warriors have made several barbarous incursions on the
Illinois and Miamies.*

BIG MOUTH: We plundered none of the French but those
that carried guns, powder, and ball to the Twightwies and
Chictaghicks [Miami and Illinois], because those arms
might have cost us our lives. Herein we follow the example
of the Jesuits, who stove all the kegs of rum brought to
our castles, lest the drunken Indians should knock them
on the head. . . .
    We carried the English into our lakes to trade there
with the Utawawas and Quatoghies [Ottawa and Huron]
as the Andirondacks brought the French to our castles to
carry on a trade, which the English says is theirs. We are

born free. We neither depend on Yonnondio nor Corlear [the Canadian governor nor the New York governor].

We may go where we please, and carry with us whom we please. If your allies be your slaves, use them as such. Command them to receive no other but your people. This belt preserves my words.

We knocked the Twightwies and Chictaghicks on the head because they had cut down the trees of peace which were the limits of our country. They had hunted beavers on our land. . . . We have done less than either the English or French, that have usurped the lands of so many Indian nations, and chased them from their own country. This belt preserves my words.

Hear, Yonnondio: what I say is the voice of all the Five Nations: hear what they answer. Open your ears to what they speak. The Senecas, Cayugas, Onondagas, Oneidas, and the Mohawks say, that when they buried the hatchet at Cadarackui (in the presence of your predecessor) in the middle of the fort, they planted the tree of peace in the same place, to be there carefully preserved, that in place of a retreat for soldiers, that fort might be a rendezvous for merchants; that in place of arms and ammunition of war, beavers and merchandise only should enter there.

Hear, Yonnondio: take care for the future, that so great a number of soldiers as appear there, do not choke the tree of peace planted in so small a fort. It will be a great loss if after it had so easily taken root you should stop its growth, and prevent its covering your country and ours with its branches. I assure you, in the name of the Five Nations, that our warriors shall dance to the calumet of peace under its leaves, and shall remain quiet on their mats, and shall never dig up the hatchet till their brother Yonnondio, or Corlear, shall, either jointly or separately, endeavor to attack the country which the Great Spirit has given to our ancestors.

17 The Fox Indians found that Sieur Dubisson
    had been inciting the Hurons, the Illinois, and
    other tribes against them. In 1712 an unnamed
    Fox chief raged at Sieur Dubisson in Detroit.

What does this mean, my father? You did invite us to
come live near you; the word is even now fresh in our
pouches. And yet you declare war against us. What cause
have we given for it? My father, you seem no longer to
remember that there are no nations among those you call
your children who have not wet their hands with the blood
of Frenchmen. I am the only one you cannot reproach,
and yet you are enjoining our enemies to eat us. But know
that the Foxes are immortal! and that if in defending myself I shed the blood of Frenchmen, my father cannot
reproach me.

18 A Chitmachas chief spoke to the Sieur de Bien-
    ville, the governor of Louisiana Territory, who
    had held the tribe responsible for the death of
    a missionary. The Indians sued for peace, pre-
    senting the head of the culprit as evidence of
    good faith, and were welcomed back in the
    fold.

My heart laughs with joy because I am in your presence.
We have all heard the words of peace which you have
sent us. . . . We came trembling on the path until we saw
your face . . . Ah, how much more beautiful is the sun
today than when you were angry with us! How dangerous
a bad man is! You know that just one man killed the
prayer chief, whose death caused our best warriors to fall
with him. . . .
    The sun was red before, the path was full of thorns and
brambles, the clouds were black, the water troubled and
stained with our blood, our women wept constantly over
the loss of their relatives and dared not go off in search
of firewood to prepare our meals, our children cried in
fright. All our warriors sprang up at the slightest cry of
the night birds, they slept with their arms within reach,

our huts were abandoned and our fields lay fallow. We all had empty stomachs and drawn faces, game fled from us, the snakes hissed and bared their fangs; the birds, perched in trees near our villages, seemed to sing only songs of death.

19 STUNG ARM, Natchez mother of the young chief Sun, 1729, on the banks of the Mississippi River, sensed a conspiracy against the French which she hoped to forestall, believing the elders were using her son as a tool in their schemes.

Open your ears and listen to me. I have always taught you not to lie. I have always taught you that a liar is not worthy of being considered a man, and that a lying Sun deserves even the contempt of women . . . Tell me, are not all the Suns brothers? Yet all the Suns are keeping something from me as though my lips were cut and could not keep a secret. Have you ever known me to speak in my sleep? I am deeply hurt by my brothers' contempt of me, but even more by yours . . . Would you be a Sun if you were not my child? Have you already forgotten that? . . . I have told you, and so has everyone else, that you are the son of a Frenchman; but my own blood is dearer to me than strangers'. . . . I am not surprised that others avoid me, but how can you, who are my son? Have you ever seen a son distrust his mother in our nation? You alone behave this way. There is all this activity in the nation, and yet I do not know the reason for it, I, who am the chief Sun's mother.

20 The Iroquois Confederation originated before the white man came to their country. The League of the Iroquois was known also as the Five Nations, composed of the Cayuga, Mohawk, Oneida, Onondaga, and Seneca; later as the Six Nations when the Tuscarora joined

11

about 1720. Iroquois legend tells of the work of Hiawatha (not Longfellow's) and Dekanawidah in founding the Confederation. DEKANAWIDAH's words open the Iroquois Constitution.

I am Dekanawidah, and with the Five Nations confederate lords I plant the Tree of the Great Peace. . . . I name the tree the Tree of the Great Long Leaves. Under the shade of this Tree of the Great Peace we spread the soft white feather down of the globe thistle as seats for you, Atotarho and your cousin lords. There shall you sit and watch the council fire of the confederacy of the Five Nations. Roots have spread out from the Tree, and the name of these roots is the Great White Roots of Peace. If any man of any nation shall show a desire to obey the laws of the Great Peace, they shall trace the roots to their source, and they shall be welcomed to take shelter beneath the Tree of the Long Leaves. The smoke of the confederate council fire shall pierce the sky so that all nations may discover the central council fire of the Great Peace. I, Dekanawidah, and the confederate lords now uproot the tallest pine tree and into the cavity thereby made we cast all weapons of war. Into the depth of the earth, down into the deep underearth currents of water flowing into unknown regions; we cast all weapons of war. We bury them from sight forever and plant again the Tree.

21 DEKANAWIDAH, the great culture hero and lawgiver, gave the charge to the new rulers in the Confederation.

We do now crown you with the sacred emblem of the antlers, the sign of your lordship. You shall now become a mentor of the people of the Five Nations. The thickness of your skin will be seven spans, for you will be proof against anger, offensive action, and criticism. With endless patience you shall carry out your duty, and your firmness shall be tempered with compassion for your people.

Neither anger nor fear shall find lodgment in your mind, and all your words and actions shall be tempered with calm deliberation. In all your official acts, self-interest shall be cast aside. You shall look and listen to the welfare of the whole people, and have always in view, not only the present but the coming generations—the unborn of the future Nation.

22 The Iroquois Constitution gave directions for the opening of a council.

The Onondaga lords shall open each council by expressing their gratitude to their cousin lords, and greeting them, and they shall make an address and offer thanks to the earth where men dwell, to the streams of water, the pools, the springs, the lakes, to the maize and the fruits, to the medicinal herbs and the trees, to the forest trees for their usefulness, to the animals that serve as food and who offer their pelts as clothing, to the great winds and the lesser winds, to the Thunderers, and the Sun, the mighty warrior, to the moon, to the messengers of the Great Spirit who dwells in the skies above, who gives all things useful to men, who is the source and the ruler of health and life.

Then shall the Onondaga lords declare the council open.

23 The Constitution of the Five Nations provided funeral rituals for chiefs, warriors, women, children, infants.

At the funeral of a young man, say: "Now we become reconciled as you start away. In the beginning of your career you are taken away and the flower of your life is withered away. . . .

"You here present who were related to this young man and you who were his friends and associates, behold the path that is yours also. Soon we ourselves will be left in that place. For this reason hold yourselves in restraint as you go from place to place. In your actions and in your conversation do no idle thing. Speak not idle talk neither gossip . . . and do not give way to evil behavior. One year is the time that you must abstain from unseemly levity but if you can not do this for ceremony, ten days is the time to regard these things for respect." . . .

[At] the burial place, the speaker . . . shall bid the bereaved family cheer their minds once again and rekindle their hearth fires in peace. . . . He shall say that the black clouds shall roll away and that the bright blue sky is visible once more. Therefore shall they be in peace in the sunshine again.

24 Thomas Jefferson is said to have studied the Cons'itution of the Iroquois when it came time to frame the United States Constitution. Earlier, in 1754, when Benjamin Franklin was pleading the cause of political union of the American colonies at Albany, New York, Franklin referred to the Iroquois Confederation.

It would be a strange thing if Six Nations of ignorant savages should be capable of forming a scheme for such a union, and be able to execute it in such a manner as that it has subsisted for ages and appears indissoluble; and yet that a like union should be impracticable for ten or a dozen English colonies, to whom it is more necessary and must be more advantageous, and who cannot be supposed to want an equal understanding of their interests.

25 In October 1736, treaty negotiations with the Six Nations were held in Philadelphia. KA-NICKHUNGO assured the whites:

It is our Desire that we and you should be as of one Heart, one Mind, and one Body, thus becoming one People, entertaining a mutual Love and Regard for each other, to be preserved firm and entire, not only between

14

you and us, but between your Children, and our Children, to all succeeding Generations.

We who are now here, are old Men, who have the Direction of Affairs in our own Nations; and as we are old, it may be thought that the Memory of these things may be lost with us, who have not, like you, the Art of preserving it by committing all Transactions to Writing: We nevertheless have Methods of transmitting from Father to Son, an Account of all these Things, whereby you will find the Remembrance of them is faithfully preserved, and our succeeding Generations are made acquainted with what has passed, that it may not be forgot as long as the Earth remains.

26 The three metaphors of fire, road, and chain were often used by Indians to symbolize the good relationship which they hoped would exist between them and the whites. Here are two examples. The first is from a speech in 1736 at Philadelphia by KANICKHUNGO of the Six Nations. The second is from a speech in 1742 by CANASSATEGO representing the Six Nations.

We are now come down from the Towns of our several Nations to give our Answer to the great Treaty, which we and you held together, at this Place, about four Years since. . . . As you received us kindly, and at that Treaty undertook to provide and keep for us a Fire in this great City [Philadelphia], we are now come to warm ourselves thereat, and we desire and hope it will ever continue bright and burning to the End of the World.

Soon after Brother Onas [Thomas Penn], who is now here, came into this Country, he and we treated together; he opened and cleared the Road between this Place and our Nations, which was very much to our good liking, and it gave us great Pleasure. We now desire that this Road, for the mutual Accommodation and Conveniency of you and us who Travel therein to see each other, may be kept clear and open, free from all Stops and Incumbrances . . . while the Earth endureth.

One of the chief Articles of our late Treaty together, was the brightning of the Chain of Friendship between us, and the preserving it free from all Rust and Spots . . . We now assure you our Brethren, that it is our earnest Desire this Chain should continue, and be strengthened . . . until this Earth passeth away and is no more seen.

According to our Promise we now propose to return you an Answer to the several things mentioned to us yesterday. . . . On this Head [account] you yesterday put us in Mind, first, of William Penn's early and constant Care to cultivate Friendship with all the Indians; of the Treaty we held with one of his Sons [Thomas Penn], about ten Years ago; and of the Necessity there is at this Time of keeping the Roads between us clear and free from all Obstructions. . . . In Consequence of this, we, on our Part, shall preserve the Road free from all Incumbrances. . . .

You in the next Place said you would enlarge the Fire and make it burn brighter, which we are pleased to hear you mention; and assure you, we shall do the same, by adding to it more Fewel, that it may still flame out more strongly than ever. . . .

In the last Place . . . we are bound . . . to watch for each other's Preservation; that we should hear with our Ears for you, and you hear with your Ears for us. . . . We shall not fail to give you early Intelligence. . . . And to encourage you to do the same, and to nourish in your Hearts what you have spoke to us with your Tongues, about the Renewal of our Amity and the Brightening of the Chain of Friendship; we confirm what we have said with another Belt of Wampum.

27 CANASSATEGO, in this same 1742 treaty
negotiation, or renewal, had an exchange with
the white leader which poignantly illustrates
the basic clash of values, the ironies, and the
rationalizations which would plague Indian-
white relations while the Earth endureth.

CANASSATEGO: We received from the Proprietors Yesterday, some Goods in consideration of our Release of the Lands on the West-side of Sasquehannah. It is true, we have the full Quantity according to Agreement; but if the Proprietor had been here himself, we think, in Regard of our Numbers and Poverty, he would have made an Addition to them. If the Goods were only to be divided amongst the Indians present, a single Person would have but a small Portion; but if you consider what Numbers are left behind, equally entitled with us to a Share, there will be extremely little. We therefore desire, if you have the Keys of the Proprietor's Chest, you will open it, and take out a little more for us.

We know our Lands are now become more valuable: The white People think we do not know their Value; but we are sensible that the Land is everlasting, and the few Goods we receive for it are soon worn out and gone. . . . Besides, we are not well used with respect to the Lands still unsold by us. Your People daily settle on these Lands, and spoil our Hunting. We must insist on your removing them. . . .

It is customary with us to make a Present of Skins, whenever we renew our Treaties. We are ashamed to offer our Brethren so few, but your Horses and Cows have eat the Grass our Deer used to feed on. This has made them scarce, and will, we hope, plead in Excuse for our not bringing a larger Quantity. If we could have spared more, we would have given more; but we are really poor; and desire you'll not consider the Quantity, but few as they are, accept them in Testimony of our Regard.

GEORGE THOMAS: *In answer to what you say about the Proprietaries. They are all absent, and have taken the Keys of their Chest with them; so that we cannot, on their Behalf, enlarge the Quantity of Goods: Were they here, they might perhaps, be more generous; but we cannot be liberal for them. The Government will, however, take your Request into Consideration. . . .*

It is very true, that Lands are of late become more valuable; but what raises their Value? Is it not entirely

owing to the Industry and Labour used by the white Peo-
ple, in their Cultivation and Improvement? Had not they
come amongst you, these Lands would have been of no
Use to you, any further than to maintain every Thing; but
you know very well, that they cost a great deal of Money;
and the Value of Land is no more than it is worth in
Money.

28 An Assiniboin chief, traveling with the party of
Pierre Gaultier de Varrennes, December 1743,
about to go through Mandan country, tells of
a great discovery.

I am the best man to talk to you about this. You do not
rightly understand what I said to you. I don't tell lies. Last
summer I killed one of a nation who was covered with
iron. . . . If I had not killed his horse first I should not
have got the man. I saw men on horseback. I had much
difficulty in escaping. . . . I threw away everything, even
my blanket, and ran away naked. . . .
What I told you I repeat. You can't see the other side
of the mountains; the water is salt; it is mountainous country, with wide spaces between the mountains consisting of
fine land; a vast quantity of buffalo large and heavy, others
of different colors, many deer and roebuck. I have seen
their cornfields; you don't see any women in them.

29 CANASSATEGO, on July 3, 1744, after extended negotiations that day between the Six
Nations and representatives of Pennsylvania,
Virginia, and Maryland, made a not so subtle
suggestion that must have brought smiles to
the whites.

You tell us you beat the French [in a King George's War
battle]; if so you must have taken a great deal of Rum
from them, and can the better spare us some of the
Liquor to make us rejoice with you in the Victory.

30 CANASSATEGO spoke for the Iroquois at the Treaty of Lancaster, signed July 4, 1744. He replied to an offer of the Virginia Legislature to the Six Nations, inviting them to send six youths to be educated at the Williamsburg College of William and Mary.

We know you highly esteem the kind of Learning taught in these Colleges, and the maintenance of our young Men, while with you, would be very expensive to you. We are convinced, therefore, that you mean to do us Good by your Proposal; and we thank you heartily. But you who are so wise must know that different Nations have different Conceptions of things; and you will not therefore take it amiss, if our Ideas of this kind of Education happens not to be the same with yours. We have had some experience of it. Several of our young People were formerly brought up in the Colleges of the Northern Provinces; they were instructed in all your Sciences; but, when they came back to us, they were bad Runners, ignorant of every means of living in the Woods, unable to bear either Cold or Hunger, knew neither how to build a Cabin, take a deer, or kill an enemy, spoke our language imperfectly, were therefore neither fit for Hunters, Warriors, nor Counsellors, they were totally good for nothing. We are however not the less obliged for your kind Offer, tho' we decline accepting it; and to show our grateful Sense of it, if the Gentlemen of Virginia shall send us a Dozen of their Sons, we will take great care of their Education, instruct them in all we know, and make Men of them.

31 HALF-KING, the Seneca, confronted the French Commandant and party at Kuskuskas, an Indian town on Big Beaver Creek, November 25, 1753; he had at his side the youthful George Washington, whom he favored above the French, as history proved.

Fathers, I have come to hear your own speeches, what your own mouths have declared.

You, in former days, set a silver basin before us, wherein there was a leg of beaver, and desired all nations to come and eat it; to eat in peace and plenty, and not be churlish to one another. . . .

Now, fathers, it is you who are the disturbers in this land, by coming and building your towns, and taking it away unknown to us and by force.

We kindled a fire a long time ago at a place called Montreal, where we desired you to stay and not to come intrude on our land. . . .

Fathers, both you and the English are white; we live in a country between; therefore the land belongs to neither one or the other, but the Great Being above allowed it to be a place of residence for us; so fathers, I desire you to withdraw as I have done to our brothers the English, for I will keep you both at arm's length.

I lay this down as a trial for both, to see which will have the greatest regard to it, and that side we will stand by and make equal sharers with us.

32 HENDRICK, Mohawk sachem, spoke to the Albany Congress on July 2, 1754.

Brethren, you have asked us the reason of our living in this dispersed manner. The reason is your neglecting us for these three years past. [Dramatically tosses stick over his shoulder] You have thus thrown us behind your backs and disregarded us; whereas the French are a subtile and vigilant people, ever using their utmost endeavors to seduce and bring our people over to them. . . .

Brethren, the Governor of Virginia and the Governor of Canada are both quarrelling about lands which belong to us; and such a quarrel as this may end in our destruction. . . . [You] have made paths through our country to trade, and built houses, without acquainting us with it. They should first have asked our consent to build there, as was done when Oswego was built.

Brethren, it is very true, as you told us, that the clouds hang heavy over us, and it is not very pleasant to look up.

But we give you this belt to clear away all clouds, that we may all live in bright sunshine, and keep together in strict union and friendship.

33 ONGEWASGONE, of the Norridgewock tribe, spoke before Maine's Governor Shirley in 1754, when all the land—between the Kennebec River to Sheepscot and as high up as Norridgewock—was claimed by the owners of New Plymouth, to the obvious dismay of the men in the area.

Here is a river belonging to us; you have lately built a garrison there; we wish you would be content to go further up the river from the fort. We live wholly on this land and live but poorly; the Penobscots hunt on one side of us, and the Canada Indians hunt on the other side; therefore do not turn us off this land. . . .

I am an old man, and never heard any of them [his elders] say these lands were sold. We don't say these deeds are false, but we apprehend you got the Indians drunk, and so took advantage of them, when you bought the lands.

34 HENDRICK, the Mohawk who reluctantly threw in his lot with the British in the French and Indian War, at the Battle of Lake George, 1755, riding behind Colonel Ephraim Williams, looked despairingly at his warriors.

If they are to fight they are too few; if they are to die they are too many.

35 TEEDYUSCUNG, Delaware sachem, in the fall of 1756, was vehemently against the fighting powers and the treaty signing at Easton, which was not binding on the Ohio Indians, the Mingo, or the Shawnee.

The kings of France and England have settled this land so as to coop us up in a pen. This very ground under me was my land and inheritance, and is taken from me by fraud.

36 TICHOU MINGO, an Acolapissa Indian of the Osage nation, and their most expert hunter, killed a Choctaw, 1756. The French demanded his death. His father arose in council and offered himself in his son's place, in a touching plea at once accepted.

My son is dying valiantly. But since he is young and vigorous, he is more capable than I to feed his mother, his wife and four small children. He must live in order to take care of them. I am at the end of my life, I have lived enough. I wish that my son may live to be as old as I am so he can raise my grandchildren properly. I am no longer good for anything. A few years more or less will make no difference. I have lived like a man; I want to die the same way. That is why I am going to take the place of my son.

37 The Moravian missionary, Christian Frederic Post, volunteered to carry a British message of peace to the hostile, pro-French Shawnee and Delaware during the French and Indian War. He talked with them at their village of Kushkushkee the last of August 1758, and they replied on September 1. SHINGIS, Delaware chief, was one of the spokesmen.

Before you came, they all agreed together to go and join the French; but since they have seen you, they all draw back; though we have great reason to believe you intend to drive us away, and settle the country; or else, why do you come to fight in the land that God has given us? . . . It is plain that you white people are the cause of this war; why do not you and the French fight in the old country, and on the sea? Why do you come to fight on our land?

This makes every body believe you want to take the land from us by force and settle it. . . .

Brother, your heart is good, you speak always sincerely; but we know there are always a great number of people that want to get rich; they never have enough; look, we do not want to be rich, and take away that which others have. God has given you the tame creatures; we do not want to take them from you. God has given to us the deer, and other wild creatures, which we must feed on. . . .

It is told us, that . . . the French and the English intend to kill all the Indians, and then divide the land among themselves. . . . Look now, my brother, the white people think we have no brains in our heads; but that they are great and big, and that makes them make war with us: we are but a little handful to what you are; but remember, . . . when you hunt for a rattlesnake, you cannot find it; and perhaps it will bite you before you see it.

38   WHITE EYES, Delaware peace chief, accompanying the missionary, Christian Frederic Post, to Fort Duquesne with his band of Indians in 1758, rebuked an aged Onondaga who argued that all the Ohio lands belonged to the Six Nations.

That man speaks not as a man. He endeavors to frighten us by saying the ground is his; he dreams; he and his father [the French] have certainly drunk too much liquor; they are drunk; pray let them go to sleep till they are sober. You do not know what your nation does at home, how much they have to say to the British. You are quite rotten. You stink! You do nothing but smoke your pipe here. Go to sleep with your father, and when you are sober we will speak with you.

39   PONTIAC, Ottawa chief, tried to enlist the French to his cause, and the Indians to the French cause, May 23, 1760.

Until now I have avoided urging you on the subject, in the hope that, if you could not aid, you would not injure us. I did not wish to ask you to fight with us against the English, and I did not believe you would part from them. You will say that you are not with them. I know it; but your conduct amounts to the same thing. You tell them all we do and say. You carry our councils and plans to them. Now take your choice. You must be entirely French like ourselves, or entirely English. If you are French, take this belt for yourselves and your young men, and join us. If you are English, we declare war against you.

40 In 1762, Alexander Henry, against the advice of his friends, went to Michilimackinac to trade in furs. PONTIAC, pretending to be Menehwehna the Chippewa, confronted Henry.

Englishman, it is to you that I speak, and I demand your attention. Englishman, you know that the French king is our father. He promised to be such; and we, in return promised to be his children. This promise we have kept. Englishman, it is you that have made war with our father. You are his enemy; and how then could you have the boldness to venture among us, his children? You know that his enemies are ours. . . .

Englishman, although you have conquered the French, you have not yet conquered us. We are not your slaves. These lakes, these woods, and mountains were left us by our ancestors. They are our inheritance; and we will part with them to none. Your nation supposes that we, like the white people, cannot live without bread and pork and beer. But you ought to know that He, the Great Spirit and Master of Life, has provided food for us in these spacious lakes, and on these woody mountains. . . .

As for you, we have taken in consideration that you have ventured your life among us in the expectation that we should not molest you. You do not come armed, with the intention to make war; you come in peace to trade with us, and supply us with the necessaries, of which we are much in want. We shall regard you, therefore, as a brother; and you sleep tranquilly, without fear of the Chippewas.

41 PONTIAC, at a council fire by the River Ecores near Detroit in May 1763, incited the Indians to massacre. In his tirade he repeated the alleged words of the Master of Life to a Delaware chief of his acquaintance.

I am the Maker of heaven and earth, the trees, lakes, rivers, and all else. I am the Maker of all mankind; and because I love you, you must do my will. The land on which you live I have made for you and not for others. Why do you suffer the white man to dwell among you? My children, you have forgotten the customs and traditions of your forefathers. Why do you not clothe yourselves in skins, as they did, use bows and arrows and the stone-pointed lances, which they used? You have bought guns, knives, kettles and blankets from the white man until you can no longer do without them; and what is worse you have drunk the poison firewater, which turns you into fools. Fling all these things away; live as your wise forefathers did before you.

42 WAWATAM, an Ojibwa, had adopted Alexander Henry as friend and brother. When the Massacre of Old Fort Mackinac took place, June 1763, he made a touching appeal at a council lodge where Henry was being held captive.

Friends and relations, what is it that I shall say? You know what I feel. You all have friends and brothers and children, whom as yourselves, you love; and you—what would you experience, did you, like me, behold your dearest friend—your brother—in the condition of a slave; a slave exposed every moment to insult, and to the men-

25

aces of death? This case, as you know, is mine. See there my friend and brother, among slaves, himself a slave! . . .

He is my brother; and because I am your relation he is therefore your relation too. And how, being your relation, can he be your slave? On the day on which the war began, you were fearful lest on this account, I should reveal your secret. You requested, therefore, that I should leave the fort and cross the lake. I did so; but did it with reluctance . . . notwithstanding that you, Minavavana [Ojibwa war chief], who had command in this enterprise, gave me your promise that you would protect my friend, delivering him from all danger, and giving him safely to me.

The performance of this promise I now claim. I come not with empty hands to ask it. You, Minavavana, best know whether or not, as it respects yourself, you have kept your word, but I bring these goods to buy off any claim which any man among you may have on my brother, as his prisoner. [Minavavana acknowledged his promise and released Henry to Wawatam.]

43 SHINGIS, Delaware chief, was being forced by Pontiac into alliance with the French, though he was an advocate of peace. In July 1763, he appealed to Captain Simeon Ecuyer, a Swiss mercenary for the British, hoping to turn back the Indians poised to attack Fort Pitt, but Ecuyer threatened to blow Shingis to bits if he showed his face again.

Brothers: we wish to hold fast the chain of friendship—that ancient chain which our forefathers held with their brothers the English. You have let your end of the chain fall to the ground, but ours is still in our hands. Why do you complain that our young men have fired on your soldiers, and killed your cattle and your horses? You yourselves are the cause of this. You marched your armies into our country and built forts here, though we told you again and again that we wished you to remove.

My brothers, the land is ours and not yours. If you

leave this place immediately and go home to your wives and children, no harm will come of it; if you stay you must blame yourselves alone for what may happen.

44 PONTIAC, by July 1763, was in despair, trying to hold the siege of Detroit in the face of imminent disaster. A message from the commandant at Fort de Chartres suggesting they "bury the hatchet" was answered with acquiescence.

The word which my father has sent me to make peace, I have accepted. All my young men have buried their hatchets. I think you will forget the bad things which has taken place for time past. Likewise I will forget what you have done to me, in order to think of nothing but good. I, the Chippewas, and the Hurons, we are ready to speak with you when you ask us.

45 Benjamin Franklin presented in plain, unsparing words his opinion of the murders of the Conestoga and Moravian Indians during the Conspiracy of Pontiac, 1763.

There are some (I am ashamed to say it) who would extenuate the enormous wickedness of these actions by saying: "The inhabitants of the frontiers are exasperated with the murder of their relations in the present war." It is possible. But though this might justify their going out into the woods, to seek for their enemies and avenge upon them those murders, it can never justify turning into the heart of the country and murdering their friends. If an Indian injures me, does it follow that I may revenge that injury on all Indians? . . . It is well known that Indians are of different tribes, nations, and languages, as well as the white people. In Europe, if the French, who are white people, should injure the Dutch, are they (the Dutch) to revenge it on the English, because they, too, are white people? . . . I beg that I may not be misunderstood as framing apologies for all Indians. . . . I can only observe that the Six Nations, as a body, have kept faith with the English ever since we knew them, now near an hundred years; and that their governing body have notions of honour, whatever may be the case with the rum-debauched, trader-corrupted vagabonds and thieves on the Susquehanna and Ohio, at present in arms against us. . . .

What could old Shehaes, so old he had been present at Penn's Treaty in 1701, done that he should have been cut to pieces in bed? What could he or the other poor old men and women do? What had the little boys and girls done? What could children of a year old, babes at the breast, what could they do that they must be shot and hatcheted? And in their parents' arms! This is done by no civilized nation in Europe. Do we come to America to learn and practice the manners of barbarians? But this, Barbarians as they are, they practice against their enemies only, not against their friends.

46 Alexander Henry, young American trader, lived among the Indians in 1763-64.

Henry's favorable reaction towards the Indian mode of life is in agreement with the reports of many white people who lived among the tribesmen for a while. In fact, there were many whites, who, after having tried it, expressed a preference for the free but hazardous life of savagery to the more restrained life of civilization. . . .

Yet, while there were whites who preferred to live like Indians, there were few, if any, Indians who regarded a completely civilized form of living as superior to their own way of life. This is true even of Indian children who were educated in the schools of the white colonists and who were later permitted to return to their own people. With the opportunity of choosing between the two ways of life, they rarely cast their lot with civilization. This was because the Indian was convinced that the white man's style of life, with its lack of freedom; innumerable laws and taxes; extremes of wealth and poverty; snobbish class divisions; hypocritical customs; private ownership of land; pent-up communities; uncomfortable clothing; many diseases; slavery to money and other false standards, could not possibly bring as much real happiness as their own way of doing things. . . .

The great mass of white people and the great mass of Indians realized that their two ways of life were directly opposed. Each race looked upon the other as inferior; neither felt inclined to adopt the ways of the other; and that is why the Indians and the whites could not get along together. . . .

One or the other of the two groups of people had to give up their accustomed mode of existence. And the longer the whites were in the country the plainer it became that the Indians [were] . . . a race of hunters and small farmers doomed to be strangers in their own country.

47   LAWOUGHQUA, a Shawnee chief, was one of those of many tribes who listened in June 1765, when Colonel George Croghan visited Kaskaskia and the Wabash Valley for the purpose of conciliation and trade.

We of these Indian nations representing numerous tribes have let slip the chain of friendship held by the King of Great Britain and the chief [Pontiac] of the Indian nation. A high wind sprang up and raised heavy clouds over the land and almost put out the ancient Council Fire, but the fire is renewed again, some dry wood is thrown upon it so that the blaze might ascend to the clouds, and all nations will see that they live again in peace and tranquility with the settlers.

48 A Potawatomi chief, with a party of Ottawa and Chippewa, traveled from the Portage of Chicago to Detroit, to meet with Pontiac and the nations and Colonel George Croghan, to effect a general peace with the English, September 13, 1765.

Father, you sent me a belt from the Miami, and as soon as I received it I set off to meet you here. On my way I heard what has passed between you and the several tribes that met you here. You have had pity on them; and I beg, in behalf of myself and the people of Chicago, that you will have pity on us also. It is true we have been foolish, and listened to evil reports and the whistling of bad birds. We red people are a very jealous people; and, father, among you white people there are bad people also, that tell us lies and deceive us, which has been the occasion of what is past.

49 DRAGGING CANOE, Cherokee chief and son of the famous Attakullakulla (the Little Carpenter), was chagrined to learn that his aged father would consider selling land, at The Treaty of Fort Stanwix councils, 1768.

Where now are our grandfathers, the Delawares? We had hoped the white man would not be willing to travel beyond the mountains; now that hope is gone. They have passed the mountains, and have settled on Cherokee lands. . . . Finally, the whole country, which the Cherokees and their fathers have so long occupied, will be demanded, and the remnant of the *Ani-Yunwiya,* "The Real People," once so great and formidable, will be obliged to seek refuge in some distant wilderness . . . until they again behold the advancing banners of the same greedy host . . . Such treaties may be all right for men who are too old to hunt or fight. As for me, I have my young warriors about me. We will have our lands. *A-Waninski.* I have spoken.

50 CORNSTALK, Shawnee chief, headed a confederation of Ohio Indians to keep the whites from planting corn north of the Ohio River. After losing a battle at Point Pleasant October 10, 1774, he ruled against continuing the warfare.

What shall we do now? The Big Knife is coming on us, and we shall all be killed. Now we must fight or we are done. Then let us kill all our women and children and go fight until we die? I shall go and make peace!

51 METHOATASKE, a Muskogee Creek, was the imaginative mother of Tecumseh. Her Shawnee husband, Puckeshinwa, was slain in 1774. She fostered in her young sons, particularly Tecumseh, a hatred for all settlers, because of the one who had shot their father.

Tecumseh, you shall avenge the death of your father and appease the spirits of his slaughtered brothers. Already you are elected chief of many tribes. . . . Your feet shall be as swift as the forked lightning; your arm shall be as the thunderbolt, and your soul fearless as the cataract that dashes from the mountain precipice. . . .

[Later] Today you saw a deer bounding through the forest, he was lovely in strength and beauty, and fleeter than the winds. . . . Suddenly the hunter crossed his path, and an arrow cleft his heart. I led you to the spot and bade you look at the dying animal. . . . The warm blood that flowed from the wound grew dark and chill. He was stiff and cold, and his beauty had departed. Such is death, and such was the death of your father. . . .

[Still later] Time rolls on without ceasing. The winter passes quickly away, and the summer is here again. You shall soon glory in the strength of your manhood, and your enemies afar shall hear your name and tremble.

52 LOGAN (Tachnechdorus), a Mingo chief, took his name in honor of John Logan, the Quaker Indian agent and later Pennsylvania governor, deeply respected by the Indians. Logan was for years intensely loyal to the whites, until 1774, when neighboring white villagers (at Baker's Bottom, near present-day Steubenville, Ohio) treacherously killed about a dozen of Logan's tribe, among them his mother, sister, and brother. He vowed vengeance and with a band of Mingo and Shawnee exacted it all along the frontier from the Allegheny to Cumberland Gap. War resulted; when peace negotiations later began, Logan spurned the invitation to participate from Lord Dunmore, Governor of Virginia. Instead he sent to the council a message which for generations afterward was as famous in schoolboy exercises and declamation contests as was the Gettysburg Address later. Controversy has raged over the speech's origin, but opinion, from Thomas Jefferson's imprimatur on, seems to favor its basic authenticity.

I appeal to any white man to say if he ever entered Logan's cabin hungry and he gave him not meat; if he ever came cold and naked and he clothed him not. During the course of the last long and bloody war, Logan remained idle in his cabin, an advocate for peace. Such was my love for the whites that my countrymen pointed as I passed and said, "Logan is a friend of the white man." I had even thought to have lived with you but for the injuries of one man. Colonel Cresap, the last spring in cold blood and unprovoked, murdered the relatives of Logan, not even sparing his wives and children. There runs not a drop of my blood in the veins of any living creature.

This called on me for revenge. I have sought it. I have killed many. I have fully glutted my vengeance. For my country I rejoice in the beams of peace; but do not harbor a thought that mine is the joy of fear. Logan never felt fear. He will not turn on his heel to save his life. Who is there to mourn for Logan? Not one.

53 BUCKONGAHELAS, a Delaware chief, was spokesman for his people when many tribes met at Fort Pitt in 1775 with the commissioners, who were striving to have the Indians sign a treaty favorable to the Americans. Buckongahelas pointed up the dilemma of the red man in choosing sides between the British and the Americans.

Friends! Listen to what I have to say to you! You see a great and powerful nation divided! You see the father fighting against the son, the son against the father. The father has called on his Indian children to assist him in punishing his children, the Americans, who have become refractory. I took time to consider what I should do—whether or not I should receive the hatchet of the father to assist him. At first I looked upon it as a family quarrel, in which I was not interested. At length it appeared to me that the father was right, that his children deserved to be punished a little. That this must be the case, I concluded, from the many cruel acts his offspring has committed from time to time against his Indian children, by encroaching on their lands, stealing their property, shooting at and even murdering, without cause, men, women, and children. Yes, even murdering those who, at all times, had been friendly to them. Look back at the murders committed by the Long Knives on many of our relations, who lived peaceably as neighbors to them on the Ohio. Did not they kill them without the least provocation? Are they now, do you think, better men than they were?

54 BLACKFISH, the Shawnee chief who captured Daniel Boone outside Boonesborough, later adopted him into the tribe at Detroit in the spring of 1775. He never forgot the rite of adoption.

My son, you are now flesh of our flesh and bone of our bone. By the ceremony which was performed this day every drop of white blood was washed from your veins;

you were taken into the Shawnee nation and initiated into a warlike tribe; you were adopted into a great family, and now received in the place of a great man [a dead son].

You are now one of us by an old strong law and custom. My son, you have nothing to fear; we are now under the same obligation to love, support and defend you that we are to love and defend one another. Therefore you are to consider yourself one of our people.

55 A Mohawk chief, during General John Burgoyne's march southward from Canada, met in June 1776 with Sir William Johnson and Colonel John Butler. Their mission: to persuade him to join the British against the Americans.

I stand up in the name of all relations present, to assure our father that we have listened to his discourse. We receive you as our father beyond the waters. . . . We have been tried and tempted by the people of Boston; but we have loved our father, and our hatchets have been sharpened on our affections.

56 OLD TASSEL of the Cherokee tribe met at Long Island of Holston, July 1777, with U.S. Commissioners to negotiate a treaty. His band listened intently.

Much has been said of the want of what you term "Civilization" among the Indians. Many proposals have been made to us to adopt your laws, your religion, your manners, and your customs. We do not see the propriety of such a reformation. We should be better pleased with beholding the good effects of these doctrines in your own practices than with hearing you talk about them, or of reading your newspapers on such subjects. You say, "Why do not the Indians till the ground and live as we do?" May we not ask with equal propriety, "Why do not the white people hunt and live as we do?"

57 JOSEPH BRANT (Thayandangea), the Mohawk, educated in English mission schools in Philadelphia and frequent visitor to England, fought in the Revolutionary War against the Americans. In 1777 he led an attack on Fort Hunter. His retreating warriors carried away a child, who was returned by messenger the next morning to the commandant with a note.

Sir, I send you by one of our runners the child which we will deliver, that you may know whatever others do, I do not make war on women and children. I am sorry to say that I have those engaged with me in the service, who are more savage than the savages themselves. [Many believe that Brant had reference to Walter Butler and his blood-crazed rangers who scourged New York's Schoharie Valley.]

58 Warfare loomed between the Iroquois and white settlers. The English urged them to attack the Americans, warning of encroachment, while offering them gifts and promises of plunder, which brought on the tragedy of Cherry Valley and Wyoming in New York. In 1779 President George Washington ordered troops to secure the frontier.

The first of May, 1779, the troops [under General John Sullivan] commenced their march, but did not arrive at Wyoming until the middle of June. . . . On the twelfth from the date of their march, [they] reached Tioga. Here they entered the Indian settlements, and the work of devastation began. Here also, Clinton, coming down the Susquehanna, joined them with his brigade. . . .

Sullivan, in the meantime, had destroyed the village of Chemung; and Clinton, on his passage, had laid waste the settlement of Onondaga. The whole army, now amounting to nearly five thousand men, marched on the 26th of August up the Tioga River, destroying as it went. At New-

town the Indians made a stand . . . but being at length attacked in the rear by General Poor, they broke and fled.

The village was immediately set on fire, and the rich fields of corn were cut down and trodden underfoot. On the first of September the army left the river, and struck across the wilderness, to Catherine's Town. . . . This town also was burned and the fields ravaged. Having reached Seneca Lake, they followed its shores northward to Kendaia, a beautiful Indian village, with painted houses, and monuments for the dead, and richly cultivated fields. It smiled like an oasis there in the wilderness; but the smoke of the conflagration soon wrapped it, and when the sun again shone upon it, a smouldering heap alone remained —the waving corn had disappeared with the dwellings, and the cattle lay slaughtered around. Our troops moved like an awful, resistless scourge through this rich country —open and fruitful fields and smiling villages were before them—behind them a ruined waste.

Now and then, detachments sent off from the main body were attacked, and on one occasion seven were slain; and once or twice the Indians threatened to make a stand for their homes, but soon fled in despair, and the army had its own way. The capital of the Senecas, a town consisting of sixty houses, surrounded by beautiful cornfields and orchards, was burned to the ground and the harvest destroyed. Canandaigua fell next, and then the army stretched away for the Genesee flats. The fourth day it reached a beautiful region, then, almost wholly unknown to the white man. The valley, twenty miles long and four broad, had scarce a forest tree in it, and presented one of the most beautiful contrasts to the surrounding wilderness that could well be conceived. As the weary columns slowly emerged from the dark forest and filed into this open space . . . they seemed suddenly to be transported into an Eden.

The tall, ripe grass bent before the wind—cornfield on cornfield, as far as eye could reach waved in the sun— orchards that had been growing for generations, were weighted down under a profusion of fruit—cattle grazed on the banks of a river, and all was luxuriance and beauty.

. . . [All about] were scattered a hundred and twenty-eight houses—not miserable huts huddled together, but large airy buildings, situated in the most pleasant spots, surrounded by fruit trees, and exhibiting a cultivation on the part of the Indians never before witnessed.

Soon after sunrise immense columns of smoke began to rise the length and breadth of the valley, and in a short time the whole settlement was wrapped in flame from limit to limit; and before night those one hundred and twenty-eight houses were a heap of ashes. The grain had been gathered into them, and thus both were destroyed together. The orchards were cut down, the cornfields uprooted, and the cattle butchered and left to rot on the plain. A scene of desolation took place of the scene of beauty, and the army camped that night in a desert.

The next day, having accomplished the object of their mission, Sullivan commenced a homeward march. . . . The thanks of Congress was presented to Sullivan and his army for the manner in which they had fulfilled their arduous task.

59 CORNPLANTER, noted Seneca, was sired by an Irishman and raised by his Iroquois mother. As a lad he had visited his father. But in the spring of 1780, he led a raid on the Schoharie Valley, capturing his father, among others.

My name is John O'Bail, commonly called Cornplanter. I am your son. You are my father. You are now my prisoner and subject to the customs of Indian warfare; but you shall not be harmed. . . . Have no fear, I am a warrior. Many have I killed; many scalps have I taken. I was anxious to see you, to greet you in friendship. . . . I went to your cabin and took you by force, but your life was spared.

Indians love their friends and kindred, and treat them with kindness. If you do now choose to follow the fortunes of your yellow son, and live with our people, I will cherish you in age with plenty of venison; you shall live at ease.

If your choice is to return to your fields, to live with your wife and white children, I will send a party of trusty young men to conduct you safely back. . . . I respect you, my father, you have acted kindly towards the Indians, and they are your friends. [The father chose to return to his white family.]

60 A Delaware chief spoke to David Heckewelder about the Gnadenhutten Massacre, 1782, when ninety Christian Indians were slain by 200 whites, led by Colonel David Williamson, because two renegade Indians had done injury to a white man many miles away.

And yet these white men would be always telling us of their great Book which God had given them. They would persuade us that every man was bad who did not believe in it. They told us a great many things which they said was written in the Book; and wanted us to believe it. We would likely have done so, if we had seen them practice what they pretended to believe—and acted according to the good words which they told us. But no! While they held the big Book in one hand, in the other they held murderous weapons—guns and swords—wherewith to kill us poor Indians. Ah! And they did too. They killed those who believed in their Book as well as those who did not. They made no distinctions.

61 Benjamin Franklin in 1786 wrote to a French friend:

Almost every war between the Indians and the whites has been occasioned by some injustice of the latter towards the former.

62 BLUE JACKET, famed Shawnee, in April 1789:

From all quarters we receive speeches from the Americans, and not one is alike. We suppose they intend to deceive us.

63 GAYASHUTA, aged Seneca chief, living on the Pennsylvania border, sent a young sachem to deliver his speech at a 1790 meeting of the Friends at Philadelphia, to honor the memory of William Penn (Brother Onas).

When I was young and strong our country was full of game which the Great Spirit sent us to live upon. The lands that belonged to us were extended far beyond where we hunted. . . . Hunting was then not tiresome—it was a diversion—it was a pleasure. . . . When your fathers asked us for land, we gave it to them, for we had more than enough. Gayashuta was among the first to say give land to our Brother Onas.

Your fathers saw Gayashuta when he was young. When he had not even thought of old age or weakness—but you are too far off to see him now; he is grown old; he is very old and feeble, and he wonders at his own shadow, it has become so little. . . . We are men and therefore need only tell you that we are old and feeble and hungry and naked, and we have no other friends but the children of our beloved Brother Onas.

64 CORNPLANTER, the Seneca, spoke before President George Washington in 1790, six years after the Treaty of Fort Stanwix. Once more he feared the spectre of having to cede land.

When your army entered the country of the Six Nations, we called you *Caunotaucarius,* the Town Destroyer; and to this day when that name is heard, our women look behind them and turn pale, and our children cling to the knees of their mothers. Our councilors and warriors are men and cannot be afraid; but their hearts are grieved with the fears of their women and children, and desire that it may be buried so deep as to be heard no more. When you gave us peace, we called you father, because you promised to secure us in possession of our lands. Do this, and so long as the lands shall remain, the beloved name will remain in the heart of every Seneca.

65 In early 1793, a group of Indians from the Northwest Territory came to visit President George Washington in Philadelphia. Thomas Jefferson, Secretary of State, was present and recorded their speeches. The first to speak, on February 1, was JOHN BAPTIST DE COIGNE, Kaskaskia chief. He began by referring to some of their party who had died from the effects of the wintry trek.

I am about to open to you my heart. I salute first the Great Spirit, the Master of Life, and then you. I present you a black pipe on the deaths of the chiefs who have come and died in your bed. It is the calumet of the dead—take it and smoke it in remembrance of them. . . . This pipe is white. The sky is now cleared.

Your people of Kentucky are like mosquitoes, and try and destroy the red men. The red men are like mosquitoes, and try to injure the people of Kentucky. But I look to you as a good being. Order your people to be just. They are always trying to get our lands. They come on our lands, they hunt on them; kill our game and kill us. Keep them on one side of the line, and us on the other. Listen, my father, to what we say, and protect the nations of the Wabash and the Mississippi in their lands.

The English have spoken to us, but I shut my ears to them. I despise their money, it is nothing to me. I am attached to my lands. I love to eat in tranquility, and not like a bird on the bough. . . . The hatchet has long been buried. I have always been for peace. I have done what I could, given all the gifts I had to procure it. . . . I look upon you, my heart is white again, and I smile.

66 COMO, Potawatomi chief, addressed President Washington on February 4, 1793.

I am opening my heart to speak to you—open yours to receive my words. I first address you from a dead chief, who, when he was about to die, called us to him and charged us never to part with our lands. . . . For what have we come so far? Not to ruin our nation, nor yet to carry goods home to our women and children; but to procure them lasting good, to open a road between them to the whites. . . .

I have buried the hatchet forever, so must your children. I speak the truth and you must believe me. . . .

Father, I am happy to see you. The heavens have cleared, the day is bright, and I rejoice to hear your voice. These beads are a road between us. Take hold at one end, I will at the other, and hold fast. I will visit this road every day and brush it clean. If any blood is on it I will cover it up; if stumps be on it, I will cut them out. Should your children and mine meet on this road they shall shake hands and be friends. . . .

I love the land on which I was born, the trees which cover it, and the grass growing on it. It feeds us well. I did not come here to ask [for] gifts. I am young, and by hunting on my land, can kill what I need, and sustain my women and children in plenty. I come not to beg.

67 LITTLE BEAVER, a Wyandotte, spoke in behalf of Crooked Legs, who was too old to make the trip to Philadelphia.

You have spoken words of comfort to us, and I am happy to have heard it. The sun has shone out and all is well. This makes us think the Great Spirit was speaking truth

41

through you. Do then what you said, restrain your people if they do wrong.

Be assured that when we return, the Indians and the Americans will be as one people, will hunt and play and laugh together. . . . Here I will cease. The Father of Life might otherwise think I babble too much, and so might you. I finish then by giving you this pipe. I give it to you to smoke. Let its fumes ascend to the Great Spirit in heaven.

68 Little Beaver's wife addressed President Washington in place of her uncle, recently deceased.

I take you by the hand with all my heart because you have spoken words of comfort to us. I am but a woman, yet you must listen. The village chiefs and chiefs of war have opened their bodies and laid naked their hearts to you. . . . We have come, men and women, from afar to beseech you to let no one take our lands. . . .

We know you are strong, have pity on us. Be firm in your words. They have given us courage. The Father of Life has opened our hearts on both sides for good. He who was to have spoken to you is dead, Great Joseph. If he had lived you would have heard a good man, and good words flowing from his mouth. He was my uncle, and it has fallen on me to speak for him. But I am ignorant. Excuse, then, these words, it is but a woman who speaks.

69 The Seven Nations of Canada and a dozen other tribes, "in general council at the foot of the Miami Rapids, the 13th day of August, 1793," drew up a letter of protest about white encroachment north of the Ohio River.

Brothers, how then was it possible for you to expect to enjoy peace, and quietly hold these lands, when your Commissioner was informed . . . that the consent of a general council was absolutely necessary to convey any part of these lands to the United States? . . . [He] nevertheless persisted in collecting a few chiefs of two or three nations only, and with them held a treaty for the cession of an immense country.

Brothers, money to us is of no value, and to most of us unknown; and as no consideration whatever can induce us to sell the lands, on which we get sustenance for our women and children, we hope we may be allowed to point out a mode by which your settlers may be easily removed, and peace obtained.

Brothers, we know that these settlers are poor, or they would never have ventured to live in a country which has been in continual trouble ever since they crossed the Ohio. Divide therefore this large sum of money, which you have offered to us, among these people; . . . and we are persuaded they would most readily accept of it in lieu of the lands you sold to them. . . .

Brothers, you make one concession to us by offering to us your money, and another by having agreed to do us justice, after having long and injuriously withheld it. . . . And you want to make this act of common justice a great part of your concession, and seem to expect that because you have at last acknowledged our independence, we should for such a favor surrender to you our country.

70 LITTLE TURTLE, Miami chief, 1794, after twice defeating an American army, saw his nemesis in General Anthony Wayne's strategy.

We have beaten the enemy every time under separate commanders, we cannot expect the same good fortune always to attend us. The Americans are now led by a chief who never sleeps. . . . The day and the night are alike to him during the times he has marched on our villages. In spite of the watchfulness of our braves, never have we been able to surprise him. Think well of it! There is something that whispers to me it would be prudent to listen to offers of peace.

71   LITTLE TURTLE's allies rejected his peace suggestion. The Battle of Fallen Timbers soon followed and the Indian confederacy was crushed. At Fort Greenville on July 22, 1795, Little Turtle addressed General Anthony Wayne.

It is well known by all my brothers present that my forefather kindled the first fire at Detroit; from thence he extended his lines to the headwaters of the Scioto; from thence to its mouth; from thence down the Ohio to the mouth of the Wabash; and from thence to Lake Michigan. . . . I have now informed you of the boundaries of the Miami nation where the Great Spirit placed my forefather a long time ago, and charged him not to sell or part with his lands, but to preserve them for our children.

72   MASSAS, a Chippewa chief, who had signed the Treaty of Fort Harmar (never fully sanctioned by the Confederated Indian nations), spoke at The Treaty of Greenville in Ohio, 1795.

When you yesterday read to us the treaty of Muskingum, I understood you clearly: at that treaty we had not good interpreters, and we were left unacquainted with many particulars of it. I was surprised when I heard your voice, through a good interpreter, say that we have received presents and compensations for those lands which were thereby ceded. I tell you, now, that we, the three fires, never were informed of it. If our uncles, the Wyandots, and grandfathers, the Delawares, have received such presents, they have kept them to themselves. I always thought that we, the Ottawas, Chippewas, and Potawatomis, were the true owners of those lands, but now I find that new masters have undertaken to dispose of them; so that, at this day, we do not know to whom they, of right, belong. We have never received any compensation for them.

73 BIG CAT, a Delaware, in the midst of treaty signing and prisoner exchange at Fort Defiance, 1795, addressed young John Brikell, a white captive of four years, offering him a choice of going or staying.

My son, there are men the same color as yourself! There may be some of your kin here, or your kin may be a great way off from you. You have lived a long time with me. I call on you to say if I have not used you as a father would use a son? . . . You have lived with me; you have hunted for me; but our treaty says you must be free. If you choose to go with the people of your own color, I have no right to say a word; but if you choose to stay with me, your people have no right to speak. . . .

You are a good hunter—you have been better to me than my own sons . . . I leaned on you like a staff. Now it is broken. You are going to leave me and I have no right to say a word, but I am ruined. [Brikell decided to go home; both the red man and the white wept at parting.]

74 DOUBLEHEAD, a Creek chief, addressed Benjamin Hawkins, U.S. Commissioner at the Treaty of Colerain, on St. Mary's River, June 14, 1796, which meant for the Creeks *Ulawistu Nunnehi,* the end of the trail.

On this land there is a great deal of timber, pine and oak, which are of much use to the white man. They send it to foreign countries, and it brings them a great deal of money. On the land there is much grass for cattle and horses, and much good food for hogs. On this land there is a great deal of tobacco raised, which likewise brings much money. Even the streams are valuable to the white man, to grind the wheat and corn that grows on this land. The pine trees which are dead are valuable for tar.

All these things are lasting benefits; but if the Indians have a little goods for their lands, in one or two seasons they are all rotted and gone for nothing. We are told that our lands are of no service to us, but still, if we hold our lands, there will always be a turkey, or deer, or a fish in the streams, for those young who will come after us. We are afraid if we part with any more of our lands the white people will not suffer us to keep as much as will be sufficient to bury our dead.

75 HANDSOME LAKE, Seneca orator, half-brother of Cornplanter, evolved a code of conduct which won high praise from President Thomas Jefferson. An excerpt:

Whiskey [is] a great and monstrous evil and has reared a high mound of bones. . . . You lose your minds and whiskey causes it all. . . . So now all must now say, "I will use it nevermore." . . .

The married should live together and . . . children should grow from them. . . . Man and wife should rear their children well, love them and keep them in health. . . .

Love one another and do not strive for another's undoing. Even as you desire good treatment, so render it.

76 De Witt Clinton, U.S. Senator, New York City mayor, Governor of New York, early 19th century:

Popular, or free governments have, in all ages, been the congenial soil of oratory. And it is, indeed, all important in institutions merely advisory; where persuasion must supply the place of coercion; where there is no magistrate to execute, no military to compel; and where the only sanction of law is the controlling power of public opinion. Eloquence being, therefore, considered so essential, must always be a great standard of personal merit, a certain road to popular favor, and an universal passport to public honors. These combined inducements operated with powerful force on the mind of the Indian; . . . oratory was studied with . . . much care and application. . . . It was attainment to which they devoted themselves, and to which they bent the whole force of their faculties. Their models of eloquence were to be found, not in books, but in the living orators of their local and national assemblies.

77 President Thomas Jefferson, on January 4, 1806, addressed "My friends and children, Chiefs of the Osages, Missouris, Kanzas, Ottos, Panis, Ayowas, and Sioux" visiting Washington, D.C.

The French, the English, the Spaniards have now agreed with us to retire from all the country which you and we hold between Canada and Mexico. . . . Be assured you shall find advantage in this change of your friends. . . .

My children, we are strong, we are numerous as the stars in the heavens, and we are all gunmen. Yet we live in peace with all nations; and all nations esteem and honor us because we are peaceable and just. Then let my red children then be peaceable and just.

78 The Indians replied to Jefferson and his Secretary of War, Henry Dearborn, in a speech which was recorded by a clerk and signed by fourteen representatives of the tribes involved.

It is with an open heart that we receive your hands; friendship stretches ours to yours and unites them together. . . .

Fathers, we believe that you wish to pity us and to prevent our wants by sending us supplies of goods, but look sharp and tell to your men not to take too much fur for a little of goods; should they act in that way we would not be better off than we are now with our present traders. . . .

Fathers, you say that the French, English, and Spanish nations have left the waters of the Missouri and Mississippi; we are all glad of it, and we believe that the day they leave us the weather will be clear, the paths clean, and our ears will be no more affected with the disagreeable sounds of the bad birds who wish us to relinquish the words of our good fathers whose words we keep in our hearts. . . .

Fathers, our hearts are good. Though we are powerful and strong, and we know how to fight, we do not wish to fight. Shut the mouth of your children who speak war, stop the arm of those who raise the tomahawk over our heads, and crush those who strike first; then we will confess that we have good fathers who wish to make their red children happy and peace maintained among them. For when we are at peace we hunt freely, our wives and children do not stand in want, we smoke and sleep easy. . . .

Fathers, we will keep your word in our heart. The stinking cloud may rise; it will melt away when we remember the word of our fathers. The bad birds may fly over our heads with crow mischief; their flesh will be poor, their voice weak, they will hush and fly away when hearing the word of our fathers. We will be happy with your word, fathers, and never part with it.

79   JOSEPH BRANT, the Mohawk, was made sachem of the Long House in 1807. Shortly before his death that same year, he touched on the topic of law in a letter to an unknown correspondent.

Among us we have no prisons, we have no pompous parade of courts; we have no written laws, and yet judges are as highly revered among us as they are among you, and their decisions are as highly regarded.

Property, to say the least, is well-guarded, and crimes are as impartially punished. We have among us no splendid villians above the control of our laws. Daring wickedness is never suffered to triumph over helpless innocence. The estates of widows and orphans are never devoured by enterprising sharpers. In a word, we have no robbery under color of the law.

80 LITTLE TURTLE, the Miami, now aging, on a visit to Fort Dearborn in 1808, spoke in classic fashion of an enemy he had slain.

We met, I cut him down, and his shade as it passes on the wind shuns my walk.

81 A Cayuga chief made an address before the New York Historical Society about 1808.

The land of Gahnona [New York] was once laced by our trails we had trod for centuries, trails worn so deep by the feet of the Iroquois that they became your roads of travel as your possessions gradually ate into those of my people. Have we, the first holders of this region, no longer a share in your history? Glad were your fathers to sit down on the threshold of the Long House; rich did they hold themselves in getting the mere sweepings from the door. Had our fathers spurned you from it when the French were thundering from the opposite side to get a passage through and drive you into the sea, whatever had been the fate of other nations, we might still have had a nation, and I might have had a country.

82 TENSKWAUTAWA, Tecumseh's mystic brother, visited in 1808 with Governor William Henry Harrison at Vincennes, Indiana Territory, and spoke on Indian and white ways.

I told the redskins that the way they were in was not good, and they ought to abandon it; that we should consider ourselves as one man, that we ought to live agreeable to our several customs—the red men after their mode, and the white people after theirs; particularly, they should not drink whisky; that it was not made for them, and that it is the cause of all the mischiefs the Indians suffer.

83 TECUMSEH, Shawnee chief, in one of his travels, 1809-1811, deep in southern forests, in the interests of forming an Indian federation to bar the white man from further westward penetration, raged at the Creek chief, Big Warrior, for questioning his leadership.

Your blood is white! You have taken my talk, and the sticks and the wampum, and the hatchet, but you do not mean to fight! I know the reason; you do not believe the Great Spirit has sent me. You shall know. I leave Tuck-habatchee directly and go straight to Detroit; when I arrive there, I shall stamp my foot on the ground and shake down every house in Tuckhabatchee. [Oddly enough, about the time Tecumseh reached Detroit, an earthquake tumbled the lodges in Big Warrior's village.]

84 TECUMSEH in 1810 faced Governor W. H. Harrison to bitterly protest the land sales of 1805-06. He said they were effected by the use of strong liquor, a breach of The Treaty of Greenville. He refused to enter the Governor's mansion.

Houses are built for you to hold councils in; Indians hold theirs in the open air. I am a Shawnee. My forefathers were warriors. Their son is a warrior. From them I take my only existence. From my tribe I take nothing. I have made myself what I am. And I would that I could make the red people as great as the conceptions of my own mind, when I think of the Great Spirit that rules over us all. . . . I would not then come to Governor Harrison to ask him to tear up the treaty. But I would say to him, "Brother, you have the liberty to return to your own country."

You wish to prevent the Indians from doing as we wish them, to unite and let them consider their lands as the common property of the whole. You take the tribes aside and advise them not to come into this measure. . . . You want by your distinctions of Indian tribes, in allotting to each a particular, to make them war with each other. You never see an Indian endeavor to make the white people do this. You are continually driving the red people, when at last you will drive them onto the great lake, where they can neither stand nor work.

Since my residence at Tippecanoe, we have endeavored to level all distinctions, to destroy village chiefs, by whom all mischiefs are done. It is they who sell the land to the Americans. Brother, this land that was sold, and the goods that was given for it, was only done by a few. . . . In the future we are prepared to punish those who propose to sell land to the Americans. If you continue to purchase them, it will make war among the different tribes, and, at last I do not know what will be the consequences among the white people. Brother, I wish you would take pity on the red people and do as I have requested. If you will not give up the land and do cross the boundary of our present settlement, it will be very hard, and produce great trouble between us.

The way, the only way to stop this evil is for the red men to unite in claiming a common and equal right in the land, as it was at first, and should be now—for it was never divided, but belongs to all. No tribe has the right to sell, even to each other, much less to strangers. . . . *Sell a country! Why not sell the air, the great sea, as well as the earth?* Did not the Great Spirit make them all for the use of his children?

How can we have confidence in the white people?

When Jesus Christ came upon the earth you killed Him and nailed him to the cross. You thought he was dead, and you were mistaken. You have Shakers among you and you laugh and make light of their worship.

Everything I have told you is the truth. The Great Spirit has inspired me.

85 TECUMSEH, in July 1811, with twenty-four warriors, followed the Wabash River in a second attempt to engage in historic debates to persuade the Indians to unite in a southern confederation. He voiced prophetic warnings.

Where today are the Pequot? Where are the Narragansett, the Mohican, the Pocanet, and other powerful tribes of our people? They have vanished before the avarice and oppression of the white man, as snow before the summer sun. . . . Will we let ourselves be destroyed in our turn, without making an effort worthy of our race? Shall we, without a struggle, give up our homes, our lands, bequeathed to us by the Great Spirit? The graves of our dead and everything that is dear and sacred to us? . . . . I know you will say with me, Never! Never!! . . .

Sleep not longer, O Choctaws and Chickasaws, in false security and delusive hopes. . . . Will not the bones of our dead be plowed up, and their graves turned into plowed fields?

86 TENSKWAUTAWA, the Prophet, on November 6, 1811, precipitated the Battle of Tippecanoe with Harrison's troops, which ended in disaster to the Indians and to Tecumseh's dream. Over the battleground rang the Prophet's rallying cry:

O Shawnee braves! O Potawatomi men! O Miami Panthers! O Ottawa Foxes! O Miami Lynxes! O Kickapoo Beavers! O Winnebago Wolves! Lift up your hatchets; raise your knives; sight your rifles! Have no fears—your lives are charmed! Stand up to the foe; he is a weakling and a coward! O red brothers; fall upon him! Wound, rend, tear, and flay, scalp, and leave him to the wolves and buzzards! O Shawnee braves! O Potawatomi men!

87 TECUMSEH returned from his travels, February 1812, unaware that the Battle of Tippecanoe had been fought and lost, to find his lodge in ashes. Bitterly he reproached his brother for his actions in his absence. Later, he spoke of his homecoming.

My mission to my mother's land had failed. I could not induce them to come where the water turns to stone and the rain comes from the clouds in showers of white wool and buries everything in sight. I had to shut my eyes all the way so as not to see the beautiful country that would soon be trampled under the feet of the hated white men. I was going from a sunny clime to one of ice and snow, and I thought that, although they might lie deep and cold upon the roof of my wigwam, I should find a warm fire within. And that thought kept me warm through all the chilly nights of the long journey. If I were hungry, I said, I can bear it, for my people on the Wabash have plenty of corn. . . .

I stood upon the ashes of my home, where my own wigwam had sent up its fires to the Great Spirit; where I summoned the spirits of the braves who had fallen in their vain attempt to protect their homes from the grasping invaders. And as I snuffed up the smell of their blood from the earth, I swore eternal hatred—the hatred of the avenger.

88 Two Winnebago Indians, visiting Fort Dearborn shortly before the massacre of 1812, watched the wife of Captain Nathan Heald and the wife of Lieutenant Linai T. Helm playing battledore on the parade grounds. One turned to a French interpreter, remarking:

The white chiefs' wives are amusing themselves very much; it will not be long before they are hoeing in our cornfields!

89 BLACK PARTRIDGE, the famed Potawatomi, on the eve of the Fort Dearborn Massacre, August 15, 1812, advised Captain Nathan Heald to stay inside the fort for safety and returned a gift he had cherished.

Father, I come to deliver up to you the medal I wear. It was given me by the Americans, and I have long worn it, in token of our mutual friendship. But our young men are resolved to imbrue their hands in the blood of the whites. I cannot restrain them and I will not wear a token of peace while I am compelled to act as an enemy.

90 TECUMSEH, in 1813, fighting against the Americans in the War of 1812, found that white American prisoners were being tortured and killed by his Indian allies. Tecumseh halted the slaughter and turned in fury to the British commander, Colonel Henry Procter:

Go and put on petticoats. I conquer to save, and you to murder!

91 BLACK HAWK, Sauk warrior, likely saw more United States expansion and fought harder to resist it than any other Indian. In the War of 1812 he allied himself with the British against the Americans. After the engagement at Fort Stephenson on August, 1813, Black Hawk went home to visit his family.

On my arrival at the village, I was met by the chiefs and braves, and conducted to a lodge that had been prepared to receive me. After eating, I gave an account of what I had seen and done. I explained to them the manner the British and Americans fought. Instead of stealing upon each other, and taking every advantage to kill the enemy and save their own people, as we do (which, with us is considered good policy in a war chief), they march out, in open daylight, and fight, regardless of the number of warriors they may lose! After the battle is over, they retire to feast, and drink wine, as if nothing had happened; after which, they make a statement in writing, of what they have done—each party claiming the victory! and neither giving an account of half the number that have been killed on their own side. They all fought like braves, but would not do to lead a war party with us. Our maxim is, "to kill the enemy, and save our own men." Those chiefs would do to paddle a canoe, but not to steer it. The Americans shoot better than the British, but their soldiers are not so well clothed, or provided for.

92 WILLIAM WEATHERFORD, one-eighth Creek, known as Red Eagle, led an uprising in Mississippi Territory in 1813. Andrew Jackson, at the battle of Horseshoe Bend in March 1814, routed Red Eagle and his forces, bringing an end to the Creek war. In victory, Jackson issued orders to bring in all the Creek leaders, but Red Eagle could not be found. A few days later, Red Eagle appeared voluntarily and alone at Jackson's headquarters at Fort Toulouse (newly renamed Fort Jackson).

General Jackson, I am not afraid of you. I fear no man, for I am a Creek warrior. I have nothing to request in behalf of myself; you can kill me, if you desire. But I come to beg you to send for the women and children of the war party, who are now starving in the woods. Their fields and cribs have been destroyed by your people, who have driven them to the woods without an ear of corn. I hope that you will send our parties, who will safely conduct them here, in order that they may be fed. I exerted myself in vain to prevent the massacre of the women and children at Fort Mims. I am now done fighting. The Red Sticks [his warriors] are nearly all killed. . . . I have done the white people all the harm I could; I have fought them, and fought them bravely: if I had an army, I would yet fight, and contend to the last: but I have none; my people are all gone. I can now do no more than weep over the misfortunes of my nation. . . . There was a time when I had a choice, and could have answered you: I have none now—even hope has ended. Once I could animate my warriors to battle; but I cannot animate the dead. My warriors can no longer hear my voice: their bones are at Talladega, Tallushatchee, Emuckfaw, and Tohopeka. . . . If I had been left to contend with the Georgia army, I would have raised corn on one bank of the river, and fought them on the other; but your people have destroyed my nation. . . . I rely upon your generosity. [Red Eagle promised to counsel his people toward peace. For this reason, and for his bravery, Jackson drank a cup of brandy with his guest, shook his hand, and sent him away a free man.]

93   BLACK HAWK fought with Tecumseh and the British. After Tecumseh's death, unlike most Illinois Indians, he continued to harass the Americans. At a British conference at Prairie du Chien, 1815, he still expressed hope of victory, dim as it seemed.

My Father: You see this belt! When my Great Father at Quebec gave it to me on terms of friendship with all his Red Children, to form but one body to preserve our lands, and to make war against the Big Knives who want to destroy us all, my Great Father said: "Take courage, my children, hold tight to your war club, and destroy the Big Knives as much as you can. . . . Your lands shall become green, the waters green and the sky blue. When your lands change color, you shall also change". . . .

I see now the time is drawing near when we shall all change color; but, my father, our lands have not yet turned color—they are all red—the water is red with our blood, and the sky is cloudy. I have fought the Big Knives, and will continue to fight them until they go from our

56

lands. Till then, my father, your Red Children cannot be happy.

94 BIG ELK, chief of the Omahas, delivered a funeral oration, June 14, 1815, at a great council at Portage des Sioux, when death took one of the Indian leaders, Black Buffalo.

Do not grieve. Misfortunes will happen to the wisest and best of men. Death will come and always out of season. It is the command of the Great Spirit, and all nations and people must obey. What is past and cannot be prevented should not be grieved for. . . . Misfortunes do not flourish particularly in our path. They grow everywhere.

95 YE-WHELL-COME-TETSA, Okanogan chief, in August 1815, was presented with a highly prized skin of a 127-pound white wolf, by white traders who trapped near his camp.

This is the most valuable thing I have ever possessed. While I have this we have nothing to fear. Strange wolves will kill no more of our horses. I shall always love the whites. . . . I fear you will not believe me for the whites say that the Indian has two mouths and often tells lies, but I never tell lies, the whites know I have but one word and that word is truth.

96 LITTLE CROW, a Dakota chief, met with the British in 1816 at Drummond's Island in Lake Huron, ten months after Michilimackinac had been lost to the Americans. In the War of 1812, the British had recruited 300 Sioux, Menominee, and Winnebago warriors and some Sauk and Fox. Little Crow was angered when he and his band were lightly dismissed with a few gifts. He kicked them aside.

After we have fought for you, endured many hardships, lost some of our people, and awakened the vengeance of our powerful neighbors, you make a peace for yourselves, leaving us to obtain such terms as we can. You no longer need our services; you offer us these goods to pay us for having deserted us. But no, we will not take them; we hold them and yourselves in equal contempt.

97 TUM-A-TAP-UM, Owhyhee war chief, in July 1818, arrived at a council with fresh scalps hanging from his belt. Trade expeditions had called the meeting to promote peace among the Northwest tribes, to better the fur expectations. The chief was horrified at the talk of peace.

If we make peace, how shall I employ my young men? They delight in nothing but war, and besides our enemies, the Snakes, never observe a peace. Look! Am I to throw all these trophies away? Shall Tum-A-Tap-Um forget the glories of his forefathers and become a woman?

98 BIG ELK, Omaha chief, encountered Major Stephen H. Long, U.S. Army, at a council of tribes in Nebraska in October 1819.

Here I am, my father; all these young people you see arrived here are yours, although they are poor and little, yet they are your children. All my nation loves the whites and always have loved them. Some think, my father, that you have brought all these soldiers to take our lands from us, but I do not believe it. For although I am a poor simple Indian, I know this land will not suit your farmers. If I ever thought your hearts were bad enough to take this land, I would not fear it, as I know there is not enough wood on it for the use of the whites.

99 NEENGAY, Chippewa wife of John Johnston, soothed the outrage of her kinsmen when Colonel Hugh Brady, in 1820, came to Sault Ste. Marie to build a fort. His American soldiers cut down a sacred clump of mountain ash, over the protests of the Chippewas.

The soldiers do not know Indians, my brothers. They mean well but are ignorant of our ways. Our ancestral votive tree is gone—by fire from heaven; by the ax of a new people. Its fall may be a symbol. The might of my people is ended; this I have long known. Accept it, my brothers! Let us live in peace.

100 PETALASHARO, young Pawnee, in 1820 saved a Comanche maiden from human sacrifice by cutting her down from a scaffold.

Take my life if you will. The corn grows green from the sun, the rain, the earth—not because of the owl skin, the iron arrow, and the human blood! Take my life if you will, but spare this girl who has long been a guest among us.

101 PETALASHARO, while visiting Washington, D.C. two years later, was presented with a medal of valor by the girls of Miss White's Seminary, inscribed "To the bravest of the brave."

This brings rest to my heart. I feel like a leaf after a storm, when the wind is still. I listen to you. I am glad. I love the palefaces more than I ever did, I will open my eyes wider when they speak. I'm glad you heard of what I did. I did not know the deed was so good. It came from my heart; I was ignorant of its value. I know now how fine it was. You made me know—by giving me this medal.

102 METEA, Potawatomi orator of the Illinois, spoke at a treaty signing August 1821, when five million acres on the east side of Lake Michigan were ceded to the government.

My Father: a long time has passed since first we came upon our lands; and our people have all sunk into their graves. *They* had sense. *We* are all young and foolish, and do not wish to do anything that they would not approve, were they living. We are fearful we shall offend their spirits if we sell our lands; and we are fearful we shall offend you if we do not sell them. This has caused us great perplexity of thought, because we have counselled among ourselves, and do not know how we can part with our lands.

My Father, our country was given us by the Great Spirit, who gave it to us to hunt upon, to make our cornfields upon, to live upon, and to make our beds upon when we die. And he would never forgive us should we now bargain it away. When you first spoke to us for lands at St. Mary's, we said we had a little, and agreed to sell you a piece of it, but we told you we could spare you no more. Now you ask us again. You are never satisfied.

My Father, we have sold you a great tract of land already; but it is not enough! We sold it to you for the benefit of your children, to farm and to live upon. We have now but little left. We shall want it all for ourselves. We know not how long we shall live, and we wish to leave some lands for our children to hunt upon. You are gradually taking away our hunting grounds. Your children are driving us before them. We are growing uneasy. What lands you have you may retain forever; but we shall sell no more.

103 RED JACKET, Seneca chief, sent a letter to the Governor of New York, De Witt Clinton, in 1821, naming grievances of the Iroquois.

The first subject to which we would call attention of the governor, is the depredation daily committed by the white people upon the most valuable timber on our reservation. . . . This has been the subject of complaint for many years. . . .

Our next subject of complaint is the frequent thefts of our horses and cattle by the whites, and their habit of taking and eating them when they please, and without our leave.

Another evil arising from the pressure of the whites upon us, and our unavoidable communication with them, is the frequency with which our Indians are thrown into jail . . . and for the most trifling causes.

In our hunting and fishing, too, we are greatly interrupted. Our venison is stolen from the trees where we have hung it to reclaim it after the chase. . . . The fish which, in the Buffalo and Tonnewanto creeks, used to supply us with food are now—by the dams and other obstructions of the white people—prevented from multiplying, and we are almost entirely deprived of that accustomed sustenance.

The greatest source of all our grievances is, that the white men are among us.

104 SHARITARISH, Pawnee, visited Washington, D.C. and on February 4, 1822 addressed President James Monroe and Secretary of War John C. Calhoun.

My Great Father:—I have travelled a great distance to see you—I have seen you and my heart rejoices. I have heard your words—they have entered one ear and shall not escape the other, and I will carry them to my people as pure as they came from your mouth.

My Great Father— . . . If I am here now and have seen your people, your houses, your vessels on the big lake, and a great many wonderful things far beyond my comprehension, which appear to have been made by the Great Spirit and placed in your hands, I am indebted to my Father [Major Benjamin O'Fallon] here, who invited me from home, under whose wings I have been protected. . . . but there is still another Great Father to whom I am much indebted—it is the Father of us all. . . . The Great Spirit made us all—he made my skin red, and yours white; he placed us on this earth, and intended that we should live differently from each other.

He made the whites to cultivate the earth, and feed on domestic animals; but he made us, red skins, to rove through the uncultivated woods and plains; to feed on wild animals; and to dress with their skins. He also intended that we should go to war—to take scalps—steal horses from and triumph over our enemies—cultivate peace at home, and promote the happiness of each other.

My Great Father:—Some of your good chiefs, as they are called [missionaries], have proposed to send some of their good people among us to change our habits, to make us work and live like the white people. . . . You love your country—you love your people—you love the manner in which they live, and you think your people brave. I am like you, my Great Father, I love my country—I love my people—I love the manner in which we live, and think myself and warriors brave. Spare me then, my Father; let me enjoy my country, and I will trade skins with your people. I have grown up, and lived thus long without work—I am in hopes you will suffer me to die without it. We have plenty of buffalo, beaver, deer, and other wild animals—we have an abundance of horses—we have everything we want—we have plenty of land, if you will keep your people off of it. . . .

There was a time when we did not know the whites—our wants were then fewer than they are now. They were always within our control—we had then seen nothing which we could not get. Before our intercourse with the whites, who have caused such a destruction in our game, we could lie down to sleep, and when we awoke we would find the buffalo feeding around our camp—but now we are killing them for their skins, and feeding the wolves with their flesh, to make our children cry over their bones.

Here, my Great Father, is a pipe which I present you, as I am accustomed to present pipes to all the red skins in peace with us. It is filled with such tobacco as we were accustomed to smoke before we knew the white people. It is pleasant, and the spontaneous growth of the most remote parts of our country. I know that the robes, leggings, moccasins, bear claws, etc., are of little value to you, but we wish you to have them deposited and preserved in some conspicuous part of your lodge, so that when we are gone and the sod turned over our bones, if our children should visit this place, as we do now, they may see and recognize with pleasure the deposits of their fathers; and reflect on the times that are past.

105 PUSHMATAHA, Choctaw chief, served the U.S. loyally at the Battle of New Orleans. In 1824 he was invited to be part of the official group in Washington, D.C. welcoming Lafayette on his last visit to America.

Nearly fifty snows have melted since you drew sword as a champion of Washington. With him you fought the enemy of America, and proved yourself a warrior. After you finished the war you returned to your own country, and now you are come back to visit the land where you are honored by a numerous and powerful people.

You see everywhere the children of those by whose side you went to battle, crowding around you and shaking your hand, as the hand of a father. We have had these things told us in our villages, and our hearts have longed to see you.

We have come; we have taken you by the hand and are satisfied. This is the first time we have seen you; it will probably be the last. We have no more to say. The earth will part us forever. [Pushmataha himself died while in Washington and was buried there with full military honors.]

106 MONGAZID, chief of the Fond du Lac, Lake Superior Chippewa tribe, described his delight at being invited to the Prairie du Chien Council, August 29, 1825.

When I heard the voice of my Great Father [General William Clark of St. Louis] coming up the Mississippi Valley calling me to this treaty, it seemed as a murmuring wind. I arose from my mat where I sat musing, and hastened to obey it. My pathway has been clear and bright. Truly, it is a pleasant sky above our heads this day. There is not a cloud to darken it. I hear nothing but pleasant words. The raven is not waiting for his prey. I hear no eagle cry, "Come, let us go. The feast is ready; the Indian has killed his brother."

107 KANNEKUK, Kickapoo prophet, addressed General William Clark in 1827 at St. Louis, where he was called to calm down the Kickapoo who resented losing lands in south central Illinois.

Some of our chiefs make the claim that the land belongs to us. It is not what the Great Spirit told me. He told me that the lands belong to Him, that no people owns the land; that I was not to forget to tell this to the white people when I met them in council.

108 RED BIRD and Nawkaw, Winnebago warriors, surrendered after a war flutter caused by whites pilfering their reservation. At Prairie du Chien, in 1827, Red Bird made a prophecy of his death, which occurred shortly in prison.

I am ready. I do not wish to be put in irons. Let me be free. I have given away my life—it is gone! [blows vigorously on a pinch of dust] It is gone—like that!—I would not take it back.

109 DECORI, a Winnebago chief, in January 1828 spoke at the Prairie du Chien agency about a perennial problem.

Indians ought not to buy whiskey. It is hot in his heart for a little while, then it is gone; the Indian is cold, his head is sore, and he does not remember what he did when the poison was in him. Whiskey is hot poison for the Winnebagoes. My head is like the snow with age, I have seen the ruin that it has brought upon our nation, and I advise them to buy no more whiskey.

110 DAYKAURAY, a Winnebago chief, made reply to Indian agent John H. Kinzie. In 1829, at a council fire at Prairie du Chien, Kinzie proposed a plan to educate a group of Indian children in the language and habits of civilization.

Father: The Great Spirit made the white man and the Indian. He did not make them alike. He gave the white man a heart to love peace, and the arts of a quiet life. He taught him to live in towns, to build houses, to make books, to learn all the things that would make him happy and prosperous in the way of life appointed him. To the red man the Great Spirit gave a different character. He gave him love of the woods, of a free life of hunting and fishing, of making war with his enemies. . . . The white man does not like to live like the Indian—it is not his nature. Neither does the Indian love to live like the white man—the Great Spirit did not make him so.

We do not wish to do anything contrary to the will of the Great Spirit. If he had made us with white skins and characters like the white man, then we would send our children to this school to be taught like white children.

We think if the Great Spirit had wished us to be like the whites, he would have made us so. We believe he would be displeased with us to try and make ourselves different from what he thought good.

I have nothing more to say. This is what we think. If we change our minds we will let you know.

111 SPECKLED SNAKE, aged Creek chief, spoke in 1829 when the Creeks were considering the advice of President Andrew Jackson who was urging them to move beyond the Mississippi.

Brothers: We have heard the talk of our Great Father; it is very kind. He says he loves his red children. . . .

When the first white man came over the wide waters, he was but a little man . . . very little. His legs were cramped by sitting long in his big boat, and he begged for a little land. . . .

When he came to these shores the Indians gave him land, and kindled fires to make him comfortable. . . .

But when the white man had warmed himself at the Indian's fire, and had filled himself with the Indian's hominy, he became very large. He stopped not at the mountain tops, and his foot covered the plains and the valleys. His hands grasped the eastern and western seas. Then he became our Great Father. He loved his red children, but he said: "You must move a little farther, lest by accident I tread on you."

With one foot he pushed the red men across the Oconee, and with the other he trampled down the graves of our fathers. . . .

On another occasion he said, "Get a little farther; go beyond the Oconee and the Ocmulgee [Indian settlements in South Carolina and Georgia]—there is a pleasant country." He also said, "It shall be yours forever."

Now he says, "The land you live upon is not yours. Go beyond the Mississippi; there is game; there you may remain while the grass grows and the rivers run."

Will not our Great Father come there also? He loved his red children, and his tongue is not forked.

Brothers! I have listened to a great many talks from our Great Father. But they always began and ended in this—"Get a little farther; you are too near me." I have spoken.

112 SENACHWINE, venerable Potawatomi, spoke at a council fire at Indiantown in Illinois in June 1830, when Black Hawk tried to induce them to join forces to rout the whites. His dissenting speech caused Black Hawk to rise and stalk from the meeting with his band.

For more than seventy years I have hunted in this grove and fished in this stream, and for many years I have worshipped on this ground. Through these groves and over these prairies in pursuit of game our fathers roamed, and by them this land was left unto us as a heritage forever. No one is more attached to his home than myself, and none among you is so grieved to leave it. But the time is near at hand, when the red men of the forest will have to leave the land of their nativity, and find a home toward the setting sun. The white men of the east, whose numbers are like the sands of the sea, will overrun and take possession of this country. They will build wigwams and villages all over the land, and their domain will extend from sea to sea.

In my boyhood days I have chased the buffalo across the prairies, and hunted the elk in the groves; but where are they now? Long since they have left us; the near approach of the white man has frightened them away. The deer and the turkey will go next, and with them the sons of the forest.

Resistance to the aggression of the whites is useless; war is wicked and must result in our ruin. Therefore, let us submit to our fate, return not evil for evil, as this would offend the Great Spirit and bring ruin upon us. The time is near when our race will become extinct, and nothing left to show the world that we ever did exist . . . but this I do know, the monitor within my breast has taught me the will of the Great Spirit, and now tells me good Indians will be rewarded, and bad ones punished.

My friends, do not listen to the words of Black Hawk for he is trying to lead you astray. Do not imbrue your hands in human blood; for such is the work of the evil one, and will only lead to retribution upon our heads.

113 RED JACKET, Seneca, when aged and near death in 1830, tottered from lodge to lodge, paying a last ceremonial visit, to voice a final warning.

I am about to leave you, and when I am gone and my warning shall no longer be heard or regarded, the craft and avarice of the white man will prevail. Many winters I have breasted the storm, but I am an aged tree, and can stand no longer. My leaves are fallen, my branches are withered, and I am shaken by every breeze. Soon my aged trunk will be prostrated, and the foot of the exulting foe of the Indian may be placed upon it with safety; for I leave none who will be able to avenge such an injury. Think not I mourn for myself. I go to join the spirits of my fathers, where age cannot come; but my heart fails when I think of my people, who are soon to be scattered and forgotten.

114 SHAWUSKUKHKUNG was one of the last Delaware chiefs to speak before the New Jersey legislature. Most of the Delawares were out of the state by the mid 1700s, but in 1832 a claim was settled for $2,000, for Raritan River lands. It seemed a fortune to the exiled band.

Not a drop of our blood have you spilled in battle—not an acre of land have you taken but by our consent. . . . Nothing save benisons can fall upon her [New Jersey] from the lips of a Lenni-Lenape [Delaware].

There may be some who despise our Indian benedictions; but when I return to my people, and make known to them the result of my mission, the ear of the great

Master of Life, which is still open to our cry, will be penetrated with the invocation of blessing upon the generous sons of New Jersey.

115 In 1832, a Sioux chief was killed. Three white men were subsequently killed. Under severe questioning, an American Fur Company employee admitted that he had fired a random shot, for no particular purpose, into a group of Indians gathered on the far side of the river. He had been accused by a Sioux warrior himself under investigation by W. P. Hunt, fur company agent. The warrior, frowning, had pointed a finger at a man in Hunt's party and put the Indian's case succinctly.

We kill white men because white men kill us.

116 A delegation of three Nez Perce and one Flathead came to St. Louis in 1831 to see Governor William Clark. Two of them died during their stay, and the survivors took passage up the Missouri the following year on the steamboat *Yellowstone*. George Catlin was on board and painted the two Indians. Beyond these agreed-upon facts, the story is moot. Interpreters for these seldom-seen tribes in St. Louis were scarce, making understanding difficult. Why did these Indians come from so far away, from west of the Rockies? Probably for better "medicine." Protestants and Catholics alike, taking the red men's presumed request for religious instruction as a divinely inspired thirst for Christianity, seemed to let their enthusiasm run away with them; in their imaginativeness they likely invented a speech the Indians were too handicapped by language to communicate. It is included here because it does perhaps reflect something not unlike what the Indians might have thought as they departed and be-

cause the speech, as used by Christians in the East, was unusually influential in starting a missionary movement of great importance to the development of the Pacific Northwest.

I came over the trail of many moons from the setting sun. You were the friend of my fathers who have all gone the long way. I come with one eye partly open, for more light for my people who sit in darkness. I go back with both eyes closed. How can I go back blind to my blind people? I made my way to you with strong arms through many enemies and strange lands that I might carry back much to them. I go back with both arms broken and empty. Two fathers came with us. They were the braves of many winters and wars. We leave them to sleep by your great water and wigwams. They were tired of many moons and their moccasins wore out.

My people sent me to get the white man's Book of Heaven. You took me to where you allow your women to dance, as we do ours, and the Book was not there. You took me to where they worship the Great Spirit with candles and the Book was not there. You showed me the images of the good spirits and the pictures of the good lands beyond, but the Book was not among them to tell us the way. I am going back to the long sad trail to my people in the dark land. You make my feet heavy with gifts and my moccasins will grow old in carrying them, yet the Book is not among them. When I tell my poor blind people, after one more snow, in the Big Council, that I did not bring the Book, no word will be spoken by our old men or our young braves. One by one they will rise up and go out in silence. My people will die in darkness, and they will go on the long path to the hunting grounds. No white man will go with them and no white man's Book will make the way plain.

117 KOSATO, a renegade Blackfoot, living in a Nez Perce camp at Salmon River, told Captain B. L. E. Bonneville, in the fall of 1832, the reason he had forsaken his own people, and his vain attempts to get the peace-loving Nez Perce to retaliate for Blackfoot harassment.

You see my wife, she is good; she is beautiful. I love her. Yet she has been the cause of all my troubles. She was the wife of my chief. I loved her more than he did, and she knew it. We talked together, we laughed together. . . . The chief grew jealous. . . . He beat her without cause. . . . My horses were before my lodge. Suddenly the chief came . . . and called them his own. What could I do? He was the chief. . . .

As I looked down upon the meadow I saw the chief walking among the horses. I fastened my eyes upon him as a hawk's; my blood boiled; I drew my breath hard. He went among the willows. In an instant I was on my feet; my hand was on my knife—I flew rather than ran. . . . I sprang upon him and with two blows laid him dead at my feet. I covered his body with earth. . . . I hastened to her I loved, told her what I had done, and urged her to fly with me. She answered me with tears. . . . I again urged her to fly; but she only wept more, and told me to go. My heart was heavy but my eyes dry. I folded my arms, "It is well, Kosato will go alone to the desert. None will be with him but the wild beasts of the plains. The seekers of blood will follow on his trail. They may come upon him when he sleeps and glut their revenge; but you will be safe. Kosato will go alone. . . ."

I turned away. She sprang after me, seizing me in her arms, "No, Kosato shall not go alone. Wherever he goes I will go—he shall never part from me." . . .

Speeding day and night, we soon reached this tribe. They received us with welcome, and we have dwelt with them in peace. They are good and kind; they are honest; but their hearts are the hearts of women.

71

118 KEOKUK, peace chief of the Sauk nation, was host to Black Hawk in 1832, when Black Hawk tried to rally Keokuk's village to war on the settlers. Keokuk was the last to speak [overheard by Josiah Smart, concealed in a lodge near by].

Head-men, Chiefs, Braves and Warriors of the Sauks: I have heard and considered your demand to be led forth upon the warpath against the palefaces, to avenge the many wrongs, persecutions, outrages and murders committed by them upon our people. I deeply sympathise with you. . . . Few, indeed, are our people who do not mourn the death of some near and dear loved one at the hands of the Long Guns, who are becoming very numerous. Their cabins are as plenty as the trees in the forest, and their soldiers are springing up like grass on the prairies. They have talking thunder, which carries death a long way off. . . . In a contest where our numbers are so unequal to theirs we must ultimately fail. All we can reasonably expect or hope is to wreak our vengeance upon their hated heads, and fall, when fall we must, with our faces to the enemy. . . .

It is my duty as your chief to be your father while in the paths of peace, and your leader and champion while on the war path. You have decided to follow the path of war, and I will lead you to victory if the Great Spirit prevails. . . . But what shall we do with our old and infirm, our women and children? We cannot take them with us upon the war path, for they would hamper our movements and defeat us of our vengeance. We dare not leave them behind, doomed to perish of hunger or fall captive to the palefaces, who would murder the old and the young, but reserve our wives and daughters for a fate worse than death itself.

I will lead you forth upon the war path, but upon this condition: That we first put our wives and children, our aged and infirm, gently to sleep in that slumber that knows no waking this side of spirit land. . . . Our every feeling of humanity tells us we cannot take them with us and dare not leave them behind us. . . .

[Turning to Black Hawk] Your long experience upon the war path tells you I have spoken the truth; yet, with all your wonderful eloquence, you have urged upon us this terrible sacrifice. Brooding over oft-repeated wrongs committed by the palefaces upon you and your people, your mind has grown weak, until you have lent a willing ear to the whisperings of evil counselors, who cannot speak the truth, because their tongues are forked, like the viper's.

They came to you under the guise and pretense of friendship, and by the use of base flattery and hypocrisy gained your confidence, only to lead you in the crooked path of ruin and destruction. They are enemies of you and your band, instead of friends. They first told you the British Father had promised you aid and assistance, in warriors as well as guns, tomahawks, spears, knives, ammunition and provisions, as soon as you should recross the Mississippi at the head of a hostile army. . . . The British Father is at peace with our Great Father at Washington, and neither knows nor cares for you or your grievances. . . . The same evil counselors have told you that the moment you shall sound your war whoop east of the Mississippi all the Indian tribes . . . will rise as a single warrior . . . to avenge their wrongs upon the white settlers [with whom] . . . they are on terms of peace and good will. . . . Yet they have told you that these Indians across the river were not only ready but eager to join you in a general massacre . . . only waiting Saukenuk to begin the slaughter. If this be true, why are not their great war chiefs here tonight? Where are Wauponsee, the Red Devil, Big Thunder, Shaata and Meachelle? . . .

I beseech you . . . by everything you hold sacred and dear, abandon this wild visionary and desperate undertaking and return to your village. Seed time is here but your grounds have not been prepared for the planting. Go back and plant the summer's crop. Arise to the dignity and grandeur of your honored position as the father of your gallant little band, shake off the base fetters of the

Bad Spirit. . . . If you persist in going upon the war path against the white people, then indeed may we bid farewell to Black Hawk, whose protecting spirit has forsaken him in his old age and suffered his star of success—which has led him in triumph to a hundred victories on the war path—to go down behind a cloud, never to rise again; and when the Pauguk comes, his lofty spirit will depart, groping its way doubtingly along the dark and crooked path to the land of dreams.

119 TAIMAH, a Fox chief, sent a letter from Flint Hall in Iowa, dated July 22, 1832, to General William Clark. Taimah's people had moved from their Rock River village to Iowa in 1828.

Last spring, when the unfortunate, infatuated band of our people [Black Hawk followers], now at war with the white people, visited our village on the way to Rock River, I, Taimah, used my best endeavors to learn their designs; and I was only able to discover this—that their minds were greatly corrupted by various foreign fables brought, I believe, from Canada, by those of our people who visit that country. . . .

Father: We will relate one of these fables. We were told that the Americans were shortly to lay hands on all our males, both young and old, and deprive them of those parts which are said to be essential to courage; then, a horde of negro men were to be brought from the South, to whom our wives, sisters, and daughters were to be given, for the purpose of raising a stock of slaves to supply the demand in this country where negroes are scarce. . . . Influenced by a belief of the above fables, they have uniformly treated the dead bodies of the unfortunate white men who have fallen into their hands with the same indignities which they themselves so much dreaded.

120 CHAETAR, a young Winnebago, addressed agent Joseph M. Street at Prairie du Chien, after the Battle of the Bad Axe brought the Black Hawk War of 1832 to a close. Black Hawk himself, in his autobiography, claims to have *voluntarily* surrendered to the U.S. government through the Winnebagos.

I am young to make speeches. This is the second time I have spoken before the people. My father, I am no chief; I am no orator, but I have been allowed to address you. If I should not speak as well as the others, still you must listen to me. My father, when you made the talk to the chiefs, Waugh-kon Dacori, Carmenee Dacori, and the others that day—I was there and I heard you. I thought what you said to them you also said to me. You said if these two [Black Hawk and the Prophet, White Cloud] were brought to you, a black cloud would be lifted from the Winnebago. My father, your words entered my ears and my heart. I left that very night . . . I have had much trouble. I have been a great way . . . I did what you said to do. Near the Dalles of Wisconsin I took Black Hawk. No one did it but me. I say this in the ears of all present; they know it to be true. My father, I am no chief, but what I have done I have done for the benefit of my nation . . . My father, that one, Wabkishick, is my kinsman. If he is hurt I do not wish to see it. The soldiers sometimes stick the ends of their guns in the backs of prisoners. I hope this will not be done to these men.

121 BLACK HAWK addressed J. M. Street at Prairie du Chien, August 27, 1832.

You have taken me prisoner with all my warriors. I am much grieved for I expected, if I did not defeat you, to hold out much longer and give you more trouble before I surrendered. . . . Your guns were well aimed. The bullets flew like birds in the air and whizzed by my ears like the wind in trees in winter. My warriors fell around me.

It began to look dismal. The sun rose dim on us in the morning, and at night it sank in a dark cloud that looked like a ball of fire. That was the last sun that shone on Black Hawk. His heart is dead and no longer beats quick in his bosom. He is now a prisoner of the white man; they will do with him as they wish. But he can stand torture, and he is not afraid of death. He is no coward. Black Hawk is an Indian. . . .

An Indian who is as bad as a white man could not live in our nation; he would be put to death and eaten by the wolves. The white men are bad schoolmasters; they carry false looks and deal in false actions; they smile in the face of the poor Indian to cheat him; they shake him by the hand to gain his confidence, to make him drunk, to deceive him, to ruin his wife.

We told them to let us alone and keep away from us; but they followed on, and beset our paths, and they coiled themselves among us, like the snake. They poisoned us by the touch. We are not safe. We live in danger. We are becoming like them; hypocrites and liars, adulterers, lazy drones; all talkers and no workers.

We looked up to the Great Spirit. We went to our great father [the president]. We were encouraged. His council gave us fair words and big promises; but we got no satisfaction.

Things were growing worse. . . . We called a great council and built a large fire. The spirits of our fathers arose and spoke to us to avenge our wrongs or die. We all spoke before the council fire. It was warm and pleasant. We set up the war whoop and dug up the tomahawk; our knives were ready, and the heart of Black Hawk swelled high in his bosom when he led his warriors into battle. He is satisfied. He will go to the world of spirits contented. He has done his duty. His father will meet him there and commend him.

Black Hawk is a true Indian, and disdains to cry like a woman. He feels for his wife, his children and friends. But he does not care for himself. He cares for his nation, and the Indians. They will suffer. He laments their fate. The white men do not scalp the head; but they do worse

—they poison the heart; it is not pure with them. His countrymen will not be scalped, but they will, in a few years, become like the white man, so that you can't trust them. . . .

Farewell, my nation! . . . He can do no more. He is near his end. His sun is setting, and will rise no more. Farewell to Black Hawk!

122 A Nez Perce spokesman reported to B. L. E. Bonneville at a council of Nez Perce, Flatheads, and Pends Oreilles, in the Green River Valley, the winter of 1832-33, after the Captain offered to mediate with their enemies, the Blackfeet.

War is a bloody business, and always full of evil; but it keeps the eyes of the chiefs always open, and makes the limbs of the young men strong and supple. In war every one is on the alert. If we see a trail we know it must be an enemy; if the Blackfeet come to us, we know it is for war, and we are ready. Peace, on the other hand, sounds no alarms; the eyes of the chiefs are closed in sleep, and the young men are sleek and lazy. The horses stray in the mountain, the women and their little ones go about alone.

But the heart of the Blackfoot is a lie, and his tongue is a trap. If he says peace, it is to deceive. He comes to us as a brother; he smokes his pipe with us; but when he sees us off guard, he will slay and steal. We will have no such peace; let there be war!

123 SOUWAHNOCK, a Delaware chief, spoke at a council fire held at Fort Leavenworth in 1833, called to end tribal warfare among the Plains Indians.

The Pawnees met my young men on the hunt and slew them. I have had my revenge. Let them look at their town. I found it filled with lodges, I left it a heap of ashes. . . . I am satisfied. . . . I am not afraid to avow the deed I have done, for I am Souwahnock, a Delaware warrior; but I am willing to bury the tomahawk and smoke the pipe of peace with my enemies. They are brave men and fight well.

124 WILD HORSE, the Pawnee, at the same Fort Leavenworth council in 1833, spoke in his turn, after Souwahnock, agreeing to peace with his enemy.

I have promised to the Delawares the friendship of my tribe. I respect my promise, and I cannot lie, for I am a Pawnee chief.

125 ARAPOOISH, Crow chief, in late summer of 1833, spoke in eulogy of his beloved country to Robert Campbell of the Rocky Mountain Fur Company. The Crow dynasty extended from the Black Hills to the Rocky Mountains.

The Crow country is a good country. The Great Spirit put it exactly in the right place; while you are in it you fare well; whenever you are out of it, whichever way you travel, you fare worse. . . . The Crow country is exactly in the right place. It has snowy mountains and sunny plains, all kinds of climate and good things for every season. When the summer heats scorch the prairies, you can draw up under the mountains, where the air is sweet and cool, the grasses fresh, and the bright streams come tumbling out of the snowbanks. There you can hunt the elk, the deer, and the antelope, when their skins are fit for dressing; there you will find plenty of white bear and mountain sheep.

If the autumn, when your horses are fat and strong from the mountain pastures, you can go into the plains and hunt the buffalo, or trap beaver on the streams. And when winter comes on, you can take shelter in the woody bottoms along the rivers; there you will find buffalo meat for yourselves, and cottonwood bark for your horses; or you may winter in Wind River Valley, where there is salt weed in abundance.

The Crow country is exactly in the right place. Everything good is to be found there. There is no place like Crow country.

126 MUSCAHTEWISHAH, war chief of Kishko's dissident Kickapoo band, refused to peacefully settle on the Missouri River. Before a council held late in September 1833, William Clark was given the following explanation for their behavior by Muscahtewishah himself.

Our young men and chiefs do not agree as they did some time ago. Some wish one thing, some another. Some would go to the prairie, where there is game. Some would stay and raise cattle and corn. We are like fish in the water, we jump at whatever is thrown.

127 BLACK HAWK, prisoner at Jefferson Barracks, Missouri, was told by American officers in 1834 that Keokuk was now chief of the entire Sauk tribe, and he must be listened to with respect. Black Hawk's pride was affronted and he struck at Keokuk with his breechclout.

I am a man—an old man! I will not obey the counsels of anyone—no one shall govern me. I am old, my hair is grey. I once gave counsels to young men—am I to be ruled by others? I shall soon go to the Great Spirit where I shall be at rest. What I said to the Great Father in Washington, I will say again—I will listen to *him*. I am done.

128 KEOKUK, at Jefferson Barracks, 1834, had come to ask for Black Hawk's release. At first he chided him for his outburst, then defended him, offering the ultimate in diplomacy, tact, and compassion.

Why do you speak so before the white men? I will talk for you; you are shaken—you did not mean what you said. [turns to council] Our brother who has come again among us has spoken, but he has spoken in wrath—his tongue was forked—he spoke not as a man—a Sauk. He knew his words were bad; he trembled like the oak whose roots have been wasted by many rains. He is old. What he has said let us forget. He says he did not mean it—he wishes it forgotten. I have spoken for him. What I have said are his own words—not mine. Let us say he spoke in council today—that his words were *good*. I have spoken.

129 KEOKUK, despite his efforts to propitiate the whites, shortly discovered he too must depart with his people across the Mississippi River, to fulfil the Treaty of Chicago of September 26, 1833.

The many moons and sunny days we have lived here will long be remembered by us. The Great Spirit has smiled upon us and made us glad. But we have agreed to go.

We go to a country we know little of. Our home will be beyond a great river on the way to the setting sun. We will build our wigwams there in another land. . . .

The men we leave here in possession of these lands cannot say Keokuk or his people ever took up the tomahawk. . . . In peace we bid you goodbye. . . . If you come see us, we will gladly welcome you.

130 George Catlin, the American artist who traveled and painted his way through the West during the 1830s, left us, in his art, one of the most important and authentic views of the American Indian.

I have seen him shrinking from civilized approach, which came with all its vices, like the dead of night, upon him . . . seen him gaze and then retreat like the frightened deer. . . . I have seen him shrinking from the soil and haunts of his boyhood, bursting the strongest ties which bound him to the earth and its pleasures. I have seen him set fire to his wigwam and smooth over the graves of his fathers . . . clap his hand in silence over his mouth, and take the last look over his fair hunting ground, and turn his face in sadness to the setting sun. All this I have seen performed in nature's silent dignity . . . and I have seen as often the approach of the bustling, busy, talking, whistling, hopping, elated, and exulting white man, with the first dip of the ploughshare, making sacrilegious trespass on the bones of the valiant dead. . . . I have seen . . . the grand and irresistible march of civilization. I have seen this splendid juggernaut rolling on and beheld its sweeping desolation, and held converse with the happy thousands, living as yet beyond its influence, who have not been crushed, nor yet have dreamed of its approach. . . .

I love a people who have always made me welcome to the best they had . . . who are honest without laws, who have no jails and no poor-houses . . . who never take the name of God in vain . . . who worship God without a Bible, and I believe God loves them also, . . . who are free from religious animosities . . . who have never raised a hand against me, or stolen my property, where there is no law to punish either, . . . who never fought a battle with white men except on their own ground . . . and Oh, how I love a people who don't live for the love of money!

131 A Blackfoot wife, lost on the plains with a young white trapper, was rescued, June 10, 1835, by members of the Bonneville Expedition. She explained later why she had run away to a Nez Perce camp, eventually taking up with the trapper.

I was the wife of a Blackfoot warrior, and I served him faithfully. Who was so well-served as he? Whose lodge was so well provided, or kept so clean? I brought wood in the morning, and placed water always at hand. I watched for his coming; and he found his food cooked and waiting. If he rose to go forth there was nothing to delay him. I searched the thought that was in his heart, to save him the trouble of speaking. When I went abroad on errands for him, the chiefs and warriors smiled upon me, the braves spoke soft things, in secret; but my feet were in the straight path, and my eyes could see nothing but him.

When he went out to hunt, or to war, who aided to equip him but I? When he returned I met him at the door; I took his gun; and he entered without further thought. While he sat and smoked, I unloaded his horses; tied them to stakes, brought in their loads, and was quickly at his feet. If this moccasins were wet I took them off and put on others which were warm and dry. I dressed all the skins that were taken in the chase. He could never say to me, why is it not done? He hunted the deer, and the antelope, and the buffalo, and he watched for the enemy. Everything else was done by me. When our people moved their camp; it was I who packed the horses and led them on the journey. He mounted his horse and rode away; free as though he had fallen from the skies. He had nothing to do with the labor of the camp. When we halted in the evening, he sat with other braves and smoked, it was I who pitched his lodge; and when he came to eat and sleep, his supper and bed were ready.

I served him faithfully; and what was my reward? A cloud was always on his brow, and sharp lightning on his

82

tongue. I was his dog; and not his wife. Who was it scarred and bruised me? It was he.

132 MENEWA, Creek leader who had been friend to the whites, found in 1836 that he must go chained with the other "hostiles" in the march westward. He spent the night at Okfuskee alone, and in the morning he spoke tearfully to a white friend.

Last night I saw the sun set for the last time, and its light shine upon the tree tops, and the land, and the water, that I am never to look upon again.

133 THE FOUR BEARS, a Mandan warrior, spoke to his people on the day he died, July 30, 1837, about the small pox epidemic decimating the tribe. Francis Chardon, a trader, recorded the speech in his journal.

My Friends one and all, Listen to what I have to say— Ever since I can remember, I have loved the Whites, I have lived With them ever since I was a Boy, and to the best of my Knowledge, I have never Wronged a White Man, on the Contrary, I have always Protected them from the insults of Others, Which they cannot deny. The 4 Bears never saw a White Man hungry, but what he gave him to eat. Drink, and a Buffaloe skin to sleep on, in time of Need. I was always ready to die for them, Which they cannot deny. I have done every thing that a red Skin could do for them, and how have they repaid it! With ingratitude! I have Never Called a White Man a Dog, but to day, I do Pronounce them to be a set of Black harted Dogs, they have deceived Me, them that I always considered as Brothers, has turned Out to be My Worst enemies. I have been in Many Battles, and often Wounded, but the Wounds of My enemies I exhalt in, but to day I am Wounded, and by Whom, by those same

White Dogs that I have always Considered, and treated as Brothers. I do not fear *Death* my friends. You Know it, but to *die* with my face rotten, that even the Wolves will shrink with horror at seeing Me, and say to themselves, that is the 4 Bears the Friend of the Whites—

Listen well what I have to say, as it will be the last time you will hear Me. think of your Wives, Children, Brothers, Sisters, Friends, and in fact all that you hold dear, are all Dead, or Dying, with their faces all rotten, caused by those dogs the whites, think of all that My friends, and rise all together and Not leave one of them alive.

134 TSALI, a Cherokee, caught in a roundup by General Winfield Scott's army in August 1838, killed a soldier pushing his wife with a gun barrel. Tied to a tree in the Great Smokies, waiting death, he pled with a friend to find his child lost in the fracas.

Euchela, there is one favor I wish to ask at your hands. You know I have a little boy who was lost among the mountains. I want you to find that boy, if he is not dead, and tell him the last words of his father were that he must never go beyond the Father of Waters, but die in the land of his birth. It is sweet to die in one's native land and be buried by the margins of one's native stream.

135 OSCEOLA, Seminole chief, took part in the second Seminole War in Florida. He was made prisoner while under a flag of truce and died in a cell at Fort Moultrie, Georgia in 1838.

They could not capture me except under a white flag. They cannot hold me except with a chain.

136 SHAUBENEE and BILLY CALDWELL, former Illinois aides of Tecumseh, surprisingly spoke in behalf of William Henry Harrison during his campaign for the Presidency, when his opponents branded him the coward of the Battle of the Thames, 1813.

Council Bluffs, 23rd March, 1840

To General Harrison's Friends:

The other day several newspapers were brought to us; and peeping over them, to our astonishment, we found the hero of the late war called a coward. This would have surprised the tall Braves, Tecumseh, of the Shawnees, and Round Head and Walk-In-The-Water, of the Wyandots. If the departed could rise again, they would say to the white men that General Harrison was the terror of the late tomahawkers. The first time we met with General Harrison, it was at the Council Fire of the late Tempest, General Wayne, on the headwaters of the Wabash, at Greenville, 1795, from that time until 1811, we had many friendly smokes with him; but from 1812 we changed our tobacco smoke to powder smoke. Then we found General Harrison was a brave warrior, and humane to his prisoners, as reported to us by two of Tecumseh's young men who were taken in the fleet with Captain Barclay on the 10th of September, 1813; and on the Thames, where he routed both the red men and the British; and where he showed his courage, and his humanity to his prisoners, both white and red. (See) Report of Adam Brown and family, taken on the morning of that day in this country. We hope the good white men will protect the name of General Harrison.

We remain your friends forever.

Shaub-e-nee, Aid to Tecumseh.
B. Caldwell, Captain (called the Sauganash)

137 In 1840, the Belgium missionary, Father Pierre Jean de Smet, while traveling through present-day Montana, asked a Blackfoot chief why the Indians first raised their hands to the sky and then smote the ground.

This is the happiest day of my life. For the first time we behold a man so closely allied with the Great Spirit! . . . . When we lift our hands we signify our dependence on the Great Spirit. . . . We strike the ground to signify that we are only worms and miserable creeping beings in his sight.

138 CRAZY BEAR, Assiniboin chief, in December 1843 returned to Fort William in fine clothes, carrying a jug of rum given him by a competitor of the American Fur Company to win his trade. But he reassured Alexander Culbertson that such would not be the case.

I suppose you think I have left our big house. No, I am not a child. I went below to see the chief, who treated me well. I did not ask for anything. I did not refuse his presents. But these cannot make me abandon this house, where are buried the remains of our fathers, whose tracks are yet fresh in all paths leading to this place. Do you think I am a child to be seduced by trinkets?

139 PIED RICHE, Potawatomi chief, welcomed the Mormons migrating from Illinois after the Joseph and Hyrum Smith murders in 1844, and invited them to settle near them, north of Omaha, on the banks of the Missouri River.

The Potawatomi came, sad and tired, to this unhealthy Missouri bottoms not many years back. Now you are driven away, the same way from your lodges and your lands . . . and the graves of your people. So we have both suffered. We must help one another and the Great Spirit will help us both.

140   A Crow warrior in June 1849, at Crow Creek, was outraged when he learned the boat containing food, goods, and annuities was going on to Fort Pierce instead of unloading. He spoke sharply to the young agent, Major Hatting.

I am not a chief, but I am a warrior. I see that my chiefs all hang their heads down waiting some reply from their father, as they do not know what to do nor say [strikes tomahawk violently on the table]. But I know what to do. Hold up your head when you speak to chiefs and warriors, look them in the eye! You are young, but we suppose you must have some sense, or our great father would not have sent you here. My chiefs have spoken, but it seems they have not been heard. I tell you these goods were promised here, and they will go no further. . . . Do you hear that? That is what I have to say as a warrior! [The boat was unloaded.]

141   MANGAS COLORADAS, Apache chief, took exception in 1851, when, during a Mexico-U.S. border survey, J. R. Bartlett, head of the Surveying Commission, tried to rescue two Mexican boys from the Indian camp, then attempted to buy them, to no avail.

You came into our country. You were well-received. Your lives, your property, your animals, were safe. You passed by ones, by twos, by threes through our country. You went and came in peace. Your strayed animals were always brought home to you again. Our wives,—our women and children came here and visited at your houses. We were friends—we were brothers! Believing this, we came among you and brought our captives, relying on it that we were brothers and that you would feel as we feel.

We concealed nothing. We came not secretly nor in the night. We came in open day, and before your faces, and showed our captives to you. We believed your assurances of friendship, and we trusted them. Why did you take our captives from us?

The brave who owns these captives does not want to sell. He has had one of these boys six years. He grew up under him. His heartstrings are bound around him. He is as a son in his old age. . . . Money cannot buy affection. His heart cannot be sold. He taught him to string the bow and wield the lance. He loves the boy and cannot sell him.

142 GERONIMO, Apache, absent from a hunting camp with his fellows in 1852, returned to find that the Mexican military governor of Sonora had crossed the boundary and slaughtered most in camp. Geronimo lost his wife whom he had married at seventeen, his three children, and his widowed mother. Later he described his emotions.

Without being noticed I silently turned away and stood by the river. How long I stood there I do not know, but when I saw the warriors arranging for a council I took my place among them.

That night I did not give my vote for or against any measure—without arms we could do nothing. . . . Our chief, Mangas Coloradas, gave the order to start at once in perfect silence for our homes in Arizona, leaving the dead. . . .

I stood still until all had passed, hardly knowing what I would do—I had no weapon, nor did I hardly wish to fight, nor did I contemplate recovering the bodies of my loved ones, for that was forbidden. I did not pray, nor did I resolve to do anything in particular, for I had no purpose left. I finally followed the tribe in silence, keeping just within hearing distance of the soft noise of their feet.

143 CHEQUITO, aged chief of the Liepans, was encountered on Comanche Creek by General Horace Capron, head of a U.S. Texas Expedition, August 1852. He bemoaned the dilemma of his people.

Once we were numerous in this country; plentiful was the game, and there was no sickness. Our first enemy was the Comanche from the south, then came the Spaniard with his diseases, then the Texian with guns, until our tribe was reduced. On one side was the Comanche, on the other side was the white man with his fiery spirits that debauched our young braves, and with his many sicknesses, have prostrated them in the dust.

Dare we plant corn, the white man comes upon us, and drives us on before it has ripened. All but disappeared is the game. What are we to do? Give us a country we can call our own, and we will move upon it, and always be the friend of the white man.

144 OLD BRAVE, Assiniboin warrior, spoke for Blue Thunder, his absent chief, August 1853, when Governor Isaac Stevens visited the camp while making reconnaissance along The River of Lakes. Old Brave reiterated the universal plaint of the Indian.

My father, you see us as we are. We are poor. We have but few blankets and little clothing. The great Father of Life who made us and gave us this land to live upon, made the buffalo and other game to afford us sustenance; their meat is our only food; with their skins we clothe ourselves and build our lodges. They are our only means of life—food, fuel, and clothing. . . . We soon will be deprived of these; starvation and cold will destroy us. The buffalo are fast disappearing. . . . As the white man advances, our means of life grows less. . . .

We hear a great trail is to be made through our country. We do not know what this is for; we do not understand it, but we think it will scare away the buffalo.

145 LOW HORN, Piegan chief, attended a council of Blackfeet, Piegans, and Bloods, September 21, 1853. All were dressed with ceremonial care in deerskins, elk, and antelope, fine feathers and exquisite beadwork. He was chagrined when Governor Isaac Stevens of Washington Territory arrived in soiled riding clothes.

We dress up to receive you, and why do you not wear the dress of a chief?

146 Frederick Remington:

There is a dignity about the social intercourse of old Indians which reminds me of a stroll through a winter forest.

147 SEATTLE (Seathl), Dwamish chief, spoke to Isaac Stevens, Governor of Washington Territory, in 1854.

Yonder sky that has wept tears of compassion upon my people for centuries untold, and which to us appears changeless and eternal, may change. Today is fair. Tomorrow it may be overcast with clouds. My words are like the stars that never change. Whatever Seattle says the great chief at Washington can rely upon with as much certainty as he can upon the return of the sun or the seasons. The White Chief says that Big Chief at Washington sends us greetings of friendship and goodwill. That is kind of him for we know he has little need of our friendship in return. His people are many. They are like the grass that covers vast prairies. My people are few. They resemble the scattering trees of a storm-swept plain . . . I will not dwell on, nor mourn over, our untimely decay, nor reproach our paleface brothers with hastening it, as we too may have been somewhat to blame. . . .

Your God is not our God. Your God loves your people and hates mine. He folds his strong and protecting arms lovingly about the paleface and leads him by the hand as a father leads his infant son—but He has forsaken His red children—if they really are his. Our God, the Great Spirit, seems also to have forsaken us. Your God makes your people strong every day. Soon they will fill the land. Our people are ebbing away like a rapidly receding tide that will never return. The white man's God cannot love our people or He would protect them. They seem to be orphans who can look nowhere for help. How then can we be brothers? . . . We are two distinct races with separate origins and separate destinies. There is little in common between us.

To us the ashes of our ancestors are sacred and their resting place is hallowed ground. You wander far from the graves of your ancestors and seemingly without regret. Your religion was written upon tables of stone by the iron finger of your God so that you could not forget. The Red Man could never comprehend nor remember it. Our religion is the traditions of our ancestors—the dreams of our old men, given them in solemn hours of night by the Great Spirit; and the visions of our sachems; and it is written in the hearts of our people.

Your dead cease to love you and the land of their nativity as soon as they pass the portals of the tomb and wander way beyond the stars. They are soon forgotten and never return. Our dead never forget the beautiful world that gave them being.

Day and night cannot dwell together. The Red Man has ever fled the approach of the White Man, as the morning mist flees before the morning sun. However, your proposition seems fair and I think that my people will accept it and will retire to the reservation you offer them. Then we will dwell apart in peace. . . . It matters little where we pass the remnant of our days. They will not be many. A few more moons; a few more winters—and not one of the descendants of the mighty hosts that once moved over this broad land or lived in happy homes, protected by the Great Spirit, will remain to mourn over the graves of a people once more powerful and hopeful than yours. But why should I mourn at the untimely fate of my people? Tribe follows tribe, and nation follows nation, like the waves of the sea. It is the order of nature, and regret is useless. Your time of decay may be distant, but it will surely come, for even the White Man whose God walked and talked with him as friend with friend, cannot be exempt from the common destiny. We may be brothers after all. We will see. . . .

Every part of this soil is sacred in the estimation of my people. Every hillside, every valley, every plain and grove, has been hallowed by some sad or happy event in days long vanished. The very dust upon which you now stand responds more lovingly to their footsteps than to yours, because it is rich with the blood of our ancestors and our bare feet are conscious of the sympathetic touch. Even the little children who lived here and rejoiced here for a brief season will love these somber solitudes and at eventide they greet shadowy returning spirits. And when the last Red Man shall have perished, and the memory of my tribe shall have become a myth among the White Men, these shores will swarm with the invisible dead of my tribe, and when your children's children think themselves alone in the field, the store, the shop, upon the highway, or in the silence of the pathless woods, they will not be alone. At night when the streets of your cities and villages are silent and you think them deserted, they will throng with the returning hosts that once filled and still love this beautiful land. The White Man will never be alone.

Let him be just and deal kindly with my people, for the dead are not powerless. Dead, did I say? There is no death, only a change of worlds.

148 PEOPEO MOXMOX, Yakima chief, spoke out at a council called by Governor Isaac Stevens, June 2, 1855, on the Chehalis River, Oregon, to induce the Indians to sell their lands and go to a reservation.

We have listened to all you have to say, and we desire you to listen when any Indian speaks. . . . In one day the Americans have become as numerous as grass. I know the value of your speech from having experienced it in California. . . . We had not seen in the true light the object of your speeches. . . . You have talked in a round-about way. Speak straight! Goods and the earth are not equal. Goods are for using on earth. I have ears to hear you and here is my heart. . . . You have spoken in a manner partly tending to evil. Speak plain to us.

149 EAGLE WING of the Nez Perce, because they had been promised their Wallowa country, felt he must warn Governor Isaac Stevens that a Cayuse tribe, egged on by Peopeo Moxmox, planned a massacre of the whites at the 1855 council.

I will come with my family and pitch my lodge in the midst of your camp, that those Cayuses may see that you and your party are under the protection of the head chief of the Nez Perces.

150 LITTLE CROW, a Dakota Sioux in Minnesota, led a reservation tribe from 1851 to 1862; tension was high due to white harassment and trickery. When government provisions and annuities failed to arrive in the summer of 1862, agency trader Andrew Myrick refused credit, saying, "Let them eat grass or their own dung." This became a war cry of the young Sioux who called Little Crow a coward for trying to quiet them.

We are only little herds of buffalo left scattered; the great herds that once covered the prairies are no more. See!—the white men are like the locusts when they fly so thick that the whole sky is a snowstorm. You may kill one—two—ten; yes, as many as the leaves in the forest yonder, and their brothers will not miss them. Kill one, kill two, kill ten, and ten times ten will come to kill you. Count your fingers all day long and white men with guns in their hands will come faster than you can count.

Yes, they fight among themselves [the Civil War]—away off. Do you hear the thunder of their big guns? No, it would take you two moons to run down to where they are fighting, and all the way your path would be among white soldiers as thick as tamaracks in the swamps of the Ojibways. Yes, they fight among themselves, but if you strike at them they will all turn on you and devour you and your women and little children just as the locusts in their time fall on the trees and devour all the leaves in one day.

You are fools. You cannot see the face of your chief; your eyes are full of smoke. You cannot hear his voice; your ears are full of roaring waters. Braves, you are little children—you are fools. You will die like the rabbits when the hungry wolves hunt them in the Hard Moon of January.

Little Crow is not a coward. He will die with you.

151 WOWINAPA, son of Little Crow, remained at large with his father after General H. H. Sibley ended the Sioux uprising in 1862. Little Crow was shot by deer hunters in July 1863. His young son, picked up later, told about it.

I am the son of Little Crow; my name is Wowinapa. I am sixteen years old. . . . Father hid after the soldiers beat us last fall. . . . There were no horses. . . . We were hungry. . . . Father and I were picking berries near Scatter Lake. . . . It was near night. He was hit the first time in the side, just above the hip. . . . He was shot the second time near the shoulder. This was the shot that killed him. He told me he was killed and asked for water. He died.

152 RED CLOUD, great Sioux leader, aroused at the sight of Union Pacific Railroad surveyors laying out a route through buffalo country in 1866 and incensed that a few small tribes welcomed them, spoke with vigor at an Indian council fire on Powder River.

Hear ye, Dakotas! When the Great Father at Washington sent us his chief soldier [Gen. W. S. Harney] to ask for a path through our hunting grounds, a way for his iron horse to the mountains and the western sea, we were told they merely wished to pass through our country, not to tarry among us, but to seek for gold in the far west. Our old chiefs thought to show their friendship and good will, when they allowed this dangerous snake in our midst. They promised to protect the wayfarers.

Yet before the ashes of the council fire are cold, the Great Father is building his forts among us. You have heard the sound of the white soldier's ax upon the Little Piney. His presence here is an insult and a threat. It is an insult to the spirits of my ancestors. Are we then to give up their sacred graves to be plowed for corn? Dakotas, I am for war!

153 RAIN-IN-THE-FACE, noted Hunkpapa Sioux, in 1905, not long before his death, related a youthful exploit—a daring attack on Fort Totten in North Dakota during the summer of 1866.

Hohay . . . was the leader in this raid. Waupaypay, the Fearless Bear, who was hanged afterwards at Yankton, was the bravest man among us. He dared Hohay to make the charge. Hohay accepted the challenge, and in turn dared the other to ride with him through the agency and right under the walls of the fort, which was garrisoned and strong.

Waupaypay and I in those days called each other brother-friend. It was a life and death vow. What one does the other must do; and that meant I must be in the forefront of the charge, and if he is killed, I must fight until I die also.

I prepared for death. I painted as usual like the eclipse of the sun, half-black and half-red. Now the signal for the charge was given! I started even with Waupaypay, but his horse was faster than mine, so he left me a little behind as we neared the fort. This was bad for me, for by this time the soldiers had somewhat recovered from the big surprise and were aiming better.

Their big guns talked very loud, but my Waupaypay was leading on, leaning forward on his fleet pony like a flying squirrel on a smooth log! He held his rawhide shield on the right side, a little to the front, and so did I. Our warwhoop was like the coyotes singing in the evening when they smelled blood!

The soldiers' guns talked fast, but few were hurt. Their big gun was like a toothless old dog who makes himself hotter the more noise he makes.

How much harm we did I do not know. We made things lively for a time; and the white men acted as people do when a swarm of bees get into camp. We made a successful retreat.

154 WHITE SHIELD, Arikara chief, in 1867 refused to sign at the agency for goods not received by his people. His agent threatened him with jail but the good chief was not intimidated.

I am old, it is true; but not old enough to fail to see things as they are, and even, as you say, if I am now just an old fool, I still would prefer a hundred times to be a honest red fool than a thieving white scamp like you.

155   SITTING BULL, the famous Hunkpapa Sioux, in 1867 at Fort Union on the Missouri River near the mouth of the Yellowstone, replied to a suggestion that he make peace with the U.S. government.

I have killed, robbed and injured too many white men to believe in a good peace. They are bad medicine; I would rather have my skin pierced with bullet holes. I don't want anything to do with a people who makes a brave carry water on his shoulders, or haul manure.

156   WHITE SHIELD, Arikara chief, was at an 1867 council of the Gros Ventre, Mandans, and Arikaras at Fort Berthold, to welcome Colonel P. R. de Trobriand, new Army officer for Dakota Territory.

The Dakotas of the lower plains [the Sioux] have sent messengers who have said to us: "Why do you stay friends with the Pale Faces? You are weak and poor and the white men scorn you. But we who steal their mules and horses, we who kill their warriors and attack their camps on the prairies, they are afraid of us; they ask for peace. . . . Do as we do, and you will have more spoils, and more presents, and you will be richer and stronger!" This is the message of the Dakota of the low country. Did we believe their words? No. Were we tempted by their promises? No. Did we act according to their advice? No. Between the Sioux and ourselves there is no score but the score of blood. And so, since they could not induce us to join them, they make war more vindictively than ever, and in the field of the dead are stretched three of our warriors on whom the rain has not fallen, since they were surprised and killed on our hunting grounds. . . .

Let my father listen to justice and let him grant what is just to his red children. The color of the skin makes no difference; what is good and just for one is good and just for the other, and the Great Spirit made all men brothers.

. . . I have a red skin, but my grandfather was a white man. What does it matter? It is not the color of the skin that makes me good or bad.

157 CROW BELLY (or Crow Breast), a Gros Ventre chief, arrived to visit Colonel P. R. de Trobriand, March 6, 1867, at Fort Stevenson in Dakota Territory.

The Great Spirit has given the white man great fore-sightedness; he sees everything at a distance, and his mind invents and makes the most extraordinary things; but the red man has been made shortsighted. He sees only what is close around him and knows nothing except what his father knew. . . . It is the Pale Faces who have brought the horse to the plains. . . . They have given us crockery pots and pots of iron to cook our food, and furnished us with guns and powder to kill more game. . . .

The Sioux, liars, thieves and murderers, have received presents in quantity and guns which they have used to kill us, and they are rich in horses and all things, while we have remained poor because we have not received all the things our Great Father has sent us. . . . But, when the great chief came to visit us a few years ago, he said to us: "My children, be faithful to the whites, obey your Great Father, keep the peace and do not break your word, and the smoke of your fires will go straight up to the sky."

We have done as our Great Father ordered, and, in spite of all, the smoke of our fires instead of rising straight up towards the heavens, is thrown upon the ground and has been chased by all the winds.

158 TEN BEARS, Yamparika Comanche, was one of the principal chiefs at the October 1867 council at Medicine Lodge Creek (Kansas), one of the largest treaty-making gatherings in U.S. history. Ten Bears spoke to the U.S. Commissioners.

My heart is filled with joy when I see you here, as the brook fills with water when the snow melts in the spring; and I feel glad as the ponies do when the fresh grass starts in the beginning of the year. I heard of your coming when I was many sleeps away, and I made but few camps before I met you. . . .

My people have never first drawn a bow or fired a gun against the whites. There has been trouble on the line between us, and my young men have danced with war dance. But it was not begun by us. It was you who sent out the first soldier and we who sent out the second. Two years ago I came upon this road, following the buffalo, that my wives and children might have their cheeks plump and their bodies warm. But the soldiers fired on us, and since that time there has been a noise like that of a thunderstorm, and we have not known which way to go. So it was upon the Canadian [River]. Nor have we been made to cry once alone. The blue-dressed soldiers and the Utes came from out of the night when it was dark and still, and for campfires they lit our lodges. Instead of hunting game they killed my braves, and the warriors of the tribe cut short their hair for the dead. So it was in Texas. They made sorrow come in our camps, and we went out like buffalo bulls when their cows are attacked. When we found them we killed them, and their scalps hang in our lodges. The Comanches are not weak and blind, like the pups of a dog when seven sleeps old. They are strong and farsighted, like grown horses. We took their road and we went on it. The white women cried and our women laughed.

But there are things which you have said to me which I do not like. They are not sweet like sugar, but bitter like gourds. You said that you wanted to put us upon a reservation, to build us houses and make us medicine lodges. I do not want them. I was born upon the prairie, where the wind blew free and there was nothing to break the light of the sun. I was born where there were no enclosures and where everything drew a free breath. I want to die there and not within walls. I know every stream and every wood

99

between the Rio Grande and the Arkansas. I have hunted and lived over that country. I lived like my fathers before me, and, like them, I lived happily.

When I was at Washington the Great White Father told me that all the Comanche Land was ours, and that no one should hinder us in living upon it. So, why do you ask us to leave the rivers, and the sun, and the wind, and live in houses? Do not ask us to give up the buffalo for the sheep. . . .

If the Texans had kept out of my country, there might have been peace. But that which you now say we must live on is too small. The Texans have taken away the places where the grass grew the thickest and the timber was the best. Had we kept that, we might have done the things you ask. But it is too late. The white man has the country which we loved, and we only wish to wander on the prairie until we die.

159 SATANTA, Kiowa chief, called the "Orator of the Plains," also spoke at Medicine Lodge.

I love the land and the buffalo and will not part with it. I want you to understand well what I say. Write it on paper. . . . I hear a great deal of good talk from the gentlemen whom the Great Father sends us, but they never do what they say. I don't want any of the medicine lodges [schools and churches] within the country. I want the children raised as I was. . . .

I have heard that you intend to settle us on a reservation near the mountains. I don't want to settle. I love to roam over the prairies. There I feel free and happy, but when we settle down we grow pale and die. I have laid aside my lance, bow, and shield, and yet I feel safe in your presence. I have told you the truth. I have no little lies hid about me, but I don't know how it is with the commissioners. Are they as clear as I am? A long time ago this land belonged to our fathers; but when I go up to the river I see camps of soldiers on its banks. These soldiers cut down my timber; they kill my buffalo; and when I see that, my heart feels like bursting; I feel sorry. I have spoken. [A decade later, confined to prison, Satanta committed suicide.]

160 WHITE CLOUD, Sioux chief, intercepted a half-breed and his men carrying mail between Fort Berthold and Fort Stevenson in December 1867 in Dakota Territory. Gardespie related the warning he received that day.

Do not complain, and consider yourself lucky to escape with your life. We let you go because we all know you, but do not come back or you will be treated like an American. For what difference is there between you and the Long Knives if you carry their writings, and if you are paid to serve them? Do you know what you are doing? You are not working for our life but our death, for the destruction of the redskins, of our warriors, our women and children. Wherever the whites are established, the buffalo is gone, the red hunters must die of hunger. Just a few years ago, the buffalo was grazing on both sides of the Missouri in countless herds; the prairie was often black with them, and living was easy for the Indian and his family, for they always had meat to eat and furs to trade. But the white man has advanced up the river; and their warriors are building a great many forts. . . . We cannot live on our own lands until they have gone from them.

161 COCHISE, Chiricahua Apache chief, talked with Tom Jeffords, a stage driver and U.S. mail operator out of Tucson. In the late 1860s, Jeffords made his way alone to Cochise's mountain camp to ask Cochise to stop killing his mail riders. Cochise agreed and the two became close friends. Remembering his first conversation with Cochise, Jeffords later recalled this query.

This is the country of the Chiricahua Apaches. This is the country where the Chiricahua Apaches belong. The mountains and the valleys, the days and the nights belong to the Chiricahua Apaches. It was so from the memory of the oldest man, and that memory comes from the oldest man ahead of him. There was none but the Indian here and the land was filled with food. The Indians could make a living for themselves. The men with steel came and tried to take it from us and we defeated them. Now the Americans—and none is more treacherous than the Americans, and none more arrogant. The Americans think they are better than other men. They make their own laws and say those laws must be obeyed. Why?

162 U.S. Commissioners, led by N. G. Taylor, in 1868 went west to study means of solving the Indian problem.

In making treaties it was enjoined on us to remove, if possible, the causes of complaint on the part of the Indians. . . . We have done the best we could under the circumstances. . . . Nobody pays any attention to Indian matters. This is a deplorable fact. . . . Naturally the Indian has many noble qualities. He is the very embodiment of courage. Indeed, at times he seems insensible to fear. If he is cruel and revengeful, it is because he is outlawed and his companion is the wild beast. Let civilization be his companion and the association warms into life virtues of the rarest worth. Civilization has driven him away from the home he loved; it has often tortured and killed him, but it could never make him a slave. As we have so little respect for those we enslave, to be consistent, this element of Indian character should challenge our admiration. . . . It is useless to go over the history of Indian removals. If it had been done but once the record would be less revolting: from the eastern to the middle states, from there to Illinois and Wisconsin, thence to Missouri and Iowa, thence to Kansas, Dakota and the plains; where now we cannot tell. Surely the policy was not designed to perpetuate barbarism, but such has been its effect.

163 MANUELITO, Navajo chief, told about the treaty signing of June 1868 which permitted the Navajos to leave the hated reservation in east central New Mexico and return westward —home.

We promised to keep the treaty. . . . We promised four times to do so. We all said "yes" to the treaty, and he gave us good advice. He was General Sherman. We told him we would try to remember what he said. He said: "I want all you people to look at me." He stood up for us to see him. He said if we would do right we could look people in the face. Then he said: "My children, I will send you back to your homes." The nights and days were long before it came time for us to go to our homes. The day before we were to start we went a little way towards home, because we were so anxious to start. We came back and the Americans gave us a little stock to start with and we thanked them for that. We told the drivers to whip the mules, we were in such a hurry. When we saw the top of the mountain from Albuquerque we wondered if it was our mountain, and we felt like talking to the ground, we loved it so, and some of the old men and women cried with joy when they reached their homes.

The agent told us here how large our reservation was to be. A small piece of land was surveyed off to us, but we think we ought to have had more. Then we began to talk about more land, and we went to Washington to see about our land. Some backed out of going for fear of strange animals and from bad water, but I thought I might as well die there as here. I thought I could do something at Washington about the land. I had a short talk with the Commissioner. We were to talk with him next day, but the agent brought us back without giving us a chance to say what we wanted. . . . I tell these things in order that you might

103

know what troubles we have had, and how little satisfaction we got. Therefore we have told you that the reservation was not large enough.

164 SITTING BULL, Sioux, answered Father Pierre Jean de Smet, the Jesuit missionary, when, at his Powder River camp on June 20, 1868, the "black robe" advised the sale of some Sioux land to appease the whites.

Father: I wish all to know that I do not propose to sell any part of my country, nor will I have the whites cutting our timber along the rivers, more especially the oak. I am particularly fond of the little groves of oak trees. I love to look at them, and feel a reverence for them, because they endure the wintry storm and summer's heat, and, not like ourselves—seem to thrive and flourish in them. One thing more: those forts filled with white soldiers must be abandoned; there is no greater source of trouble and grievance to my people.

165 BLACK KETTLE, Cheyenne chief of the Coloradas, was startled at hearing rumors that they were to be removed from their lands. In July 1868, at Fort Larned, Kansas, he addressed the U.S. Commissioners.

Our white brothers are pulling away from us the hand they gave us at Medicine Lodge, but we will try and hold on to it. We hope the Great White Father will take pity on us, and let us have the guns and ammunition he promised us so we can hunt buffalo to keep our families from starving.

166 WASHAKIE, Shoshone chief, in 1870 heard that the lands between the Wind River and the Sweetwater—set aside for the exclusive use of the Shoshones and the Bannocks by the Peace Commission of 1864—were being demanded for white development. He tried to dissuade his young men from war.

I am not only your chief but an old man, and your father. It therefore becomes my duty to advise you. I know how hard it is for youth to listen to the voice of age. The old blood creeps with the snail, but the young blood leaps with the torrent. Once I was young, my sons, and thought as you do now. Then my people were strong and my voice was ever for war. . . .

You must not fight the whites, and I not only advise against it, I forbid it.

167 SLUISKIN, Yakima guide for General Hazard Stevens and P. B. Van Trump in an arduous ascent of Mount Ranier (Takhoma) in August 1870, refused to accompany them to the top.

We go to the top of that mountain today, and tomorrow we follow along the high backbone ridge of the mountains, now up, now down, first one side and then on the other, a long day's journey, and at last, descending far down from the mountains into a deep valley, reach the foot of Takhoma.

Takhoma Wynatchie is an enchanted mountain, inhabited by an evil spirit, who lives in a fiery lake on its summit. No human can ascend it or even attempt to climb to the top and survive. At first, indeed, the way will be easy. The broad snowfields, over which often I have hunted the mountain goat, pose no obstacles, but above that there are steeps of loose rolling stones which turn beneath the climbing feet, to cast any adventurer into the deep crevasse below. The upper snowslopes are so steep that not even a mountain goat, far less a man, can get over them. And he would have to pass below lofty walls and precipices where avalanches of snow and vast masses of rocks continually fall; and these would inevitably bury the intruder beneath their ruins. Moreover, a furious tempest continually sweeps the crown of the mountain, and the luckless adventurer even if he escapes the perils below would be torn from the mountain and whirled through the air by its fearful blast.

And the awful Spirit upon the summit would surely punish the sacrilegious attempt to invade his sanctuary. Who could hope to escape his vengeance? Many years ago, my grandfather, a great chief and warrior, ascended high up the mountain, and encountered some of the dangers, but fortunately he turned back in time to escape destruction; and no other Indian has gone so far. [Stevens and Van Trump reached the summit and found all the conditions Sluiskin had warned them about.]

168 In June 1870, Chief RED CLOUD and a group of his Oglala Sioux visited President U. S. Grant in Washington. From there the party went to New York City where Red Cloud and Red Dog delivered speeches to an enthusiastic Cooper Union audience.

My Brothers and my Friends who are before me today: God Almighty has made us all, and He is here to hear what I have to say to you today. The Great Spirit made us both. He gave me lands and He gave you lands. You came here and we received you as brothers. When the Almighty made you, He made you all white and clothed you. When He made us He made us with red skins and poor. When you first came we were very many and you were few. Now you are many and we are few. You do not know who appears before you to speak. He is a representative of the original American race, and first people of this continent. We are good, and not bad. The reports which you get about us are all on one side. You hear of us only

106

as murderers and thieves. We are not so. If we had more lands to give to you we would give them, but we have no more. We are driven into a very little island, and we want you, our dear friends, to help us with the Government of the United States. The Great Spirits made us poor and ignorant. He made you rich and wise and skillful in things which we know nothing about. The good Father made you to eat tame game and us to eat wild game. Ask any one who has gone through to California. They will tell you we have treated them well. You have children. We, too, have children, and we wish to bring them up well. We ask you to help us do it. At the mouth of Horse Creek, in 1852, the Great Father made a treaty with us. We agreed to let him pass through our territory unharmed for fifty-five years. We kept our word. We committed no murders, no depredations, until the troops came there. When the troops were sent there trouble and disturbance arose. Since that time there have been various goods sent from time to time to us, but only once did they reach us, and soon the Great Father took away the only good man he had sent us, Col. Fitzpatrick. The Great Father said we must go to farming, and some of our men went to farming near Fort Laramie, and were treated very badly indeed. We came to Washington to see our Great Father that peace might be continued. The Great Father that made us both wishes peace to be kept; we want to keep peace. Will you help us? In 1868 men came out and brought papers. We could not read them, and they did not tell us truly what was in them. We thought the treaty was to remove the forts and that we should then cease from fighting. But they wanted to send us traders on the Missouri. We did not want to go on the Missouri, but wanted traders where we were. When I reached Washington the Great Father explained to me what the treaty was, and showed me that the interpreters had deceived me. All I want is right and justice. I have tried to get from the Great Father what is right and just. I have not altogether succeeded. I want you to help me to get what is right and just. I represent the whole Sioux nation, and they will be bound by what I say. I am no Spotted Tail, to say one thing one day and be bought for a pin the next. Look at me. I am poor and naked, but I am the Chief of the nation. We do not want riches, but we want to train our children right. Riches would do us no good. We could not take them with us to the other world. We do not want riches, we want peace and love.

The riches that we have in this world, Secretary [of the Interior Jacob] Cox said truly, we cannot take with us to the next world. Then I wish to know why Commissioners are sent out to us who do nothing but rob us and get the riches of this world away from us! I was brought up among the traders, and those who came out there in the early times treated me well and I had a good time with them. They taught us to wear clothes and to use tobacco and ammunition. But, by and by, the Great Father sent out a different kind of men; men who cheated and drank whisky; men who were so bad that the Great Father could not keep them at home and so sent them out there. I have sent a great many words to the Great Father but they never reached him. They were drowned on the way, and I was afraid the words I spoke lately to the Great Father would not reach you, so I came to speak to you myself; and now I am going away to my home. I want to have men sent out to my people whom we know and can trust. I am glad I have come here. You belong in the East and I belong in the West, and I am glad I have come here and that we could understand one another. I am very much obliged to you for listening to me. I go home this afternoon. I hope you will think of what I have said to you. I bid you all an affectionate farewell.

169 RED DOG, Oglala Sioux, also spoke on June 16, 1870 at the Cooper Union.

I have but a few words to say to you, my friends. When the good Great Spirit raised us, he raised us with good men for counsels, and he raised you with good men for counsels. But yours are all the time getting bad, while ours

Two Strikes. A member of Spotted Tail's delegation to Washington, D.C., photographed by Alexander Gardner, 1872.

Indian Delegation of 1867. Dakota and other Indians at the White House with President Andrew Johnson. Photograph probably by Alexander Gardner, 1867.

Smithsonian Institution National Anthropological Archives

The Treaty Council of 1868. U.S. Commissioners and Indians meet in council at Fort Laramie. Photograph by Alexander Gardner, 1868.

Dakota Tree Burial. Photograph by Alexander Gardner, taken during the Treaty Council of 1868 at Fort Laramie, Dakota Territory.

Omaha Indians in costume. Photograph from the Fred R. Meyer Collection.

Indians gathered for a dance in front of the trading post at Fort Peck (Poplar), Montana. By an unknown photographer, about 1882.

Indians at Fort Laramie, Wyoming, 1868. Left to right: Spotted Tail (Brule), Roman Nose (Miniconjou), Old Man Afraid of His Horses (Oglala), Lone Horn (Miniconjou), Whistling Elk, Pipe and an unidentified Indian. Photograph attributed to Alexander Gardner.

Sitting Bull with two wives and three children. Photograph taken at Fort Randall, South Dakota, 1882.

Smithsonian Institution National Anthropological Archives
Three Apache warriors, ready for battle. Photograph by T. H.
O'Sullivan, Wheeler Expedition, 1873.

Family group of the sheep-eater band (Bannock), encamped near the head of Medicine Lodge Creek, Idaho. Photograph by William H. Jackson, 1871.

Kiowa or Arapaho camp near Fort Dodge or Camp Supply. Photograph by William S. Soule, about 1867–74.

A GALLERY OF INDIAN PORTRAITS

Manuelito, Navaho war chief 1855–72, photographed while visiting Washington, D.C. with a Navaho delegation in 1874.

Sitting Bull, medicine man and warrior of the Hunkpapa Sioux. Photograph by David F. Barry, 1885.

"I have killed, robbed and injured too many white men to believe in a good peace...."

Standing Bear, chief of the Brule Sioux:
"*I seem to stand on the brink of a ruin....In front the river is wide and impassable, and behind me are perpendicular cliffs. No man of my race had ever stood there before....*"

Museum of the American Indian, Heye Foundation

Running Antelope, Hunkpapa Sioux. In 1868 the U.S. Government acknowledged the Black Hills to belong to the Indians forever. But in 1870, white men discovered gold there.

"The land known as the Black Hills is considered by the Indians to be the center of their land...."

Museum of the American Indian, Heye Foundation

Rain in the Face, Hunkpapa Sioux:
"*I prepared for death. I painted as usual like the eclipse of the sun, half black and half red....*"

Chief Joseph, Nez Perce:

"Words do not pay for my dead people. I am tired of talk that comes to nothing...."

Ten Bears, Comanche Chief (1792-1872), photographed in
the last year of his life by Alexander Gordon, Washington, D.C.
*"I was born upon the prairie, where the wind blew free and
there was nothing to break the light of the sun. I want to die
there and not within walls...."*

Museum of the American Indian, Heye Foundation

General George Armstrong Custer, killed in the Battle of the Little Big Horn, June 17, 1876.

"For strength and visions." A Crow Indian undergoing self-torture. The thongs from the pole are attached to skewers embedded in his flesh. Photograph by Edward S. Curtis.

Skin lodges of the Nez Perce in temporary encampment on the banks of the Yellowstone River. Woman in foreground is making pemmican, a form of dried meat. Photograph by William H. Jackson, 1871.

A Cheyenne woman, photographed by William S. Soule, around 1867–74.

Smithsonian Institution National Anthropological Archives

Two Indian girls, photographed on the Kiowa Reservation, Oklahoma Territory, 1891. The girl on the left is Wanda Parker, daughter of the Comanche war chief, Quanah Parker.

Acoma woman with child in cradleboard. Photograph taken in 1899 by Adam Clark Vroman at the Pueblo of Acoma, New Mexico.

Nez Perce baby in buckskin and cloth cradleboard. An unknown photographer took this picture around 1900.

Soldiers of Wounded Knee. On the banks of Wounded Knee Creek in South Dakota, 350 men, women and children of the Sioux, arrested for practicing the Ghost Dance religion, were fired upon by soldiers of the U.S. Seventh Cavalry. It was the morning of December 29, 1890. There were few survivors.

Smithsonian Institution National Anthropological Archives

Smithsonian Institution National Anthropological Archives

A mounted trooper surveys the Indian encampment at Wounded Knee where 153 bodies were counted in the snow.

Smithsonian Institution National Anthropological Archives

Burial of the dead at Wounded Knee, January 1, 1891. An unknown cameraman took this photograph for the North-western Photographic Co., Chadron, Nebraska.

Blue Whirlwind and her children, survivors of the Wounded Knee Massacre. This woman received 14 bullet wounds; both children were also wounded. Photograph by James Mooney, sometime prior to 1896.

These five Blackfoot warriors were photographed by R. W.
Reed in 1915. The camera shows what the mind sees: The
Indian as Vanishing American.

Wovoka, the Paiute "Messiah" who founded the religion of the Ghost Dance, photographed with T. J. McCoy at Walker Lake, Nevada, 1926.
"The dead are all alive again.... When the time comes there will be no more sickness and everyone will be young again...."

remain good. These are my young men. I am their Chief. Look among them and see if you can find any among them who are rich. They are all poor because they are all honest. Whenever I call my young men together in counsel, they all listen to what I say. Now you have come together in counsel, I want you and your children to listen to what I say. When the Great Father first sent out men to our people, I was poor and thin; now I am large and stout and fat. It is because so many liars have been sent out there, and I have been stuffed full with their lies. I know all of you to be men of sense and men of respect, and I therefore ask you confidently to see that when men are sent out to our country, they shall be right men and just men, and will not do us harm. I don't want any more men sent out there who are so poor that they think only of filling their pockets. We want those who will help to protect us on our reservations, and save us from those who are viciously disposed toward us.

170 DONEHOGAWA, or Ely Samuel Parker, Seneca chief, was appointed Commissioner of Indian Affairs in 1868. Parker entertained Red Cloud and Red Dog during their Washington visit. He was, however, too honest for the whites political enemies plotted his downfall and succeeded in forcing his resignation in 1871. From a report by Parker on Indian Peace Policy and Grants:

The white man has been the chief obstacle in the way of Indian civilization. The benevolent measures attempted by the government for their advancement has been almost uniformly thwarted by the agencies employed to carry them out. The soldiers, sent for their protection, too often carried demoralization and disease into their midst. The agent appointed to be their friend and counselor, business manager, and the almoner of government bounties, frequently went among them only to enrich himself in the shortest possible time, at the cost of the Indians, and spend the largest available sum of the government money with the least ostensible beneficial result.

171 OLD JOSEPH, revered Nez Perce leader, called his thirty-one-year-old son, Heinmot Tooyalaket, to him in 1871 as he lay dying. His death words were to his son who came to be known as Chief Joseph.

My son, my body is returning to my mother earth, and my spirit is going very soon to see the Great Spirit Chief. When I am gone, think of your country. You are the chief of these people. They look to you to guide them. Always remember that your father never sold his country. You must stop your ears whenever you are asked to sign a treaty selling your home. A few more years and the white men will be all around you. They have their eyes on this land. My son, never forget my dying words. This country holds your father's body. Never sell the bones of your father and your mother.

172 CHIEF JOSEPH met with a U.S. Commission sent to the Nez Perce Wallowa Valley country in Oregon to introduce the idea of a Nez Perce removal to Idaho. Chief Joseph was asked why churches were not allowed on his reservation.

They will teach us to quarrel about God, as Catholics and Protestants do on the Nez Perce Reservation and other places. We do not want to do that. We may quarrel with men sometimes about things on earth, but we never quarrel about the Great Spirit. We do not want to learn that.

173 SATANK, Kiowa chief, after a raid against an Army train in May 1871, was put into a prison wagon, with Satanta and Big Tree in a second wagon, to be taken from Oklahoma to Texas for trial. Satank cried out to the Indian guard, then began his death chant.

I wish to send a little message by you to my people. Tell them that I am dead. I died the first day out, and my bones will be lying on the side of the road. I wish my people to gather them up and take them home. [See that tree ahead?] I shall never go beyond that tree.

I hahyo oya iya iya o iha yaya yoyo
Aheya aheya yaheyo ya eya heyo eheyo
Kaitsenko anaobahema haaipaidegi obaika
Kaitsenko anaobahema hadamgagi obaika

O sun, you remain forever, but we Kaitsenko must die.
O earth, you remain forever, but we Kaitsenko must die.

[Satank then tore the manacles and flesh from his wrists and stabbed a white guard. He was shot dead.]

174 COCHISE, Chiricahua Apache chief, met in September 1871 with General Gordon Granger to discuss a peace settlement and a reservation location for Cochise and his band.

I speak straight and do not wish to deceive or be deceived. I want a good, strong and lasting peace. When God made the world he gave one part to the white man and another to the Apache. Why was it? Why did they come together? . . .

When I was young I walked all over this country, east and west, and saw no other people than the Apaches. After many summers I walked again and found another race of people had come to take it. . . . The Apaches were once a great nation; they are now but few, and because of

111

this they want to die and so carry their lives on their finger nails. Many have been killed in battle. You must speak straight so that your words may go as sunlight to our hearts. Tell me, if the Virgin Mary has walked throughout all the land, why has she never entered the wigwam of the Apache? Why have we never seen or heard her? . . .

I want to live in these mountains; I do not want to go to Tularosa. That is a long ways off. The flies on those mountains eat out the eyes of the horses. The bad spirits live there. I have drunk of these waters and they have cooled me; I do not want to leave here.

175 OURAY, Uncompahgre Ute chief in Colorado, was angered at a meeting with the McCook Commission in 1872 when a member disparaged the Utes as a lazy people.

We work as hard as you do. Did you ever try skinning a buffalo?

176 George P. Belden, "The White Chief," wrote in 1872 about the plight of the Indians of the Wind River area.

The face of the white man, like an insatiable fiend, presents itself constantly before the Indian, and a voice cries, "Back, back to the setting sun. I want your land, your game, your home, and even the graves of your people; and I will have it all! all!"

Some nations fight, some implore; but the result is the same—the white man becomes the oppressor. So the beautiful valleys of the Snake land will soon teem with population; towns will spring up, and the iron and the coal, plaster and copper, be dug from the hills; mills will be heard on the clear streams of the Popoagie; church bells will ring along the silent waters of Wind River; and poor Wash-a-kee and his children, where will they be. . . . Gone to the happy hunting grounds of their fathers—with King Philip and his people, the Pawnee, the Minnetaree, the Mohican, the Mandan, and all who have gone before.

177 KINTPUASH, or Captain Jack, was a Modoc chief friendly to the whites in California. But after Kintpuash and his people were removed to a reservation in Oregon with Klamaths, they rebelled and left. A small group of the Modocs exchanged killings with white settlers and the whole Modoc band retreated to the California Lava Beds, where they were followed and penned up by hundreds of Army troops. Kintpuash sent a letter on March 6, 1873 to those besieging him, though it did not end the fighting.

I am very sad. I want peace quick, or else let the soldiers come and make haste to fight. . . . Let everything be wiped out, washed out, and let there be no more blood. I have got a bad heart about those murderers. I have got but a few men and I don't see how I can give them up. Will they give up their people who murdered my people while they were asleep? I never asked for the people who murdered my people. . . . I can see how I could give up my horse to be hanged; but I can't see how I could give up my men to be hanged. I could give up my horse to be hanged, and wouldn't cry about it, but if I gave up my men I would have to cry about it. . . . I have given up now and want no more fuss. I have said yes and thrown away my country.

178 BIG MOGGASEN, aged Navajo chief, received wo d in 1875 that all Navajo children must attend school. He trekked for three days out of his mountain fastness to Fort Defiance to defy the edict, though he was promised gifts and rations if he would agree. To his own people he said, about the offers of food, "I have trapped deer by such methods." To the whites he said:

No, my children shall not come. I do not believe in the white man or his ways. I am old and I have seen many things. The white man makes our young men drunk. He steals away our daughters. He takes away their hearts with sweet drinks and clothes. He is a wolf. . . . I did not come to beg of the white man. I did not come to ask anything for myself. I came because my people in council decided to send me. I have come. I am old and I have not departed from the ways of my fathers. I have lived thus far without the white man's help. I will die as I have lived. I have spoken.

179 An Arapaho Indian guide explained to Colonel William "Buffalo Bill" Cody in 1875 why 200 young braves left the reservation, only to be rounded up and returned by the army in a matter of hours.

The land to the north and west is the land of plenty. There the buffalo grows larger, and his coat is darker. There the antelope comes in droves, while here there are but a few. There the whole region is covered with short, curly grass our ponies like. There grows the wild plum. . . . There are the springs of the Great Medicine Man, Tel-ya-ki-y. To bathe in them gives new life; to drink them cures every bodily ill.

In the mountains beyond the river of the blue water there is gold and silver, the metals that the white man loves. There lives the eagle, whose feathers the Indian must have to make his war bonnet. There the sun always shines.

It is the *Ijis* of the red man. My heart cries for it. The hearts of my people are not happy when away from the *Eithity Tugala* [Big Horn Basin].

180 CHARLOT, Flathead chief, spoke to his people in 1876 about the white man, when the whites were attempting to oust them from their ancestral home in the Bitterroot Valley of Montana.

Since our forefathers first beheld him, more than seven times ten winters have snowed and melted. . . . We were happy when he first came. We first thought he came from the light; but he comes like the dusk of the evening now, not like the dawn of the morning. He comes like a day that has passed, and night enters our future with him. . . .

To take and to lie should be burned on his forehead, as he burns the sides of my stolen horses with his own name. Had Heaven's Chief burnt him with some mark to refuse him, we might have refused him. No; we did not refuse him in his weakness. In his poverty we fed, we cherished him—yes, befriended him, and showed him the fords and defiles of our lands. . . .

He has filled graves with our bones. His horses, his cattle, his sheep, his men, his women have a rot. Does not his breath, his gums stink? His jaws lose their teeth and he stamps them with false ones; yet he is not ashamed. No, no; his course is destruction; he spoils what the spirit who gave us this country made beautiful and clean . . .

His laws never gave us a blade, nor a tree, nor a duck, nor a grouse, nor a trout. . . . How often does he come? You know he comes as long as he lives, and takes more and more, and dirties what he leaves. . . .

The white man fathers this doom—yes, this curse on us and on the few that may see a few days more. He, the cause of our ruin, is his own snake which he says stole on his mother in her own country to lie to her. He says his story is that man was rejected and cast off. Why did we not reject him forever? He says one of his virgins had a son nailed to death on two cross sticks to save him. Were all of them dead when that young man died, we would all be safe now, and our country our own.

181 In 1868, the U.S. government by treaty acknowledged the Black Hills to be the Indians' forever and agreed that no white man could set foot there without Indian permission. In the early 1870s white miners were allegedly finding gold in the sacred hills, without permission. In 1874 General George Armstrong Custer and his 7th Cavalry entered the Black Hills, without permission, and confirmed the abundance of gold. Then, of course, the real invasion by whites began. The Indians quickly and clearly saw how valuable the Black Hills were to the gold-lusting whites, but for the original owners the land had a different value and a different reverence.

RUNNING ANTELOPE: The land known as the Black Hills is considered by the Indians as the center of their land.

WOLF NECKLACE: I never want to leave this country; all my relatives are lying here in the ground, and when I fall to pieces I am going to fall to pieces here.

CROW FEATHER: My friends, for many years we have been in this country; we never go to the Great Father's country and bother him about anything. It is his people who come to our country and bother us, do many bad things, and teach our people to be bad. . . . Before you people ever crossed the ocean to come to this country, and from that time to this, you have never proposed to buy a country that was equal to this in riches. My friends, this country that you have come to buy is the best country that we have; . . . this country is mine, I was raised in it; my forefathers lived and died in it; and I wish to remain in it.

LONG MANDAN: We have sat and watched them pass here to get gold out and have said nothing. . . . My friends, when I went to Washington I went into your money-house and I had some young men with me, but none of them took any money out of that house while I was with them.

At the same time, when your Great Father's people come into my country, they go into my money-house [the Black Hills] and take money out.

WHITE GHOST: You have driven away our game and our means of livelihood out of the country, until now we have nothing left that is valuable except the hills that you ask us to give up. . . . The earth is full of minerals of all kinds, and on the earth the ground is covered with forests of heavy pine, and when we give these up to the Great Father we know that we give up the last thing that is valuable either to us or the white people.

CRAZY HORSE: One does not sell the earth upon which the people walk.

182 Yet, the Indians were not blind to the inevitable. In September 1875, a special commission came to Red Cloud agency to treat with the Sioux for their relinquishment of the Black Hills. In light of the great value placed upon the area by both the whites and the Indians, one can wonder whether the Indians' demands were actually "extra-ordinary." Here is how the commission's own report summarized three days of meetings:

The commission listened to propositions from the leading chiefs of the various tribes, which were a mixture of complaints and demands, the latter of so extra-ordinary a character as to make it manifest that it was useless to continue the negotiations. We quote from most of these speeches to show the character and extent of their requirements.

RED CLOUD: There have been six nations raised, and I am the seventh, and I want seven generations ahead to be fed.

RED DOG: We want to get pay for seven generations

ahead, the same subsistence that you have been giving us. All our chiefs are here. They want to get back pay from what our Great Father has promised us, in horses and light wagons with six yokes of oxen. . . . Our Great Father asked for the Black Hills, and our chiefs said, "We don't want to give the whole Hills; we will just give where there is gold, in the center, not to include the pine; just the Black Hills." We don't want to have any more roads through the country to run over us here.

LITTLE BEAR: Our Great Father has a house full of money. Suppose a man walks right into the house and takes the money, do you suppose that would suit everybody? The Black Hills are the house of gold for our Indians. We watch it to get rich. For the last four years the Great Father's men are working at that hill, and I want our Great Father to remember that and not to forget it. . . .

SPOTTED BEAR: Our Great Father has a big safe, and so have we. This hill is our safe. That is the reason we can't come to a conclusion very quick. Before our Great Father does anything for us, these people go and steal from us, and I want that made good. As long as we live I want our Great Father to furnish us with blankets and things that we live upon. We want seventy millions of dollars for the Black Hills. Put the money away some place at interest so we can buy live stock. That is the way the white people do.

FAST BEAR: The beef-cattle that the Great Father has issued to me, no doubt each steer has been weighed twice and called two, and some of them have been put away somewhere else, and I wish the Great Father would track them up. It seems that all this back pay is due me and some of it has been lost and I didn't know it, and I wish that it would all be tracked up and put in with this payment for the Black Hills. This land that you want to buy is not a small thing. It is very valuable and therefore I am going to put a big price on it.

118

DEAD EYES: You have put all our heads together and covered them with a blanket. That hill there is our wealth, but you have been asking it from us. It is not a very small thing, you must remember; therefore, at our Great Father's house, we asked for a great deal, but it is not very much when we will ask equal shares. You white people, you have all come in our reservation and helped yourselves to our property, and you are not satisfied; you went beyond to take the whole of our safe. These tribes here all spoke with one word in saying that they look after their children for seven generations to come, and I think it is right.

CROW FEATHER: Our Great Father has asked me to give up the heart of this land where I was born and raised, and the heart of this land is big and good, and I have camped all around it and watched and looked after it. Our people here speak of seven generations to come. Now, remember, I hope that our Great Father will not be so stingy with his money as not to grant that. We wish our Great Father to feed people of my color hereafter as long as the race lasts. We want from our money different kinds of live stock such as the white people have. We want clothes for the Indian race as long as it lasts. Even if our Great Father should give a hundred different kinds of live stock to each Indian house every year, it seems that that would not pay for the Black Hills. I was not born and raised on this soil for fun.

FLYING BIRD: There is gold all over this hill out here which our people own. You can see it with your naked eyes. What our people ask for the Black Hills, the amount that we ask from our Great Father, will grow small year by year, and the Black Hills will grow richer. As long as our Indian race lasts we hope that our Great Father will not forget us.

183 The Sioux finally rejected all offers made by the commission in 1875 for the Black Hills; they would neither lease nor sell. Reaction in Washington, D.C. was to rely upon force: forced sale of the lands and forced removal of the Indians to designated reservations. 1876 was the year of intense Indian wars along the Powder and the Rosebud Rivers; it was the year of Little Big Horn.

CRAZY HORSE, young Oglala Sioux, is said to have yelled as he rode into battle at Rosebud in June 1876:

Hoka hey! Follow Me! Follow me! Today is a good day to fight, today is a good day to die!

184 WHITE BULL, Sioux chief, gave an account of the Battle of the Little Big Horn, June 17, 1876, in which he claimed to have killed General George A. Custer.

I charged in. A tall, well-built soldier with yellow hair and mustache saw me coming and tried to bluff me, aiming his rifle at me. But when I rushed him, he threw his rifle at me without shooting. I dodged it. We grabbed each other and wrestled there in the dust and smoke. It was like fighting in a fog. This soldier was very strong and brave. He tried to wrench my rifle from me, and nearly did it. I lashed him across the face with my quirt, striking the *coup*. He let go, then grabbed my gun with both hands until I struck him again.

But the tall soldier fought hard. He was desperate. He hit me with his fists on jaw and shoulders, then grabbed my long braids with both hands, pulled my face close and tried to bite my nose off. I yelled for help: "Hey, hey, come over and help me!" I thought that soldier would kill me.

Bear Lice and Crow Boy heard me call and came running. These friends tried to hit the soldier. But we were whirling around, back and forth, so that most of their blows hit me. They knocked me dizzy. I yelled as loud as I could to scare my enemy, but he would not let go. Finally I broke free.

He drew his pistol. I wrenched it out of his hand and struck him with it three or four times on the head, knocked him over, shot him in the head and fired at his heart. I took his pistol and cartridge belt. Hawk-Stays-Up struck second on his body.

Ho hechetu! That *was* a fight, a *hard* fight. But it was a glorious battle, I enjoyed it. . . .

On the hill top, I met my relative, Bad Juice [Bad Soup]. He had been around Fort Abraham Lincoln and knew Long Hair by sight. When he came to the tall soldier lying on his back naked, Bad Soup pointed him out and said, "Long Hair thought he was the greatest man in the world. Now he lies there."

"Well," I said, "if that is Long Hair, I am the man who killed him."

185   1876 also saw the performance of a special Presidential commission which manifested a curious ambivalence toward the American Indian. One face of the commission produced a report full of moral and self-critical judgments.

While the Indians received us as friends, and listened with kind attention to our propositions, we were painfully impressed with their lack of confidence in the pledge of the Government. At times they told their story of wrongs with such impassioned earnestness that our cheeks crimsoned with shame. In their speeches, the recital of the wrongs which their people had suffered at the hands of the whites, the arraignment of the Government for gross acts of injustices and fraud, the description of treaties made only to be broken, the doubts and distrusts of present professions of friendship and good-will were portrayed in colors so vivid and language so terse, that admiration and sur-

prise would have kept us silent had not shame and humiliation done so. That which made this arraignment more telling was that it often came from the lips of men who were our friends, and who have hoped against hope that the day might come when their wrongs would be redressed.

186   The 1876 Commission heard comments by two chiefs which summarized sharply the Indians' point of view.

If you white men had a country which was very valuable, which had always belonged to your people, and which the Great Father had promised should be yours for ever, and men of another race came to take it away by force, what would your people do? Would they fight?

I am glad to see you, you are our friends, but I hear that you have come to move us. Tell your people that since the Great Father promised that we should never be removed we have been moved five times. I think you had better put the Indians on wheels and you can run them about wherever you wish.

The Indian was forgotten. It did not occur to any man that this poor, despised red man was the original discoverer and the sole occupant for many centuries of every mountain seamed with quartz and every stream whose yellow sand glittered in the noonday sun. He asked to retain only a secluded spot where the buffalo and elk could live, and that spot he would make his home. The truth is, no place was left for him. [Thus it was when the same Commission, showing its other face, met at Red Cloud agency in September 1876 to impose a treaty already written:]
    We came here to bring a message to you from your Great Father, and there are certain things we have given to you in his exact words; we cannot alter them, even to the scratch of a pen. [Two weeks later time was running

out for the Sioux and patience was running out for the Commissioners:]

When we go back, which must be very soon, we must take back a paper signed by you to the Great Father saying what you will do. . . . We want you to sign this paper just as soon as you decide what you will do, and we ask you to determine that this afternoon, if you can.

187 The end was near. But not yet. There were a few more protests and hopes expressed by the Indians, such as LITTLE WOUND's elegiac utterance.

Yesterday I heard something that made me almost cry. I always considered that when the Great Father borrowed the country for the overland road that he made an arrangement with us that was to last fifty years as payment for that privilege, and yesterday another arrangement was mentioned concerning the Black Hills, and the words that I heard from the Great Father and from the commissioners from the Great Council made me cry. The country upon which I am standing is the country upon which I was born, and upon which I heard that it was the wish of the Great Father and of the Great Council that I should be like a man without a country. I shed tears.

188 Then it was over. Red Cloud and his followers touched the pen. The Commissioners then visited the Spotted Tail, Standing Rock, Cheyenne River, Crow Creek, Lower Brulé, and Santee agencies and pressured those Sioux into signing the paper. Negotiations everywhere were similar and prolonged. For example, Standing Elk and Spotted Tail elaborated a wisdom and caution born of deceit long experienced. STANDING ELK's talk was a direct response to a statement by Commissioner A. S. Gaylord. SPOTTED TAIL's remarks are combined from two speeches.

GAYLORD: *Now the Great Council [U.S. Congress] has made a law stating the things which must be done by you in order that more food shall be given you. They have sent us to you to tell you their words, and we cannot change them. . . . Now we cannot take the paper back without your signatures. . . . The Great Father desires you should go to the country [Indian Territory] he has selected for you and look at it. . . . But before this is done we must have the treaty signed here.*

STANDING ELK: My friend, your speech is as if a man has knocked me in the head with a stick. A person who is friendly, who wishes to consider a matter that is very difficult, takes time to consider it. I have often signed papers before. I have taken account of the many persons that have come here with papers to sign, and now it is more than ten. It seems these men are considered chiefs in vain, that it is in vain we try to live in peace with the whites. By your speech you have put great fear upon us. I have been brought up among a great many things that are very hard, very difficult, but I never thought, when I came to shake hands, that the Missouri River would be mentioned to me as the place to go to. At the time when you made away with a great many old women and children, those who were not strong, I went to the Missouri River. . . . All of our good people went over there, carrying their burdens. They had a very hard time of it. Therefore our people consider for our good; but it seems that hard words are placed upon us and bend down our backs. Whatever the white people say to us, wherever I go, we all say, "Yes" to them—"Yes," "Yes," "Yes." Whenever we don't agree to anything that is said in council, they give the same reply—"You won't get any food;" "You won't get any food." Since the old treaty was made, it was to be for thirty-five years. Now there are twenty-five years of that passed, and there are nearly ten years left. Before that time was passed we were all to be as white men and support ourselves, but were given no implements. What are we to do if you simply go on feeding us without giving us cattle and other animals and implements? We want to be like white people. I thought when I came to sell the Black Hills we would receive some very fat cattle and something that would make our hearts glad. Instead of that we hear some words that are very severe.

SPOTTED TAIL: This is the fifth time that you have come. At the time of the first treaty that was made on Horse Creek—the one we call the "great treaty"—there was provision made to borrow the overland road of the Indians, and promises made at the time of the treaty, though I was a boy at the time; they told me it was to last fifty years. These promises have not been kept. All the Dakotas that lived in this country were promised these things together at that time. All the words have proved to be false. The next conference was the one held with General Manydear, when there was no promises made in particular, nor any amount to be given to us, but we had a conference with him and made friends and shook hands. Then after that there was a treaty made by General Sherman, General Sanborn, and General Harney. At that time the general told us we should have annuities and goods from that treaty for thirty-five years. He said this, but yet he didn't tell the truth. At that time General Sherman told me the country was mine, and that I should select any place I wished for my reservation and live in it. . . . When these promises failed to be carried out, I went myself to see the Great Father, and went into his house and told him these things. . . . When we went to Washington to give up our hunting privilege south for $25,000 we were asked to sign a paper. We received for that $25,000 only eighty horses. The Secretary of the Interior told us then we would get $25,000 more, but it didn't come to pass. . . . The Great Father told me to go home, to select any place in my country I choose, and to go there and live with my people. I came home and selected this place to move here and settle. Then persons came to me, after I had settled, and said I must move from this place, and I came back here again and located the agency. You told me to come here and locate my agency and I should receive the fulfillment of these promises. You gave me some very small cows, and some very bad cattle, and some old wagons that were worn out. Again: you came last summer to talk about the country, and we said we would consider the matter; we said we would leave the matter to the Great Father for settlement. In answer to that reply of ours, he has sent you out this summer. You have now come to visit our land, and we now ask you how many years there are for us to live? My friends, you that sit before me are traders and merchants. You have come here to trade. You have not come here to turn anything out of the way without payment for it. When a man has a possession that he values, and another party comes to buy it, he brings with him such good things as the people that own it desire to have. My friends, your people have both intellect and hearts. You use these to consider in what way you had best live. My people, who are here before you to-day, are precisely the same. If you have much of anything you use it for your own benefit and in order that your children shall have food and clothing, and my people also are the same. I see that my friends before me are men of age and dignity. Men of that kind have good judgment to consider well what they do. I infer from this you are here to consider what shall be good for my people for a long time to come. I think that each of you have selected somewhere a good piece of land for himself, with the intention of living on it, that he may there raise up his children. My people, that you see here before you, are not different; they also live upon the earth and upon the things that come to them from above. We have the same thoughts and desires in that respect that white people have. The people that you see before you are not men of a different country, but this is their country, where they were born and where they have acquired all their property; their children, their horses, and other property were all raised here in this country. You have come here to buy this country of ours, and it would be well if you came with the things you propose to give us—the good price you propose to pay for it in your hands, so we could see the price you propose to pay for it, then our hearts would be glad. . . .

My friends, this seems to me to be a very hard day.

You have come here to buy our country, and there is, at the time you come, half our country at war, and we have come upon very difficult times. This war did not spring up here in our land; this war was brought upon us by the children of the Great Father who came to take our land from us without price, and who, in our land, do a great many evil things. The Great Father and his children are to blame for this trouble. . . . This war has come from robbery—from the stealing of our land. My friends, I wish to tell the Great Father "Let us consider this matter." There are on both sides a great many widows and a great many orphans. Let us consider who is to take care of these. This matter has not been begun with judgment; and I think it is displeasing to the Great Spirit—the Great Spirit is very much displeased at it. The Great Father sent you out here to buy our land and we have agreed together to that, but with one understanding: That it shall be the end, also, of this war. We all live in this country, and have always been peaceful friends of the Great Father, and shall remain at peace with him; but all at once a whirl-wind has passed over our land, and the ammunition has been locked up so that we cannot get it to hunt game to live upon. Now we shake hands and make peace and wish it to be unlocked so we can buy ammunition. . . . We have here a storehouse to hold our provisions the Great Father sends us, but he sends very little provision to put in our storehouse. When our people become displeased with their provision and have gone north to hunt in order that they might live, the Great Father's children are fighting them. It has been our wish to live here in our country peaceably, and do such things as may be for the welfare and good of our people, but the Great Father has filled it with soldiers who think only of our death. Some of our people who have gone from here in order that they may have a change, and others who have gone north to hunt, have been attacked by the soldiers from this direction, and when they have got north have been attacked by soldiers from the other side, and now when they are willing to come back the soldiers stand between them to keep them from coming home. It seems to me there is a better way than this. When people come to trouble, it is better for both parties to come together without arms and talk it over and find some peaceful way to settle it.

You have come here in the first place to buy a part of our country, and we said, "Yes." You came, in the next place, to say the Great Father wanted some of our young men to go down and look at another country [Indian Territory], and we said, "Yes." I say the names of these young men should be written on that paper, and you can take it to the Great Father and say, "These men have gone to see the country." . . . I also said I would go down myself with the delegation to look at the country and when I came back I would look over all the country occupied by my people and consider everything that was necessary to be considered in regard to that, and when I made up my mind what was best, I would go to the Great Father and talk about it, and when he told me what goods he was going to give me, and what cattle he was going to give me, and for how many years, I would consider the matter all over with him, and touch the pen. . . . I only wish now that my name shall be attached to that paper without my signing it . . . It has been said to us that there is no deceit in touching the pen to sign a treaty, but I have always found it full of deceit. We know it is not the Great Father who deceives us; we know that, therefore we wish to go and see him and sign it in his presence, and then we will both of us understand it. . . . If I should sign the paper now, you would take it back to the Great Father, and then this commission would be discharged and go to their several homes, and there would be nobody to see that we got these things. Therefore I said I would go myself to see that no mistake was made. When I go to Washington I wish you all go with me, and when we get in the presence of the Great Father we will spread out these papers, and spread out all the talk that has been made on both sides, and there we will finish it without doubt.

189 While talking of large issues and of a future into seven generations, the Sioux chiefs did not forget immediate individuals at hand. Time and again, for instance, a plea was made for the government to include as recipients of annuities the non-Indians who were members of the tribes.

SPOTTED TAIL: My people have grown up together with these white men, who have married into our tribe. A great many of them have grown up with their children; a great many of us have learned to speak their language; our children are with theirs in our school, and we want to be considered all one people with them.

STANDING ELK: There are a great many whites and persons of mixed blood that speak our language that live with the tribes over there that are well taken [care] of, but it seems you don't wish to give rations to the whites that live with us.

TWO STRIKE: There is another thing that troubles us: We want it understood that none of these white men who speak our language and are married to Dakota women shall be sent away.

RUNNING ANTELOPE: In respect to the white men that are living in our country and are married to our women, I consider them as my own. Their wishes are our wishes, and what we get I hope they will get.

SPOTTED TAIL: There is an old man living among the Brules who has been brought up with them and is now very poor. In the business necessary to be done at the agency I wish him to have some employment and pay.

190 SITTING BULL, Sioux, a refugee over the Canadian line after the Custer Massacre, was asked by a friendly trader at Wolf Point why he did not surrender and go live on a reservation, since he and his people were near starvation that bitter winter of 1876-77.

Because I am a red man. If the Great Spirit had desired me to be a white man he would have made me so in the first place. He put in your heart certain wishes and plans, in my heart he put other and different desires. Each man is good in his sight. It is not necessary for eagles to be crows. Now we are poor but we are free. No white man controls our footsteps. If we must die we die defending our rights.

191 The 1860s brought disputes between the U.S. government and the Nez Perce about the use of Wallowa Valley, which was claimed as home by Old Joseph and his followers. In 1871 Old Joseph died. In 1873, in response to a petition from Old Joseph's successor, his son, Chief Joseph, President U. S. Grant issued an executive order excluding Wallowa Valley from white settlement. In 1875, Grant revoked the order and the Nez Perce were told to move to the Lapwai reservation. They did not, and in May of 1877 General Oliver Otis Howard was sent to encourage the move. Howard met with Chief Joseph at Fort Lapwai; among others accompanying Joseph who had not signed the earlier treaty was TOOHULHULSOTE, a Nez Perce prophet who acted for a while as spokesman at the meeting. Howard, in his official report summarizing the meeting, also summarized some key attitudes. He referred to Toohulhulsote as "the old 'dreamer' . . . a large, thick-necked, ugly, obstinate savage of the worst type." Howard then indicated how the opening exchanges went.

[I said] we were all children of a common government, and must obey. The old man replied that he had heard about a trade between Indians and white men, bargaining away the Indians' land, but that he belonged to the land out of which he came. . . . The old man declared I had no right to compare him and grown-up Indians to small children. . . . This sort of talk was continued at some length. [The meeting adjourned for the weekend and reconvened the following Monday.]

We then called upon the Indians, as they had plenty of time to consider the instructions, to complete what they had to say. The same old "dreamer," Too-shul-hul-sote, was put forward again to talk. His manner was loud, harsh, and impudent. He had the usual words concerning the earth being his mother, and the wrong that was done to attempt to separate the Indians from the land which was theirs by inheritance, and that no decision should be arrived at till it be done in the right manner. He repeats what he had said at the other council about chieftainship—chieftainship of the earth—and that he wanted Mr. Monteith and me to tell the truth. I answer, "I don't want to offend your religion, but you must talk about practicable things; twenty times over I hear that the earth is your mother and about chieftainship from the earth. I want to hear it no more, but come to business at once." The old man then began to speak about the land and became more impudent than ever, and said, "What the treaty Indians talk about was born to-day; wasn't true law at all. You white people get together and measure the earth and then divide it, so I want you to talk directly what you mean."

The agent, Monteith, said, "The law is, you must come to the reservation. The law is made in Washington; we don't make it."

Other positive instructions are repeated. Too-shul-hulsote answers, "We never have made any trade. Part of the Indians gave up their land; I never did. The earth is part of my body, and I never gave up the earth."

I answer, "You know very well that the government has set apart a reservation, and that the Indians must go on it. . . . The government has set apart this large reservation

131

for you and your children, that you may live here in peace and prosper."

The old man, in a surly way, asked, "What person pretended to divide the land and put me on it?"

I answered, with emphasis, "I am the man. I stand here for the President, and there is no spirit, good or bad, that will hinder me. My orders are plain, and will be executed. I hoped the Indians had good sense enough to make me their friend and not their enemy." . . . *I then turned to the old man, and say,* "Then you do not propose to comply with the others?" *He answers,* "So long as the earth keeps me, I want to be left alone; you are trifling with the law of the earth." *I reply, "Our old friend does not seem to understand that the question is, will the Indians come peaceably on the reservation, or do they want me to put them there by force?"*

192 CHIEF JOSEPH counseled peace, but a small band of his young warriors killed almost a dozen whites in June 1877 and there was no chance then that the Nez Perce could "come peaceably on the reservation."

I would have given my own life if I could have undone the killing of white men by my own people. I blame my young men and I blame the white man. . . . My friends among the white men have blamed me for the war. I am not to blame. When my young men began the killing, my heart was hurt. Although I did not justify them, I remembered all the insults I had endured, and my blood was on fire. Still, I would have taken my people to buffalo country [Montana] without fighting, if possible.

I could see no other way to avoid war. We moved over to White Bird Creek, sixteen miles away, and there encamped, intending to collect our stock before leaving; but the soldiers attacked us and the first battle was fought.

193 WOUNDED HEAD, young Nez Perce brave, was injured when Colonel John Gibbon and his men caught up with Chief Joseph's band at Big Hole during their flight to Canada. About thirty dead warriors and fifty dead women and children were left in the wake of battle.

I still had a strip of wolf's hide with which I tied my hair at the time I was shot in the fight. The hide I have had since a boy old enough to know anything. I have kept it all my life, kept it for the purpose of going to war and engaging in battle. Up to the present this hide is my possession. . . . This animal *hemene* once gave me by its spirit the strength and power to face battle and go through it without danger, which I have done time and time again. . . . When I went back to camp many of the tepees were ashes—some of the blackened poles still standing. . . . On reaching the tepee escaped from burning . . . my wife and baby had both been shot. . . . I did not leave the tepee. I had to care for my wounded wife and child. . . . Four days later my little one died. . . . We lost many warriors in battle and a number of women and children killed.

194 CHIEF JOSEPH, after some of the finest battle strategy ever witnessed, tragically surrendered only fifty miles from Canada, at Eagle Creek in Montana under the shadow of Bear Paw Mountains, October 5, 1877, to Generals O. O. Howard and Nelson A. Miles.

I am tired of fighting. Our chiefs are killed. Looking Glass is dead. Toohulhulsote is dead. The old men are all dead. It is the young men who say yes or no. He [Ollokot, Joseph's brother] who led the young men is dead. It is cold and we have no blankets. The little children are freezing to death. My people, some of them, have run away to the hills and have no blankets, no food; no one knows where they are—perhaps freezing to death. I want to have time to look for my children and see how many of them I can find. Maybe I shall find them among the dead. Hear me, my chiefs. I am tired; my heart is sick and sad. From where the sun now stands I will fight no more forever.

195 CHIEF JOSEPH later told of the promises made to him at the time of his surrender and of his bitter disillusionment when the agreement was promptly forgotten and his people were shipped to Kansas where many died, and then to Indian Territory where many more died.

General Miles said to me in plain words, "If you will come out and give up your arms, I will spare your lives and send you back to the reservation." General Miles had promised we might return to our country with what stock we had left. . . . I believed General Miles, or I never would have surrendered.

196 CHIEF JOSEPH was never permitted to live again in his beloved hills, though he did visit Wallowa Valley briefly in 1900. He was first taken to Fort Leavenworth, then to Indian Territory, then to Washington, D.C., twice, again to Indian Territory, and finally in 1885 to Colville Reservation in the state of Washington, where he died in 1904.

I have heard talk and talk, but nothing is done. Good words do not last long unless they amount to something. Words do not pay for my dead people. They do not pay for my country, now overrun by white men. . . . Good words will not give my people good health and stop them from dying. Good words will not get my people a home where they can live in peace and take care of themselves. I am tired of talk that comes to nothing. It makes my heart sick when I remember all the good words and broken promises. . . .

You might as well expect the rivers to run backward as that any man who was born a free man should be contented when penned up and denied liberty to go where he pleases. . . .

Let me be a free man—free to travel, free to stop, free to work, free to trade where I choose, free to choose my own teachers, free to follow the religion of my fathers, free to talk and think and act for myself—and I will obey every law, or submit to the penalty.

197 CRAZY HORSE, last of the Sioux war chiefs at large, finally was confined to a reservation in May 1877. Angered over the many Sioux he saw taking up white men's ways and discontented about the unfulfilled promise of a reservation of his own, Crazy Horse never adjusted to his new life. By September he found himself being ushered into the guardhouse at Fort Robinson, Nebraska. Resisting, he was stabbed. His dying words were:

I was hostile to the white man. . . . We preferred hunting to a life of idleness on our reservations. . . . At times we did not get enough to eat and we were not allowed to hunt. All we wanted was peace and to be let alone. Soldiers came . . . in the winter . . . and destroyed our villages. Then Long Hair [Custer] came. . . . They said we massacred him, but he would have done the same to us. . . . Our first impulse was to escape . . . but we were so hemmed in we had to fight. After that I . . . lived in peace; but the government would not let me alone. . . . I came back to the Red Cloud Agency. Yet I was not allowed to remain quiet. I was tired of fighting. . . . They tried to confine me . . . and a soldier ran his bayonet into me. I have spoken.

198 CROWFOOT, a Blackfoot chief in Canada, talked of the Northwest Mounted, who began their duties in 1874. Treaty 7, 1877, was generally admired by the Indians, because it suppressed American traders, with their rum, from Indian trade.

If the police hadn't come to the country, where would we all be now? Bad men and bad whisky was killing us so fast that very few, indeed, of us would have been left today. The police have protected us as the feathers of a bird protects it from the frosts of winter.

199 LITTLE WOLF and Dull Knife, Northern Cheyenne chiefs, were removed with their people from their lands in 1877 to malarial Indian Territory. In 1878, about the Fourth of July, they protested to the government agent, demanding to go home to their Powder River hunting grounds. Denied, they set out northward nonetheless, sparking the Dull Knife War.

These people were raised far up in the north among the pines and the mountains. In that country we were always healthy. There was no sickness and very few of us died. Now, since we have been in this country, we are dying every day. This is not a good country for us, and we wish to return to our home in the mountains. . . .

We cannot stay another year; we want to go now. Before another year has passed, we may all be dead and there will be none of us left to travel north. . . .

My friends, I am now going to my camp. I do not wish the ground about this agency to be made bloody, but now listen to what I say to you. I am going to leave here; I am going north to my own country. I do not want to see blood spilt about this agency. If you are going to send your soldiers after me, I wish that you would first let me get a little distance away from this agency. Then if you want to fight, I will fight you, and we can make the ground bloody at that place.

The white man, who possesses this whole vast country from sea to sea, who roams over it at pleasure and lives where he likes, cannot know the cramp we feel in this little spot, with the undying remembrance of the fact, which you know as well as we, that every foot of what you proudly call America, not very long ago belonged to the Red Man. The Great Spirit gave it to us, there was room enough for all his tribes; all were happy in their freedom.

The white man had, in ways we know not of, learned some things we had not learned: among them how to make superior tools and terrible weapons, better for war than bows and arrows, and there seemed no end to the hordes of men that followed them from other lands beyond the sea.

And so, at last, our fathers were steadily driven out, or killed. We, their sons, but sorry remnants of tribes once mighty, are cornered in little spots of the earth, all ours by right—cornered like guilty prisoners, and watched by men with guns who are more than anxious to kill us off.

201 WASHAKIE, Shoshone chief, gave Major G. A. Gordon permission in 1878 to let a starving band of Arapahoe stay on his Wind River Reservation until spring. Over bitter protests they lingered year after year. Washakie minced no words.

I don't like these people; they eat their dogs. They have been enemies of the Shoshones since before the birth of the oldest man. If you leave them here there will be trouble. But it is plain they can go no further now. Take them down to where Popo Agie walks into Wind River and let them stay until the grass comes again. But when the grass comes again take them off my reservation. I want my words written down on paper with the white man's ink. I want you all to sign as witnesses to what I have said. And I want a copy of that paper. I have spoken. [A half century later a court decision awarded the Shoshone $4.5 million for suffering the Arapahoe presence.]

202 In 1858 the U.S. negotiated a treaty with the Ponca Indians—one of the friendliest tribes the government ever knew. The Poncas relinquished a portion of their land; the U.S. agreed to a permanent home for the Poncas on the Niobrara River and promised to protect them and their property. In 1868 the U.S. negotiated a treaty with some Sioux Indians—traditional enemies of the Poncas. The government erred and gave the Poncas' Niobrara land to the Sioux. The Poncas protested, in vain. By 1879 Secretary of the Interior Carl Schurz had admitted that "the Poncas were grievously wronged by . . . a mistake in making the Sioux treaty." But by 1879 the Poncas had already suffered grievously from this wrong. In 1877 they were force-marched over 500 miles south to Indian Territory. Life in the new land proved as devastating as the trip. Many had died during the fifty-day journey; during the first year in Indian Territory over twenty percent of them died. Finally in December of 1880 the President appointed a special commission to investigate the removal of the Poncas from the Niobrara and to evaluate their present condition in Indian Territory. The Commissioners traveled south in January of 1881, met with the chiefs, and asked about their departure from Nebraska and Dakota. WHITE EAGLE replied.

A white man [Edward C. Kemble, Indian inspector] came there suddenly after Christmas to see us. We didn't get any news he was coming; he came suddenly. They called us all to the church and there they told us the purpose of his coming. This is the fifth winter since that time [1877-1881]. *"The Great Father at Washington says you are to move, and for that reason I've come,"* said he. *"These Dakotas are causing you a great deal of trouble, and they'll put you out of patience very soon."* "My friend, you have caused us to hear these things very suddenly," I said. "When the Great Father has any business to transact with us he generally sends for us to come to Washington and there we transact it. When the Great Father has any plans on foot he generally sends word to all the people, but you have come very suddenly." *"No; the Great Father says you have to go,"* said he. "My friend, I want you to send a letter to the Great Father, and if he really says this I desire him to send for us," I said. "If it be so, and I hear of it the right way, I'll say his words are straight. The Great Father can't be surpassed." *"I'll send a letter to him,"* said he. He struck the wire. He sent the message by telegraph and it reached the Great Father very soon. *"Your Great Father says you are to come with ten of your chiefs,"* said he. *"You are to go and see the land, and after passing through a part you are to come to Washington."* We consented to that proposition and went. *"You are to look at the Warm Land* [Indian Territory] *and if you see any land that is good there you are to tell him about it,"* said he, *"and also about any bad land there; tell him about both."* And so we went there to the Warm Land. We went to the terminus of the railroad and passed through the land of the Osages and on to the land full of rocks, and next morning we came to the land of the Kaws; and leaving the Kansas reservation we came to Arkansas City, and so, having visited the lands of two of these Indian tribes and seen this land full of rocks and how low the trees were, I came to this town of the whites. We were sick twice and we saw how the people of that land were, and we saw those stones and rocks, and we thought those two tribes were not able to do much for themselves. And he said to us the next morning, *"We'll go to the Shicaska River and see that;"* and I said, "My friend, I've seen these lands and I've been sick on the journey. From this on I'll stop on this journey, seeing these lands, and will go and see the great Father. Run to the Great Father. Take me with you to see the Great Father. These two tribes are poor and sick, and these lands are poor; therefore, I've seen enough of them." *"No,"* said he, *"come and see these other lands in the Indian Territory."* "My friend," said I, "take me, I beg, to see the Great Father. You said formerly we could tell him whatever we saw, good or bad, and I wish to tell him." *"No,"* said he, *"I don't wish to take you to see him. If you take part of this land I'll take you to see him; if not, not."* "If you will not take me to see the Great Father," said I, "take me home to my own country." *"No,"* said he, *"notwithstanding what you say, I'll not take you to see the Great Father. He did not say I should take you back to your own country."* "How in the world shall I act," said I; "You are unwilling to take me to the Great Father, and you don't want to take me back to my own country. You said formerly that the Great Father had called me, but now it is not so; you have not spoken the truth; you have not spoken the straight word." *"No,"* said he, *"I'll not take you to your homes; walk there if you want to."* "It makes my heart feel sad," said I, "as I do not know this land." We thought we should die, and felt that I should cry, but I remembered that I was a man. After saying this, the white man, being in a bad humor, went upstairs. After he had gone upstairs, we chiefs sat considering what to do. We said, "He does not speak of taking us to see the Great Father or of taking us to our own country. We don't think the Great Father has caused this." We had one interpreter there with us, and we said, "As he will not take us back, we want him to give us a piece of paper to show the whites, as we don't know the land." The interpreter went upstairs to see the man and came back and said, "He will not give you the paper. He does not wish to make it for you." We sent the interpreter back again and said: "We want some money due us from the Great Father, so we can make our way home." When he came back he said, "He does not wish to give you the money." He said, "The interpreter and three others, half-breeds must stay. The rest of you can go on foot." We sat talking with each other and said, "Although the Great Father has not caused this, yet if we stay here

140

what man will give us food? Let [us] go towards our own home." . . . We said, "He has behaved shamefully towards us, and now, at night let us go," and so we went towards our home. This man, Standing Bear, said "Beware, lest they say of us these men have stolen off." We did not know the land; we were without food; we were without moccasins, and we said, "Why should we die? What have we done?" I thought we should die. Passing on, I was sick on the way—very sick. At last we came to the land of the Otoes, and on the way we lived on corn. For ten days we staid with the Otoes and they gave us food. Passing on our homeward way, we reached the Omahas, and from that place we soon reached our home [500 miles and forty days later]. When we got home we found that he [Kemble] anticipated us and was there in advance of us. When we reached home we found that he had ordered the Poncas who were there to get ready to move. Having called us, we went there to him. *"Move ye,"* said he; *"prepare to remove."* We were unwilling. Said I, "I've come back weary; every one of us is unwilling to move; this removal is difficult. Much money will be lost, fall to the ground. Stop your speaking; that is enough," said I. *"No,"* said he, *"the Great Father wishes you to remove at once, and you must move to the Indian Territory."* "If you wish to speak saucy to us and scold us, scold us," said I. Some soldiers came there. *"Only this day will I speak about it,"* said he. *"I will leave this matter in the hands of the leader of the soldiers,"* said he, *"surrender my charge to him."* I said, "There are white people traveling around and some of them may come here and look at my body and say, 'Why did they kill him?' and they will say 'Because he did not go.' And I wish the Great Father to know it. I want no trouble with the white soldiers. If the soldiers should shoot at me, I'd not take revenge; I'll not shoot back." *"My friend, stop saying that; I do not want it that way,"* said he. They separated the half-breeds from the pure bloods and talked separately to them, and suddenly they were carried away. The white man came with the rations intended for us, but we did not take and eat of them. They

141

had taken away some of our people in advance and we sat without eating. We commenced plowing our land, thinking of the affair as ended, so we commenced to dig up our land. I wanted to see some of the leading men of the whites, but I could not see any of them. On the other side of the Niobrara River, at the town of Niobrara, was a white man, one who was a lawyer. I went to see him. "Alas, my friend, I want to find out—I want you to send a message to the Great Father, but I haven't any money. If you will send to him quickly, I'll give you this horse." He sent the message, but none ever came back, although I'd given him the pony. Then I said to this lawyer, "My friend, I want you to go to the Great Father." *"I have no money,"* said he. "My friend, I have thirty-two horses, I'll give them to you." *"Well, bring them to me,"* said the white man. Driving the horses before me, I took them to the white man and gave them to him. He sold the ponies and went to the Great Father and returned. This white man sent a letter to me. In it he said, *"I've been to see the Great Father."* He sent the first letter before he returned and he was on his way home when he sent a second letter, saying, *"My friend, I am sick and on my way home."* It came to pass a person came there. A white man came with a half-breed interpreter. . . . He spoke gently and softly to us. *"My friend, I've come back to you that we may go; that we may remove."* At that time we were very tired. Before we returned home a young man came to us and said, "The soldiers have come to the lodges." We had not yet seen them. Buffalo and myself said to the young men, "Come to decision; if you say we are to remove we are to remove." The Ponca women were afraid of the soldiers. The soldiers came to the borders of the village and forced us across the Niobrara to the other side, just as one would drive a herd of ponies; and the soldiers pushed us on until we came to the Platte River. They drove us on in advance just as if we were a herd of ponies, and I said, "If I have to go, I'll go to that land. Let the soldiers go away, our women are afraid of them." And so I reached the Warm Land, and so I've been there up to this time. And this is the end.

203 General George Crook asked WHITE EAGLE if he were satisfied after he got to Indian Territory.

We found the land there was bad and we were dying one after another, and we said "What man will take pity on us?" And our animals died. O, it was very hot. "This land is truly sickly, and we'll be apt to die here, and we hope the Great Father will take us back again." That is what we said. There were one hundred of us died there.

204 One of those who died in Indian Territory was the son of Standing Bear. He and his band left the hated Warm Land in January 1879 and walked as a funeral party to bury the chief's son in their homeland. In March, Standing Bear was arrested for leaving Indian Territory and was held in jail at Fort Omaha. Friendly white lawyers, with the aid of General Crook himself, arranged a suit. The U.S. district attorney denied Standing Bear's right to a writ of *habeas corpus* on grounds that Indians were "not persons within the meaning of the law." In one court appearance before U.S. District Court Judge Elmer S. Dundy, STANDING BEAR lifted his arm and said:

That hand is not the color of your hand, but if I pierce it I shall feel pain. The blood that will flow from mine will be the same color as yours. I am a man. The Great Spirit made us both.

I seem to stand on the bank of a river. . . . In front the river is wide and impassable, and behind me are perpendicular cliffs. No man of my race had ever stood there before. There is no tradition to guide me. The flood rises, looking upward I see a steep, stony path. . . . I lead the way up the sharp rocks while the water rises behind us. Then I saw a rift in the rocks and felt the prairie breeze strike my cheek.

I turn with a shout that we are saved. We will return

to the Swift Running Waters that pours between the green Islands. There are the graves of my fathers. There we will pitch our teepees and build our fires.

But a man bars the passage. He is a thousand times more powerful than I. Behind him I see soldiers as numerous as the leaves on the trees. If he says I cannot pass, I cannot.

You are that man!

205 In April 1879, Judge Dundy ruled that an Indian was a "person" with legal rights, that he could not be held in custody without just cause, and that as an individual Indian separating himself from his tribe could not be moved from one part of the country to another without his consent or confined to a particular reservation against his will.* This decision encouraged the Poncas in Indian Territory who wanted to return home to the Niobrara. Standing Bear's brother, Big Snake, still in Indian Territory, made preliminary test of Judge Dundy's ruling by moving a hundred miles within the Territory to a Cheyenne reservation. He was returned to the Ponca reservation and it appeared that the matter was closed—the law and the Poncas forgotten. However, on October 31, 1879, Ponca Indian agent William H. Whiteman, fearing "a very demoralizing effect upon the other Indians" by troublemaker Big Snake, imported a detail of soldiers to arrest and imprison him. In the confrontation, Big Snake was killed. On March 12, 1880, in response to some public outcry, the U.S. Senate passed a resolution calling for an investigation of Big Snake's death. The testimony of HAIRY BEAR, a Ponca chief, tells the story.

I was present when the officer tried to arrest Big Snake. I stood by the door of the office, inside the door. The of-

* See Appendix for full text of Judge Dundy's decision.

ficer was in about the middle of the room. He told Big Snake, *"I have come to arrest you."* Big Snake said he did not want to go without an interpreter went; then he would go along. Big Snake said, "If the interpreter don't go, I want to take one of my wives along." The officer said he could not do that; that he came to arrest only him. The agent told Big Snake he had better go, and said he would give him a blanket to sleep on. The officer told Big Snake to come along, to get up and come. Big Snake would not get up, and told the officer he wanted him to tell him what he had done. He said he had killed no one, stolen no horses, and that he had done nothing wrong. After Big Snake said that the officer spoke to the agent, and then told Big Snake he had tried to kill two men, and had been pretty mean. Big Snake denied it. The agent then told him he had better go, and could then learn all about it down there. Big Snake said he had done nothing wrong; that he carried no knife; and threw off his blanket and turned around to show he had no weapon. The officer again told him to come along. Big Snake said he had done nothing wrong, and that he would die before he would go. I then went up to Big Snake and told him this man was not going to arrest him for nothing, and that he had better go along, and that perhaps he would come back all right; I coaxed all I could to get him to go; told him that he had a wife and children, and to remember them and not get killed. Big Snake then got up and told me that he did not want to go, and that if they wanted to kill him they could do it, right there. Big Snake was very cool. Then the officer told him to get up, and told him that if he did not go, there might something happen. He said there is no use in talking; I came to arrest you and want you to go. The officer went for the handcuffs, which a soldier had, and brought them in. The officer and a soldier then tried to put them on him, but Big Snake pushed them both away. Then the officer spoke to the soldiers, and four of them tried to put them on, but Big Snake pushed them all off. One soldier, who had stripes on his arms, also tried to put them on, but Big Snake pushed them all off. They tried several times, all of them, to get hold of Big Snake

145

and hold him. Big Snake was sitting down, when six soldiers got hold of him. He raised up and threw them off. [Even agent Whiteman testified that although *the soldiers say that at this time Big Snake drew a knife . . . I did not see Big Snake have any weapon.*"] Just then one of the soldiers, who was in front of him, struck Big Snake in the face with his gun, another soldier struck him along side the head with the barrel of his gun. It knocked him back to the wall. He straightened up again. The blood was running down his face. I saw the gun pointed at him, and was scared, and did not want to see him killed. So I turned away. Then the gun was fired and Big Snake fell down dead on the floor.

206 SITTING BULL, Sioux, abandoned his freezing sanctuary in Canada to return to the U.S. in 1881. The Fort Buford commander received him courteously, but told him his orders were to take him as a military prisoner to Fort Yates, then to Standing Rock Reservation. Sitting Bull bristled, then softened.

I do not come in anger toward the white soldiers. I am very sad. My daughter went this road. Her I am seeking. I will fight no more. I do not love war. I never was the aggressor. I fought only to defend my women and children. Now all my people want to return to their native land. Therefore I submit. . . .

[Later] I do not wish to be shut up in a corral. It is bad for young men to be fed by an agent. It makes them lazy and drunken. All agency Indians I have seen were worthless. They are neither red warriors nor white farmers. They are neither wolf nor dog. But my followers are weary of cold and hunger. They wish to see their brothers and their old home, therefore I bow my head.

207 Tom Wilson, in charge of a pack train for the Canadian Pacific Railroad, made camp August 23, 1882, at Pipestone Creek. During a violent storm he asked his Indian guide what caused such vibrations, and the guide promised to take him to what the white man later called Lake Louise in Alberta, Canada.

The Great Spirit speaks at the Lake of the Little Fishes, five miles at the foot of the ice mountain where the blue picture is painted, the picture that the Great Spirit made for the Indians. White man's pictures all fade, the Indian's pictures last forever.

208 DELCHE, aging Apache chief of the Chiricahuas, surrendered April 27, 1883, at Camp Verde, eleven years after Cochise, leaving only Geronimo, who held out until 1886, ending the long Apache war against the whites.

There was a time we could escape the white soldiers. But now the very rocks have become soft. We cannot put our feet anywhere. We cannot sleep, for if a coyote or fox barks, or a stone moves, we are up—the soldiers have come.

209 SITTING BULL, Sioux, in 1883 replied to a Senate Investigating Committee, who asked questions and demanded immediate answers, by saying the Indian habit was to discuss a question then answer through a spokesman. One committeeman asked who did Sitting Bull think he was—he was only an Indian like the rest of them.

I am here by the will of the Great Spirit, and by his will I am a chief. My heart is red and sweet, because whatever passes near me puts out its tongue to me; and yet you have come here to talk to us, and you say you don't know who I am. I want to tell you if the Great Spirit had chosen anyone to be chief of this country, it is myself.

210 Chief CHARLES JOURNEYCAKE of the Delawares was one of the founders of Bacone College, the Indian school in Oklahoma. Inscribed on the cornerstone of the college's chapel are Chief Journeycake's words he addressed to the Indian Defense Association meeting in Washington, D.C. in 1886.

We have been broken up and moved six times. We have been despoiled of our property. We thought when we moved across the Missouri River and had paid for our homes in Kansas we were safe. But in a few years the white man wanted our country. We had good farms. Built comfortable houses and big barns. We had schools for our children and churches where we listened to the same gospel the white man listens to. The white man came into our country from Missouri. And drove our cattle and horses away and if our people followed them they were killed. We try to forget these things. But we would not forget that the white man brought us the blessed gospel of Christ. The Christian hope. This more than pays for all we have suffered.

211 SITTING BULL in 1889 talked to a white man he trusted—John Carnigan, a school teacher at Standing Rock Reservation.

Our religion seems foolish to you, but so does yours to me. The Baptists and Methodists and Presbyterians and the Catholics all have a different God. Why cannot we have one of our own? Why does the agent seek to take away our religion? My race is dying. Our God will soon die with us. If this new religion is not true then what matters? I do not know what to believe? If I could dream like the others and visit the spirit world myself, then it would be easy to believe, but the trance does not come to me. It passes me by. I help others to see their dead, but I am not aided.

212 WASHAKIE, Shoshone chief, following enactment of The Dawes Allotment Act of 1887, met in council with Indian Bureau officials to discuss small truck farming for the Indians. For hours he listened to the officials and his minor chiefs discuss the subject. Rising, he cut short the debate with majestic simplicity.

God damn a potato!

213 WOVOKA, son of an earlier Paiute Messiah, Tavibo, in 1889 began the Ghost Dance "medicine" which spread like wild fire among the Plains Indians as a last protection against the white man's invasion of their beloved lands.

Grandfather [the messiah] says, when your friends die you must not cry. You must not hurt anybody or do harm to anyone. You must not fight. Do right always. It will give you satisfaction in life.

Do not tell the white people about this. Jesus is now upon the earth. He appears like a cloud. The dead are all alive again. I do not know when they will be here; maybe this fall or in the spring. When the time comes there will be no more sickness and everyone will be young again.

Do not refuse to work for the whites and do not make any trouble with them until you leave them. When the earth shakes [at the coming] do not be afraid. It will not hurt you.

The whole world is coming,
A nation is coming, a nation is coming,
The Eagle has brought the message to the tribe.
The father says so, the father says so.
Over the whole earth they are coming.
The buffalo are coming, the buffalo are coming,
The Crow has brought the message to the tribe,
The father says so, the father says so.

215 WOVOKA to his followers:

My people, before the white man came you were happy.
You had many buffalo to eat and tall grass for your
ponies—you could come and go like the wind. When it
grew cold you could journey to the valleys of the south,
where healing springs are; and when it grew warm, you
could return to the mountains of the north. The white
man came. He dug up the bones of our mother, the earth.
He tore her bosom with steel. He built big trails and put
iron horses on them. He fought you and beat you, and put
you in barren places where a horned toad would die. He
said you must stay there; you must not go hunt in the
mountains.

216 MANY HORSES, Oglala Sioux, helped promote a Ghost Dance at Standing Rock Reservation in 1890, to dance the white soldiers
away. At dawn, seeing the white tipis of the
army still there, he knew with profound grief
the magic had failed. Later, he confided to a
white friend:

I will follow the white man's trail. I will make him my
friend, but I will not bend my back to his burdens. I will

be cunning as a coyote. I will ask him to help me understand his ways, then I will prepare the way for my children. Maybe they will outrun the white man in his own
shoes. . . . There are but two ways. One leads to hunger
and death, the other leads to where the poor white man
lives. Beyond is the happy hunting ground where the white
man cannot go.

217 FOUR GUNS, Oglala Sioux Indian judge, with
two other judges, Pine Tree and Running Wolf,
were guests in 1891 at a dinner given by anthropologist Clark Wissler. Four Guns' after
dinner speech:

I have visited the Great Father in Washington. I have
attended dinners among white people. Their ways are not
our ways. We eat in silence, quietly smoke a pipe and depart. Thus is our host honored. This is not the way of the
white man. After his food has been eaten, one is expected
to say foolish things. Then the host feels honored. Many
of the white man's ways are past our understanding, but
now that we have eaten at the white man's table, it is
fitting that we honor our host according to the ways of his
people.

Our host has filled many notebooks with the sayings of
our fathers as they came down to us. This is the way of
his people; they put great store upon writing; always there
is a paper. But we have learned that though there are many
papers in Washington upon which are written promises to
pay us for our lands, no white man seems to remember
them. However, we know our host will not forget what he
has written down, and we hope that the white people will
read it.

But we are puzzled as to what useful service all this
writing serves. Whenever white people come together there
is writing. When we go to buy some sugar or tea, we see
the white trader busy writing in a book; even the white
doctor as he sits beside his patient writes on a piece of

paper. The white people must think paper has some mysterious power to help them on in the world. The Indian needs no writings; words that are true sink deep into his heart where they remain; he never forgets them. On the other hand, if the white man loses his papers, he is helpless. I once heard one of their preachers say that no white man was admitted to heaven unless there were writings about him in a great book.

218 A reservation chief at Pine Ridge answered Major D. F. Royer when told of an 1891 order from Washington that Indians must cease their drumming, because it was a waste of time and unnecessary.

My father, the Great Father is not at fault, but his foolish advisors hide from him the true state of affairs. The white man makes use of the drum, when soldiers come together and even at a burial. Why is the Great Father so unmindful of his children? In order that he might know their hearts a letter should be written telling how much the drum means to the Indian, but should the Great Father in accordance with his infinite wisdom, decide that all drums should be put away forever, and require that the white people do so, then his Red Children will not hold back, but they will sound the drum no more.

219 SIMON POKAGON, Potawatomi chief and son of the man who sold the site of Chicago and environs to the United States in 1833, reminisced about life as it was once.

In early life I was deeply hurt as I witnessed the grand old forests of Michigan, under whose shades my forefathers lived and died, falling before the cyclone of civilization as before a prairie fire. In those days I traveled thousands of miles along our winding trails, through the unbroken solitudes of the wild forest, listening to the songs of the woodland birds, as they poured forth their melodies from the thick foliage above and about me.

Very seldom now do I catch one familiar note from these early warblers of the woods. They have all passed away. . . . I now listen to the songs of other birds which have come with the advance of civilization . . . and, like the wildwood birds which our fathers used to hold their breath to hear, they sing in concert, without pride, without envy, without jealousy—alike in forest and field; alike before wigwam or castle; alike before savage or sage . . . alike for chief or king.

220 PLAYFUL CALF, Osage, in the early 20th century related to anthropologist Francis La Flesche, himself an Omaha, the rites and customs of the Osage.

My son, the ancient No-ho-zhi-ga have handed down to us, in songs, wi-gi-e, ceremonial forms, symbols, and many things they learned of the mysteries that surround us on all sides. All these things they learned through their power of wa-thi-gtho, the power to search with the mind. They speak of the mysteries of the light of day by which the earth and all living things that dwell thereon are influenced; of the mysteries of the darkness of night that reveal to us all the great bodies of the upper world, each of which forever travels in a circle upon its own path, unimpeded by the others. They searched, for a long period of time, for the source of life and at last came to the thought that it issues from an invisible creative power to which they applied the name Wa-ko-da. [Later, in 1910, during another interview session, Playful Calf paused for a long, long silence, then, "when he had composed himself," turned to La Flesche and explained:]

My son, a sudden remembrance of the old No-ho-zhi-ga brought tears to my eyes. They were kind to me, those old men, when I was working hard to learn from them these sacred songs. As they sat around the fireplace I fed the fire to make it shed light and warmth and I ran to the spring to fetch water for them when they were thirsty. By these little services I won their affection and they were gentle and patient with me when they taught me.

221 In 1909, 261 of Geronimo's Apaches were still prisoners of war at Fort Sill, Oklahoma, having been herded from Arizona to Florida to Alabama to Oklahoma during the past quarter century. Now the government proposed to move them yet again (the Army needed their land for an artillery firing range). Some Indians wanted to stay in Oklahoma, some wanted to go back to their ancestral home at Warm Springs, and some wanted to go join the Mescalero Apaches on their reservation in New Mexico. On August 22, 1909, Lt. George A. Purington, in charge of the Fort Sill Apaches, discussed the matter with them, calling first on Asa Daklugie (son of Juh, Nednhi Apache chief), who had recently journeyed to the Mescalero Reservation to arrange a transfer.

Asa Daklugie: We want to go there but not all of us— maybe a little more than half. Counting the men, women, and children, one hundred and fifty-two of us want to go to Mescalero. Just want to go there because we have friends and relatives among those people and they want to see them and be with them. It is true that the Mescaleros there are willing to have us come. I was there and saw them, saw their mouths move when they talked, and they saw mine. When I gave them the words of these Apaches they said we could come there and live. . . .
There are mountains there and all kinds of timber that can be used. They can cut the timber to make lumber and build houses, or make fence posts and railroad ties. There is lots of water all over, and streams and springs. Dig a well three hundred feet and get water that never fails. It is that way all over the reservation. There are places on the reservation, valleys in the mountains and along the

streams, good for farming where one can get a farm of ten, twenty, fifty, or even a hundred acres. The Indians said that whatever was planted would grow, whether vegetables or grain. I went down there to see what kind of a country it was and if we could make a living on it. The white man first goes and looks at a country and if a certain spot, whether trees or rocks, suits him and he thinks a living can be made, that is where he wants to go. We are the same way ourselves now. . . . It might not rain, the same as it has not rained in this country this year, and then nothing would grow, however rich the land. But we don't depend entirely upon farming to make a living. We have cattle, horses, sheep, pigs, and chickens from which to make a living. Lots of us may not have learned yet but we all have brains and are anxious to work. Some of us are old and crippled and not able to work; we who are strong can take care of them. You white people, when a family is poor and unable to earn a living, others will give them something to feed them, also build a house. We are that way now ourselves. The meanness that was in us is all out now—all gone, none have any more.

A great many years ago the government commenced feeding us and clothing us. Do they want to keep it up until our children's children and their children's children are old men and women? No, we don't want it so. We think we have been given enough, meaning rations and clothing. We want to be free now. We want to be turned over to the Interior Department. When this paper goes to Washington we want its words to set us free. Those who want to stay here, let them stay; those who want to go, send them. . . .

I told them [Mescalero Apaches] . . . What do you think about it? Are you willing for us to come? Can it be done soon, or don't you want us? It is with you. This is your reservation, you have been here a long time. We live some other place, but we have nothing. We have no home, no land. We have been moved about among white people, caused to work here and there and other places while you have lived here always. You are born here and you die

155

here. You must like it for you stay here so long. You think a great deal of your land but we would like to come and live with you and bring all our property. Do you want us?

LIEUT. PURINGTON: *What did the Indians say when you asked them, "Do you want us?"*

ASA DAKLUGIE: "Come to us." . . .

LIEUT. PURINGTON: *Now we will hear from the people who do not want to go to Mescalero to live.*

ROGERS TOOKLANNI: My people long ago had something that belonged to them; that is why I think and act good. Ojo Caliente! [Warm Springs in west central New Mexico] I was born close to there and raised there. That is a good country. There are mountains on this side and on that side. In the middle there is a wide valley. There are springs in that valley, fine grass, and plenty of timber around. Dig a well and get water in forty feet. These people who want to go there will get old pretty soon. They want to be there and get settled so their children can grow up there.

The soil is good there—you can raise anything. Even when I lived there and planted seeds by digging a hole in the ground with a stick the corn grew up very high and pumpkins got very large. Horses and cattle will not freeze there. It is a healthy place for man and beast. Women nor children get sick there. Neither do animals. Don't send me any place except there. For years I have been on other people's ground and trouble has always come of it. Somebody has always bothered me. That is why I want to go to ourselves in our own country. That is why I have always been a friend to the white people. I thought that when the time came and I would ask for something I would not be refused. Since I was a small boy I have been a friend to the white. The white people have accomplished many things that were hard—that were difficult; I ask for something that is not hard for them to grant. I beg it may be granted

156

me. If what I say here will be the cause of my removal to my old home I will be very grateful. Food and water will taste good to me. I will be happy again in my old home.

TALBOT GOODY: Ojo Caliente is my home. All of my people so far as I can remember have lived there. It has been a great many years since I was taken away from there. . . .

From San Carlos they took me to Fort Apache. We had trouble at San Carlos and Fort Apache both. Both of those times we were on land belonging to other Indians. From Fort Apache I was sent to St. Augustine, Florida. At St. Augustine I was told that my way was a bad one, that my thoughts and life had been bad, to put it away from me, get away from it and go to school and learn the ways of the white people. They sent me to Carlisle, Pennsylvania. At Carlisle I learned to talk English and learned something about books. From Carlisle they sent me to my people in Alabama. When I got back to Alabama I found lots of my people from Ojo Caliente there. In Alabama lots of them died. They brought us from Alabama to Fort Sill and there was lots of them died here. But they gave us strong words, strong thoughts, and some of their writings, and they stayed in our hearts and are there today. From what they gave us we have been able to learn to work and are able to work intelligently. We are not afraid to work and we are not afraid to do right. We are like the white people. We have talked with many generals who have visited Fort Sill and have pleaded with them all to send us back to our old homes. We plead once more to be sent back to our old home. I talked to Secretary [of War William H.] Taft when he was here, held him by the wrists, and with tears running from my eyes begged him to send me back to my own country. . . . Most all of the Indians originally from Ojo Caliente are dead. Just a few of us left now and we beg to be sent back there.

LIEUT. PURINGTON: *Does anybody else want to say anything?*

157

JASON BETZINEZ: These few men that are here want to stay here—fourteen of us want to stay at Fort Sill. We are poor and want something for ourselves, that is why we want to stay here. I talked before and asked to be left here. I talked with President Taft who was then Secretary of War and asked to be left here. He made a note on paper of what I said and may have it yet. I told him then that I wanted my farm here at Fort Sill. I didn't want to go to Arizona nor New Mexico. And now that these Indians have asked for different places, I still ask to be left here at Fort Sill and given land here for myself and these few people who are with me. I like this country; I like to live here.

222 Lieutenant Purington immediately recommended to Washington that the problem be disposed of basically the way the Indians had proposed, but four years later Asa Daklugie and his group were still trying to find a wider welcome in New Mexico. New Mexico Senator Albert B. Fall (later of Teapot Dome infamy) argued as follows to his fellow Senators on February 25, 1913:

It is an outrage upon the people of New Mexico, and it is bad faith upon the part of the Secretary of the Interior . . . to insist that he will misapply these funds and take these Indians back, despite the protest of the legislature and of the people of New Mexico and of their Representatives in Congress. . . . The entire people of New Mexico are protesting against this action. . . . We do object most seriously to receiving them back in New Mexico, where they themselves and their fathers made the ground run red with the blood of Americans, descendants of whom are yet living around the Mescalero Reservation.

223 BLACK ELK, shaman of the Oglala Sioux, at Harney Peak in the Dakota Black Hills, in 1912, facing west, holding the sacred pipe before him in his right hand, sang his swan song to Wakan Tanka, the Great Mystery.

Hey-a-a-hey! Hey-a-a-hey! Hey-a-a-hey! Hey-a-a-hey! Grandfather, Great Spirit, once more behold me on earth and lean to hear my feeble voice. You lived first, and you are older than all need, older than all prayer. All things belong to you—the two-legged, the four-legged, the wings of the air and all green things that live. You have set the powers of the four quarters of the earth to cross each other. The good road and the road of difficulties you have made me cross; and where they cross, the place is holy. Day in, day out, forevermore, you are the life of things.

Therefore I am sending you a voice, Great Spirit, my Grandfather, forgetting nothing you have made, the stars of the universe and the grasses of the earth.

You have said to me when I was still young and could hope, that in difficulty I could send a voice four times, once for each quarter of the earth, and you would hear me.

Today I send a voice for a people in despair.

You have given me a sacred pipe, and through this I should make my offering. You see it now!

From the west you have given me the cup of living water and the sacred bow, the power to make life and to destroy it. You have given me the sacred wind and the herb from where the white giant lives—the cleansing power and the healing. The daybreak star and the pipe, you have given me from the east; and from the south the nation's sacred hoop and the tree that was to bloom. To the center of the world you have taken me and showed the goodness and the beauty and the strangeness of the greening earth, the only mother, and there the spirit-shapes of things, as they should be, you have shown me, and I have seen. At the center of the sacred hoop you have said that I should make the tree to bloom.

With tears running, O Great Spirit, my Grandfather—

with running eyes I must say now that the tree has never bloomed. A pitiful old man, you see me here, and I have fallen away and done nothing. Here at the center of the world, where you took me when I was young and taught me; here, old I stand, and the tree is withered, my Grandfather.

Again, and maybe the last time on earth, I recall the great vision you sent me. It may be that some little root of the sacred tree still lives. Nourish it, then, that it may leaf and bloom and fill with singing birds. Hear me, not for myself but for my people; I am old. Hear me, that they may once more go back into the sacred hoop and find the good road and the shielding tree.

224 In 1870, four-year-old WASSAJA, a Mohave Apache, was captured by the Pima Indians in Arizona and sold for $30 to Charles Gentile, a prominent Chicago photographer, who was visiting the Southwest. Wassaja received some schooling, but was put out on his own when Mr. Gentile's business failed in 1877. The Apache, as Carlos Montezuma, later received a BS degree from the University of Illinois (1884) and an MD from Northwestern University (1889). For almost eight years he served as government physician on Indian reservations and at the Indian school in Carlisle; he then established a private practice in Chicago. On September 30, 1915, Dr. Montezuma delivered a fiery address to the Society of American Indians meeting in Lawrence, Kansas. The speech reflects what today could be called a combination of "Red Power" and a policy of assimilation.

In the bloody and gloomy days of Indian history public sentiment was against the Indians, that they could not be civilized; they could not be educated; they were somewhat like human beings, but not quite within the line of human rights; the only hope was to let the bullets do the work, cover up the bloody deeds, and say no more—God and humanity were forgotten. . . .

Patient, silent, and distant the Indian race has been these many years. There comes a time in human events when abandonment of racial responsibilities becomes very oppressive, unbearable, intolerable, and there seems to be no hope—then man must exert himself, speak, and act. . . .

Brothers, that time has come to our race. The society of American Indians is not free. We are wards; we are not free! In a free country we are not free; our heritage is freedom, but we are not free. Wake up, Indians, all over America! We are hoodwinked, duped more and more every year; we are made to feel that we are free when we are not. We are chained hand and foot; we stand helpless, innocently waiting for the fulfillment of promises that will never be fulfilled in the overwhelming great ocean of civilization. . . .

Some well-meaning people feel very bad over this matter of taking away the support of the Indians. They pass their hands over their foreheads, take a long sigh, sadly look into space, and wonder how we are going to free the Indians and what will become of the poor Indians then. This going here and there seeking to find a solution of the Indian problem is all nonsense. It has been a problem so long that it has become a problem. . . .

It is all in our mind. To free the Indian is to free the Indian. There is nothing complicated about that. It is so simple that we cannot believe it.

Common sense teaches us that when you free the Indian in civilization, the Indian will civilize himself—it is automatic and involuntary—and that to free the Indian from bureauism is to free him from bureauism. . . .

The question of abolishing the Indian Bureau is not a new idea. . . . Gen Pratt ["Lieut. R. H. Pratt (founder of the United States Indian School, Carlisle, Pa., 1879), now our most beloved and honored benefactor, a brigadier general"] sounded the keynote when he said [1904]:

"I believe that nothing better could have happened to the Indians than the complete destruction of the bureau,

161

which keeps them so carefully laid away in the dark of its numerous drawers, together with all the varied influences, which only serve to bolster and maintain tribal conditions.

"The early death of the 'Freedmen's Bureau' was an infinite blessing to the negro himself and to the country as well. If you say the turning loose of this large number of ignorant and unprepared people would threaten the peace of our communities, I say that not a year within the last 30 but we have imported from foreign countries and turned loose in the United States a much greater number of no less unprepared and ignorant people. . . .

"Better, far better for the Indians had there never been a bureau. Then self preservation would have led the individual Indian to find his true place, and his real emancipation would have been speedily consummated." . . .

The Indian Bureau could dissolve itself and go out of business, but what is the use? Just think, 8000 employees would be jobless and there would be no $11,000,000 appropriation. By dissolving it would be killing its hen that lays the golden egg. Having nursed the Indians for so long, they might be lonesome living without Indians. . . .

[How did we come to be "wards of the Government"? It is as if the Government said:]

"Say, Sitting Bull, I know you are a good fellow, but you are as a child in looking after your business, you are easily cheated and robbed. I know it, because I have done it myself. Now, my good friend, Sitting Bull, I will tell you what to do. You give everything over to me, and I will do everything for you." . . .

It is a psychological fact that by everlastingly harping and pointing that *"you are an Indian,"* that *"you are a ward,"* that *"you are a child and must be protected,"* that *"you must not do anything without your superintendent's approval,"* that *"you are not ready to live as a free man,"* it is a scientific fact that after a while you will actually believe that it is all true, that you are different from other races, that you have "Washington" for your father, that he feels your weakness as a child, and that the Government is so good as to protect you, that the superintendent and "Washington" will attend to your rights. . . .

To-day the Indian Bureau is founded on a wrong basis. It is un-American. . . .

Keep in mind that Indian Bureau, Indian reservations, Indian schools, Indian college, Indian art, Indian novels, Indian music, Indian shows, Indian movies, and Indian everything create prejudice and do not help our race. To tackle prejudice it is better to do it face to face in the busy world. To play the same card as the other fellow we must know him. . . .

To fight is to forget ourselves as Indians in the world. To think of oneself as different from the mass is not healthy. Push forward as one of them, be congenial, and be in harmony with your environments and make yourselves feel at home as one of the units in the big family of America. Make good, deliver the goods, and convince the world by your character that the Indians are not as they have been misrepresented to be. . . .

Would-be friends of the Indians discovered the Indian to be an ideal and fit subject to be exploited by the Indian Bureau, by the missionaries, by the philanthropists, by the anthropologists, by the sociologists, by the psychologists, by the archaeologists, by the artists, by the novelists, and, O Lord, no telling how many can use the Indian. Scientifically, the native child of the forest is so useful. They rushed in pell-mell, tumbling over one another, and the Indian was used as an Indian—as a man he was lost sight of. . . .

The reservation is a hothouse, the wrong "melting pot," a demoralizing prison of idleness, beggary, gambling, pauperism, and ruin, where the Indians remain as Indians, a barrier against enlightenment and knowledge. There is not one redeeming feature on the Indian reservations for the Indians. . . .

Some may ask, Can we not adjust or reform the Indian Bureau so that it will accomplish something for the Indians? The Indian Bureau system is wrong. The only way to adjust wrong is to abolish it, and the only reform is to let my people go. . . .

What did the Indians get for their land that is flooded?

How much did the Indians get for the land that irrigation ditches pass through? How much did the Indians get from the forest reserve and the natural park reserve? . . .

Has the Indian no right to express himself or to be consulted and give his approval and disapproval of the construction of a dam on his domain?

Has he no right to say what part of his reservation may be sold?

Coming down to the fine point, has the Indian any right to open his mouth, to think for himself, or to do for himself, or even to live and breathe for himself?

Not at all; not at all! The Indian Bureau—the Indian Bureau does it all. If there is such a place as hell, O, it's like hell! O, it's like hell to me. . . .

The iron hand of the Indian Bureau has us in charge. The slimy clutches of horrid greed and selfish interests are gripping the Indian's property. Little by little the Indian's land and everything else is fading into a dim and unknown realm. . . .

In behalf of our people, with the spirit of Moses, I ask this—the United States of America—"Let my people go."

225 ANAQUONESS, Ojibway, served in France during World War I as a member of the Canadian Army. Wounded, he was sent to a hospital in England. Upon his return to Canada, he wrote a letter to the English nurse who cared for him while he recovered from his war injuries.

February 3, 1918

Dear Miss Nurse:

Nearly four months now the Canada geese flew south and the snow is very deep. . . . The wee sorryful animals I tol you about sit around me tonight. . . . I seen my old old trees and the rocks that I know and the forest that is to me what your house is to you. . . . I wisht youd been here to see when I got back. The Injuns were camped and had their tents at the Head of the lake. I went up. They come out and looked at me and the chief took me by the hand and said How, and they all come one at a time and shake hands and say How. They ast me nothin about the War but said they would dance the Morning Wind dance, as I just come from the East and that is the early morning wind on the lakes. Then they dance the next night the Neebiche, meanin the leaves that are blown and drift before the wind in the empty forest. . . . Gee I'm lucky to travel the big woods agen. To us peple the woods and the big hills and the Northern lights and the sunsets are all alive and we live with these things and live in the spirit of the woods like no white person can do. The big lakes we travel on, the little lonely lakes we set our beaver traps on with a ring of big black pines standin in rows lookin always north, like they were watchin for somethin that never comes, same as the Injun, they are real to us and when we are alone we speak to them and are not lonesome, only thinkin always of the long ago days and the old men. So we live in the past and the rest of the world keeps goin by. For all their modern inventons they cant live the way we do and they die if they try because they cant read the sunset and hear the old men talk in the wind. A wolf is fierce, but he is our brother he lives the old way, but the Saganash [white man] is sometime a pup and he dies when the wind blows on him, because he sees only trees and rocks and water, only the outside of the book and cant read. We are two hundred years behind the times and dont change much. . . . I am hunting in a place called Place-where-the-water-runs-in-the-middle because the water runs in the center of the lake. . . . It is now Seegwun when the snow is all melt of the ice and it thaw in the daytime and freeze at night, making a crust so the moose breaks through and cant run. This is the days when we have hardship and our snowshoes break through the crust and get wet and heavy an our feet is wet everyday all the time wet. The crows have come back. Between now and the breakup is pleasant weather in the settlements but it is hell in the woods. White men dont travel not at all now and I dont blame him. March 20th/18 Well I lay up all day today in my camp and it is a soft moon, which is bad believe me, so I write more to your letter. I travel all day yestdy on the lakes in water and slush half way to my knees on top of the ice. It will be an early spring. My wound has kinda gone on the blink, to hard goin. . . . Well the spring birds waken me up in the morning, but they eat my meat hanging outside too, but they are welcome to it, a long time I didnt see them and I am to glad too be back wher I can get meat and be wher there is birds. . . . I caught a squirrell in a trap by accident I had set for a fisher. He was dead and I felt sorry. I made my dinner in the snow right there an sat an think an smoke an think about it and everything until the wind changed and blow the smoke in my face and I went away then. An I wondered if the tall black trees standing all aroun and the Gweegweechee [whisky-jacks] in the trees and the old men that still travel the woods, thats dead long long ago I wondered if they knowed what I was thinkin about, Me, I kinda forgotten anyhow. Theys a bunch of red birds outside feeding. I guess youd find them pretty, red with stripes on their wings. Well Miss Nurse this is somewheres around the last of March. Half of the snow is went now and the lakes are solid ice about 4 or 3 ft thick. That all has to go in about one month. The sun is getting warm. . . . Did I ever tell you about my throwin knife I had, well I got it back it lays along side of me as I write, the edge all gapped from choppin moose bones with. I would sure like to show you this country with its big waters and black forests an little lonely lakes with a wall of trees all around them, quiet, never move but just look on an on an you know as you go by them trees was there ahead of you and will be there after you are dead. It makes a person feel small, ony with us, that is our life to be among them things. I killed that lynx today and somehow I wisht I hadnt. His skin is only worth $10 an he didnt act cross an the way he looked at me I cant get it out of my mind. I dont think I will sell that skin no. . . . I was on a side hill facing south and in spots it was bare of snow and the leaves were dry under my feet and I thought of what I tol you onct, about bein sick. Once I walked amongst flowers in the spring sun and now I stand on dry leaves an the wind blows cold through the bare tree tops. I think it tells me that wind that pretty soon no one cannot ever hear me. That must be so becase I cannot see my own trail ahead of me. a cloud hangs over it. Away ahead not so awful far the trail goes into the cloud, the sun dies behind the hills, there are no more trees ony the cloud. I had a friend he is dead now. I wonder if he is lonesome. I am now. . . . Hows the wee garden and the nieces coming along. Write and tellme all about them. My ears are open. . . . I will listen to the song of a bird for a little while. Now the curtain is pulled down across the sun and my heart is black. A singing bird comes and sings an says I do this an I do that an things are so with me an I will listen an forget there is no sun, until the bird goes, then I will sit and think an smoke for hours an say to myself, that's good, *I am only an Injun and that bird sang for me.* When the morning wind rises and the morning star hangs off the edge of the black swamp to the east, tomorrow, I will be on my snoeshoe trail. Goodbye.

226   In 1915, some Yakima Indians were charged with violating a state law which the Indians claimed violated an 1855 treaty which gave them certain fishing rights "as long as the sun shines, as long as the mountains stand, and as long as the rivers run." The Yakima lost in court and about five years later they initiated a test case with the intention of carrying it to the U.S. Supreme Court. Chief MENINOCK testified during the trial.

God created this Indian country and it was like He spread out a big blanket. He put the Indians on it. They were created here in this country, truly and honestly, and that was the time this river started to run. Then God created fish in this river and put deer in these mountains and made laws through which has come the increase of fish and game. Then the Creator gave us Indians life; we awakened and as soon as we saw the game and fish we knew that they were made for us. For the women God made roots and berries to gather, and the Indians grew and multiplied as a people. When we were created we were given our ground to live on, and from that time these were our rights. This is all true. We had the fish before the missionaries came, before the white man came. We were put here by the Creator and these were our rights as far as my memory to my great-grandfather. This was the food on which we lived. My mother gathered berries; my father fished and killed the game. These words are mine and they are true. It matters not how long I live, I cannot change these thoughts. My strength is from the fish; my blood is from the fish, from the roots and the berries. The fish and the game are the essence of my life. I was not brought from a foreign country and did not come here. I was put here by the Creator. We had no cattle, no hogs, no grain, only berries and roots and game and fish. We never thought we would be troubled about these things, and I tell my people, and I believe it, it is not wrong for us to get this food. Whenever the seasons open I raise my heart in thanks to the Creator for his bounty that this food has come.

227 On December 1, 1927, the Grand Council Fire of American Indians presented a memorial to the mayor of Chicago.

You tell all white men "America First." We believe in that. We are the only ones, truly, that are 100 percent. We therefore ask you while you are teaching school children about America First, teach them truth about the First Americans.

We do not know if school histories are pro-British, but we do know that they are unjust to the life of our people— the American Indian. They call all white victories, battles, and all Indian victories, massacres. The battle with Custer has been taught to school children as a fearful massacre on our part. We ask that this, as well as other incidents, be told fairly. If the Custer battle was a massacre, what was Wounded Knee?

History books teach that Indians were murderers—is it murder to fight in self-defense? Indians killed white men because white men took their lands, ruined their hunting grounds, burned their forests, destroyed their buffalo. White men penned our people on reservations, then took away the reservations. White men who rise to protect their property are called patriots—Indians who do the same are called murderers.

White men call Indians treacherous—but no mention is made of broken treaties on the part of the white man. . . .

White men called Indians thieves—and yet we lived in frail skin lodges and needed no locks or iron bars. White men call Indians savages. What is civilization? Its marks are a noble religion and philosophy, original arts, stirring music, rich story and legend. We had these. . . .

We sang songs that carried in their melodies all the sounds of nature—the running of waters, the sighing of winds, and the calls of the animals. Teach these to your children that they may come to love nature as we love it.

We had our statesmen—and their oratory has never been equalled. Teach the children some of these speeches of our people, remarkable for their brilliant oratory.

We played games—games that brought good health and sound bodies. Why not put these in your schools? We told stories. Why not teach school children more of the wholesome proverbs and legends of our people? Tell them how we loved all that was beautiful. That we killed game only for food, not for fun. Indians think white men who kill for fun are murderers.

Tell your children of the friendly acts of Indians to the white people who first settled here. Tell them of our leaders and heroes and their deeds. . . . Put in your history books the Indian's part in the World War. Tell how the Indian fought for a country of which he was not a citizen, for a flag to which he had no claim, and for a people that have treated him unjustly.

We ask this, Chief, to keep sacred the memory of our people.

228 JESSE CORNPLANTER, Chief of the Senecas, interpreted for author Carl Carmer in the 1930s a phenomenon of sounds wafted through New York State valleys, seemingly louder in the Finger Lakes region to the west.

The New York State drums are the death drums of my people. When the British fought the Colonies my forefather, Chief Cornplanter, was a friend of George Washington. But many of the tribes joined the British armies in the fight against the white man who had taken their lands from them. And so toward the end of the war the American Congress sent an avenging army against the Senecas and the other Iroquois nations. They destroyed our villages, they burned our granaries filled with the harvest, they killed our women and children. When they were gone the Senecas who were left, starving and homeless, beat on their water drums and sang their death songs. Now the drummers are dead too, but sometimes they come back to where their villages were and beat their drums again and sing the death songs for the Senecas killed by the cruel white army.

229 HENRY STANDING BEAR, Sioux chief, in a 1939 letter to Korczak Ziolkowski made a request which inspired the sculptor to begin his mammoth project of carving a statue of Crazy Horse out of a mountain in the Black Hills.

My fellow chiefs and I are interested in finding some sculptor who can carve a head of an Indian Chief who was killed many years ago. . . .

My fellow chiefs and I would like the White man to know that the Red man had great heroes too.

230　JOE FRIDAY, a Woods Cree Indian of northern Canada, after killing geese to smoke for winter use in about 1940, expressed an Indian sentiment towards animal life.

I never kill a bird or other animal without feeling bad inside. All true hunters must have that feeling that prevents them from killing just for killing's sake. There's no fun in just destroying life, and the Great Spirit puts that shadow in your heart when you destroy his creatures.

231　ALFRED W. GILPIN, Omaha tribal council chairman, reported to his people on proposals by the Bureau of Indian Affairs made in April 1954.

What can I say to my Omaha people? That is my main question. For two nights I have stayed awake, looking for honest thoughts and true words to say. I knew my Omaha people would be afraid when they heard that the Bureau of Indian Affairs was thinking of making a great change in their lives. It is a poor life, but it is the only one they have to live. The only changes that will not frighten my Omaha people are the changes they make themselves. These respected officials of the Bureau of Indian Affairs told me my people do not have to be afraid. I stayed awake, trying to know if I could tell them there was nothing to fear. I cannot tell my people that. These honored officials met in Omaha April 15 and 16 to talk about whether it would be good administration to transfer many services to the county and state, and perhaps to move our Indian Agency away from the Reservation. When I heard that the officials were meeting about such a serious thing, I asked to be allowed to sit with them when they talked. They graciously said I could. I did, for two whole days. The officials said they would consult the people before any changes were made. They are being true to their word. They are consulting, but I have to say this: After the people have been consulted, I am afraid the changes will be made, even if the people do consent to them or not. I think, probably, in Washington, D.C., someone has already decided that the changes will make for a cheaper administration. I think these respected officials are telling my people about how their life is to be changed, not asking whether they want it changed.

I do not think Congress is going to pass a law terminating the Omaha Tribe. I think the Bureau of Indian Affairs is going to terminate the tribe by taking away the Agency services and selling our Omaha lands. I say, most humbly, to the respected officials, that cheaper administration, even better administration, is not everything. The good and happiness of the people is everything. My poor Omaha people have lived in helplessness for a long time under the Bureau of Indian Affairs. They were taken care of in a way that made them forget to take care of themselves. Today, they are just waking up . . . just rubbing their eyes . . . and beginning to hate this helplessness. Today my Omaha people are beginning to fight and to hold what is left of their land, planning how to use the land well. They are beginning to go into county and state politics and protect their American rights. They are beginning to do for themselves the things that the Bureau of Indian Affairs has always done for them. My Omaha people are just beginning to feel strong and proud, the way they used to feel before they were made humble and weak. Soon they will be able to say to the Bureau of Indian Affairs, *We can take care of ourselves, now. We do not want you.* Why does the Bureau of Indian Affairs pick this moment to say it does not want the Omaha people?

The Omaha Tribal Council has asked the Association on American Indian Affairs and the University of Nebraska to cooperate in working out a long-range plan for this Omaha community. My people want to see the day when they will not need the special services of the Bureau of Indian Affairs, and this plan will make the day come. I say to these honored officials that any transferral of services, any termination of our Agency, should be part of this long-range plan for the Omaha people, by the Omaha people; it should not be planned for them. If the Bureau of Indian Affairs makes big changes in my people's lives, they will remember the lawlessness that came after PL 280 and they will be afraid, they will sink down lower. If my Omaha people are allowed to make their own change, they will feel brave, proud, they will face the future standing up straight.

232 In June 1961, over 400 Indians representing ninety tribes met in Chicago and issued a "Declaration of Indian Purpose." This excerpt is from its conclusion.

In the beginning the people of the New World, called Indians by accident of geography, were possessed of a continent and a way of life. In the course of many lifetimes, our people had adjusted to every climate and condition from the Arctic to the torrid zones. In their livelihood and family relationships, their ceremonial observances, they reflected the diversity of the physical world they occupied.

The conditions in which Indians live today reflect a world in which every basic aspect of life has been transformed. Even the physical world is no longer the controlling factor in determining where and under what conditions men may live. In region after region, Indian groups found their means of existence either totally destroyed or materially modified. Newly introduced diseases swept away or reduced populations. These changes were followed by major shifts in the internal life of tribe and family.

The time came when the Indian people were no longer the masters of their situation. Their life ways survived subject to the will of a sominant sovereign power. This is said, not in a spirit of complaint; we understand that in the lives of all nations of people, there are times of plenty and times of famine. But we do speak out in a plea for understanding.

When we go before the American people, as we do in this Declaration, and ask for material assistance in developing our resources and developing our opportunities, we pose a moral problem which cannot be left unanswered. For the problem we raise affects the standing which our nation sustains before world opinion.

Our situation cannot be relieved by appropriated funds alone, though it is equally obvious that without capital investment and funded services, solutions will be delayed. Nor will the passage of time lessen the complexities which beset a people moving toward new meaning and purpose.

The answers we seek are not commodities to be purchased, neither are they evolved automatically through the passing of time.

The effort to place social adjustment on a money-time interval scale which has characterized Indian administration, has resulted in unwanted pressure and frustration.

When Indians speak of the continent they yielded, they are not referring only to the loss of some millions of acres in real estate. They have in mind that the land supported a universe of things they knew, valued, and loved.

With that continent gone, except for the few poor parcels they still retain, the basis of life is precariously held, but they mean to hold the scraps and parcels as earnestly as any small nation or ethnic group was ever determined to hold to identity and survival.

What we ask of America is not charity, not paternalism, even when benevolent. We ask only that the nature of our situation be recognized and made the basis of policy and action.

In short, the Indians ask for assistance, technical and financial, for the time needed, however long that may be, to regain in the America of the space age some measure of the adjustment they enjoyed as the original possessors of their native land.

MRS. JOSEPHINE C. MILLS, Shoshone, wrote a letter in March 1964, prompted by controversy over Bureau of Indian Affairs actions in Nevada.

Because the Indian culture is so different from other people, he has remained aloof. The Indian has never wanted integration, although he is too intelligent not to realize that it is inevitable. Only the Jewish people and the Indians were subjected to attempts to exterminate them. No other people have suffered in all the ways that the Indian has in the past one and a half centuries. All these years we have stood aloof, proud, and alone, trying to understand why we are being exploited.

The Indian regards all of America as his land. No other Americans can possibly have the strong feeling the Indian has toward the land he calls "Mother Earth."

In almost every instance in American history, the first act of injustice must be laid at the white man's door. Today, we Indians are experiencing one of the greatest injustices ever forced on us. We are being forced to accept the Indian Claims proposal through psychological methods employed by our own attorneys and the Bureau of Indian Affairs. This proposal, which is in legal terminology, is explained to our people in 40 minutes by our attorneys. After arguing with our own attorneys over this proposal, we are asked to vote yes on it immediately. Definite psychological methods are used to confuse us thoroughly and force us to accept something we don't understand.

There is no longer any need to shoot down Indians in order to take away their rights and lands. Legislation and the combination of three forces, our own attorneys, the Indian Claims Commission and the Indian Bureau, does the trick legally.

RAY D. MILLS, Sr., Sioux, wrote a letter in April 1964, prompted by Bureau of Indian Affairs actions in Nevada.

The Indian Reorganization Act was passed by Congress in 1934. It gave the Indian the right to organize and govern his own affairs on the colonies and reservations. He was to settle his problems as he saw fit.

When the Indian Bureau realized the councils on my reservation took their problems and settled them readily their attitude changed. It was only a matter of time before the conscientious councilmen were removed through various manipulations and replaced with the Bureau's choice. This was the procedure employed by the Indian Bureau to control the Indian's power of free speech and fair representation. When I realized how my people were still being controlled, I left the reservation in hopeless disgust. My only way to rebel was to get away from the control of the Indian Bureau and live the white man's life.

Almost 30 years have passed since I left my reservation. Most of my time was spent in Nevada working and living in the white man's society. Yet I remain an Indian. I have seen plenty and kept silent all these years. I can no longer keep silent.

The Indian Bureau kept the Indians of Nevada divided, apart and under control through puppet councils. Those they cannot control are being constantly harassed by the Bureau officials and their sympathizers.

All these years I have seen the need for an Inter-Tribal organization in Nevada. A true Inter-Tribal organization can only operate effectively when there is no interference or control by the Bureau. I considered this impossible until last Saturday when I attended the first Inter-Tribal meeting held in Nevada.

History was made in Nevada by the Indians in our centennial year. This was the first time in Nevada an Inter-Tribal meeting was sponsored by the Indians themselves and without any control or interference by the Bureau. Approximately 23 tribes were represented.

The Indian Bureau is already fighting to keep the

Indians from organizing. Several months ago . . . the Bureau came up with an Indian Bureau sponsored and controlled Nevada Inter-Tribal Council. . . .

Many legitimate Tribal Councils have been destroyed by too much Indian Bureau interference and control. We Indians in Nevada now have an opportunity that should not be overlooked. We are now capable of building our own Inter-Tribal organization without the bureau control and interference that we Indians have endured so long. Let us start our own organization consisting of Shoshones, Paiutes, Washoes and the other interested Indians of various Tribes who now call Nevada their state. An organization of this type would never be influenced or controlled by the Indian Bureau.

> *235* PATRICK KILLS CROW and MARY CRAZY THUNDER, Sioux high school freshmen in Pine Ridge, South Dakota, wrote about a new course introduced in September 1966 by Father John F. Bryde.

We've got something really different and exciting at Holy Rosary this year, and our whole class is talking about it. You'll probably be surprised when I say the exciting this is a *New Class,* but that's what it is. I never thought that I would look forward to a class period before, but we sure do now. . . .

When Father first came in and put the name of our new course on the board, we couldn't even pronounce it, much less know what it meant. It's called Acculturational Psychology, and it can also be called Modern Indian Psychology. It means a study of how to be a modern Indian. Since we are the same as the old time Indians, except in our way of making a living now, we have to learn two things—how to be like the old time Indians and yet make our living in a different way. Since this can be kind of hard, this thing called adjustment, we have to learn how. And that's what makes the course so interesting. No one ever told us this before.

Before this course, we didn't even know that Indians were important or that it was important for us to know Indian history and values and what the old time Indians did hundreds of years ago. Now we can see that it is, and it sure makes you feel good to know that you are a Sioux. It makes you really proud to see all the obstacles the old time Sioux had to overcome and to know that the Indian race is the oldest on the face of the earth today. Father says this speaks well of our values because a people is only as long lived as their values.

236 Later, at the end of the term, Father Bryde gave his students an opportunity to evaluate the course and tell what it had meant to them.

LINDA MESTETH: I never realized Indians had values and were proud of them until I took this course. It helps us to understand our race and be proud we're Indians.

FRANCIS CLIFFORD: I learned about my own people. I know their values, and many other great things about them. Now, I am glad I'm an Indian. Before I was ashamed of it. I thank you Father.

HAZEL STANDS: I didn't know Indians are written in history too.

ROBERT YOUNG: It taught me about my ancestors, and about the great things which they have done. It taught me to know and to love them for the way which they had fought to keep the land which the white men took away. . . . I think this class meant more to me than any other class I have ever taken.

MIKE GRAHAM: It means that I can be proud of my values and be proud of myself. . . . It means that I don't have to believe the image of the dominant group. . . . It means that I could judge a person by what he is and not by what he has.

DEBI ROOKS: It gets down deep in the heart of Indian culture and helps one understand and get a better insight of things. It enlightens a person such as myself to the *real* Indian ways, not just the jazz one watches on TV. . . . I think this course, if it were possible, should be taught to every American so they could derive a better understanding and be more proud of the Indian heritage.

237 **DOMINGO MONTOYA,** Pueblo leader, commented in 1967 on the treatment of Indians in movies and TV and its effect on Indian children.

I think they wonder, when are we going to win? I remember seeing such a movie when one of my boys was a kid. We came out of the movies, and he pulled my hand and said, "Daddy, we pretty near won that one."

238 **BUFFALO TIGER,** chairman of the Tribal Council of the Miccosukee Indians of Florida, testified December 14, 1967, before a U.S. Senate subcommittee studying the education of Indian children.

Before, our people needed no help from anybody, only ourselves. They wanted to live in the Everglades lands by fishing and hunting. Of course, you know, Miccosukees are proud people and independent. That is what they want to be. They do not want to be governed and have outside help. This goes on many years.

Miccosukees begin to realize the hunting lands are getting smaller each year, because development is taking over. We got together with the tribal council and all the people; we talked and asked: Could we get the United States to give us some help, because we realize this problem is not going to end the way we want? So we have councils and councils over three years before we can come to some kind of agreement, and we call on the Department of the

Interior. They came down and worked with us, and we organized in such a way that the United States will recognize the Miccosukees.

So we have adopted a constitution and bylaws. That means to us, we agree to work with the United States. In other words, we agree to be at peace with the United States. Of course, you know, Miccosukees and Seminoles have never had a treaty. Then the schools started [in 1962], but before that, this is what happened. . . .

The Indian people realized, particularly the Miccosukee realized, that they are afraid they will lose out as Indians; in other words, they do not want to lose their beliefs, their customs. We asked the United States: Could we keep this if we accept education, or to be educated, to be able to get a job in town among other people? So the United States promised the Miccosukee people, we are not going to take anything away from your people. We are not going to destroy the people. But we want you to have this new belief in the customs and show you, so you can get a job in town if you have to, or you might get educated more so you can live better and understand other people, what we need. . . .

"Could we teach the Indian children in the classroom our Indian beliefs, like our religion and history as Indians?"

They said, "Yes, you can have Indian teachers, however you want it. You can go into the classroom and teach them an hour or two hours a day. Meantime, we will be teaching the English, learn how to write or speak, learn how to speak English."

So we say this is what we want, we want to do this, but we want to make sure we keep this.

They said, "Yes, we can assure you, you can go ahead and do this."

So we did. . . . I can tell you this, I am proud today; what they are doing today is something I wish you could see. But our people realize we have to have Indian beliefs and customs to go along with English. . . .

If we do not watch, we can lose all of our youngsters. The minute they learn English, they begin to go into town, maybe have some kind of job. Before we know, they will be running contact, into some indecent people, maybe drunkards or those who go to jail, or do many wrong things. . . .

We try to teach our Indian children, do not be ashamed, even though you are Indians. You are Indians, therefore, you should realize you are Indians, nothing else but Indians. Think like Indians, be like Indians, but learn English, learn how to write, be educated. You are Indian, you have other ideas. Be educated. You have somebody else's mind. You have two minds and you can work with both. You can have three languages, if you want, or two. . . .

We do not want to lose out on being Indians.

239 ILIFF McKAY, Blackfoot leader, before the Senate subcommittee:

About the turn of the century, the Government decided, well, the Indians are not going to go away after all. . . . We will have to try another method. So they contracted with various organizations, particularly religious denominations, to educate Indian students. . . .

The policy was . . . in effect . . . to stamp out the Indian, to stamp out the culture of the Indian. . . . If you were caught in school speaking Indian, singing Indian songs, if you were caught wearing your hair long, or something like that, you were actually flogged.

240 JOHN BELINDO, Kiowa-Navajo and then executive director of the National Congress of American Indians, testified to the same Senate subcommittee on December 15, 1967.

In earlier times, Sun Chief, a Hopi, attended school first on the edge of the Hopi country and later in California. He adjusted himself fairly well to the California school until he was taken with a severe illness during which he was unconscious four times and had a vision of the Hopi Spirit Guide. During a long convalescence he concluded he should return to the way of his fathers. He said:

"As I lay on the blanket I thought about my school days and all I had learned. I could talk like a gentleman, read, write, and cipher. I could name all the States of the Union, with the capitals, repeat the names of all of the books of the Bible, one hundred verses of Scripture, sing more than two dozen hymns, debate, shout football yells, swing my partners, and tell dirty stories by the hour. It was important that I had learned how to get along with the white man. But my experience had taught me that I had a Hopi Spirit Guide, whom I must follow if I wish to live and I want to become a real Hopi again, to sing the old songs and to feel free to make love without the fear of sin or rawhide."

I think this is essentially the song of every Indian and Indian tribe, a certain feeling of freedom, a chance to be free to manage their own affairs.

241   BEN BLACK ELK, son of Sioux chief Black Elk, is the oft-photographed Indian seen by hundreds of thousands around the Visitors' Center at Mount Rushmore. However, Ben Black Elk is not just a "tourist Indian," but a thoughtful and fruitful worker for the welfare of his people.

We who are Indians today live in a world of confusion. This is the issue: the confusion in our lives. We are Indians, and we love the Indian ways. We are comfortable in the Indian ways. But to get along in this world the white man tells us we must be white men, that we cannot be what we were born to be. . . .

Our young people today . . . do not really know who they are or where they belong. So they have no pride. Today there are Indians who are ashamed they are Indians. Believe me, this is so. . . .

We would like to be proud we are Indians, but . . . many schools for Indian children make them ashamed they are Indians. . . . The schools forget these are Indian children. They don't recognize them as Indians, but treat them as though they were white children. . . . This makes for failure, because it makes for confusion. And when the Indian history and the Indian culture is ignored, it makes our children ashamed they are Indians.

I started to school when I was seven years old. I couldn't speak a word of English. I had long hair that hung to my waist, and it was in four braids. When I made progress in school a braid was cut off to mark my progress. . . .

Martin Luther King said, "I have a dream." But we Indians didn't have to dream. We had the reality. This whole continent was a paradise. We didn't know what a dollar was, what coffee was or what whiskey was. We got along fine. Then the white man came. That was our downfall. Then the persecution started. So, after many years, out of their sorrow and misery, and because they were desperate, some of the Indians danced the Ghost Dance. . . .

It was a prayer that was danced. The Indians were desperate. All they had, the great buffalo herds, everything was all gone. Then someone came along and he told the Indians, "I'm the Messiah, I'm Christ." He said the white man had sinned against him and if we would do the Ghost Dance the white man would disappear and the buffalo and all the old warriors would come back. We were to throw all our weapons away. This would happen with no warfare. We just had to dance and sing this Ghost Dance.

They thought it would come, but it never came. Instead we had the Massacre at Wounded Knee. They killed the men, women and children. The sadness of this is still in our hearts. . . .

It was there . . . that a beautiful dream died in the snow —a people's dream.

242 The Nisqually and other Indians in Washington state have long been protesting the whites' violations of the 1854 treaty which guaranteed to the Indians, as long as the grass grows, their rights "of taking fish at all usual and accustomed places, together with the privilege of hunting and gathering roots and berries." In the late 1960s the whole matter was summarized forcefully and succinctly by two Indians.

The white man, he took over, see, after he saw there was money in fish. He just took over, you know, just steal—like stealing off the Indian. And that's how they got it. And that's why they don't want the Indian to fish, because there's big money for them. Indian is nothing to the white man. He's nothing.

Now you have to have permission to gather nuts and things from the mountains and from the desert. They didn't plant these trees here. They didn't bring the deer here. They didn't bring the fish here, and yet they say: "We give you—we give you the right to fish here—we give you." They had nothing to give in the first place. They were beggars, they were paupers. They came to this country looking for freedom of speech and to worship the way they wanted to. But when they got here they forgot when it came to the Indian. This country is built on total aggression. There was room for everyone. But now he owns everything and now he wants to take the rest of us—he wants to take away everything we have. They've taken our religion. They've taken our identity. They've taken everything.

243 One of these Washington Indians, a U.S. Army sergeant, was awarded a Silver Star and a Bronze Star for his valor in Vietnam. But while home on furlough, recovering from combat wounds and attempting to provide for his large family, he was arrested three times in one month for net fishing in the old tribal way. His friend commented bitterly:

The U.S. would have accepted sacrifice of his life in Vietnam in a less legitimate cause, in fact would have honored such a death, but for fighting for his family and people they permitted a professional barber acting as a Justice of the Peace to interpret his treaty, to ignore his right, to impose punishment, and to record a criminal conviction.

244 A young Blackfoot, standing on Fisherman's Wharf waiting to ride to Alcatraz Island in San Francisco Bay:

The white man saves the whooping crane, he saves the goose in Hawaii, but he is not saving the way of life of the Indian.

245 Not only the Indian's life, *but even his death as well*, is forced into the white man's mold.

The Indian believes that he is a cannibal—all of his life he must eat his brothers and his sisters and deer and corn which is the mother, and the fish which is the brother. All our lives we must eat off them and be a cannibal, but when we die then we can give back all that we have taken, and our body goes to feed the worms that feed the birds. And it feeds the roots of the trees and the grass so that the deer can eat it and the birds can nest in the tree. And we can give back. But today we can't even do this, you know. They poison our bodies and we can't bury our people. We have to be put in boxes to wait for some life, you know, that's going to be. . . . We are all going to rise up, which is so . . . different from the way we feel about our bodies and giving back.

246 The barbed twist of serious humor is seen in this Indian's proposal.

I would say that we discovered the white man, too. At that time we hadn't known that there was land across the sea, so I think by the same token that the next time I go to England or Italy, I intend to take a flag and plant it and claim it for my Indian people, because, after all, it would be the first time that I had ever seen it, so therefore I would be discovering it.

247 Extinction, isolation and suppression, or assimilation—these have been the policies generally adopted toward the American Indian by the white world. Many Indians have other ideas.

The white people who are trying to make us over into their image, they want us to be what they call assimilated, bringing the Indians into the mainstream and destroying our own way of life and our own cultural patterns. They believe that we should be contented to become like those whose concept of happiness is two cars and a color TV, a very materialistic and greedy society which is very different from our way.

We want freedom from the white man rather than to be integrated. We don't want any part of the establishment, we want to be free to raise our children in our religion, in our ways, to be able to hunt and fish and to live in peace. We want to live off the land, to follow the sacred instructions given to us by the Creator when he put us on this land, to live with nature, the divine laws of nature which join the laws of the Creator. We don't want power, we don't want to be congressmen, bankers, we want to be ourselves. We want to have our own religion and to raise our children to be proud of our heritage, because we are the owners of this land and because we belong here.

248 JOE UPICKSOUN, president of the Arctic Slope Native Association, criticized, in January 1971, the proposed oil pipeline across Alaska.

186

My people are not concerned about a phony economy like the Caucasians. We have our land and it has been good to us. The sea has been good to us. The Bureau of Indian Affairs has given us enough education to read about what has happened in the lower forty-eight [states]. . . . Now they want to come up here and rape our land.

249 A Plains Indian put the basic issue briefly:

The white man says there is freedom and justice for all. We have had "freedom and justice," and that is why we have been almost exterminated. These are just words in the wind.

250 VINE DELORIA, Jr., Sioux, in 1969 and 1970 became a spokesman for many American Indians with his best-selling books, *Custer Died For Your Sins* and *We Talk, You Listen.*

When one examines the history of American society one notices the great weakness inherent in it. The country was founded in violence. It worships violence and it will continue to live violently. Anyone who tries to meet violence with love is crushed, but violence used to meet violence also ends abruptly with meaningless destruction.

Consider the history of America closely. Never has America lost a war. When engaged in warfare the United States has always applied the principle of overkill and mercilessly stamped its opposition into the dust. . . . No quarter, even if requested. Consider Vietnam, where the United States has already dropped more bombs that it did during the last world war—a classic of overkill.

Consider also the fascination of America's military leaders with the body count. It is not enough to kill people, bodies must be counted and statistics compiled to show how the harvest is going. . . . Yes, violence is America's sweetheart.

But name, if you can, the last peace the United States won. Victory yes, but this country has never made a successful peace because peace requires exchanging ideas, concepts, thoughts, and recognizing the fact that two distinct systems of life can exist together without conflict. . . .

As Indians we will never have the efficient organization that gains great concessions from society in the marketplace. We will never have a powerful lobby or be a smashing political force. But we will have the intangible unity which has carried us through four centuries of persecution. We are a people unified by our humanity—not a pressure group unified for conquest. And from our greater strength we shall wear down the white man and finally outlast him. . . . We shall endure.

251 An Indian grandfather:

I think we will still win, I think there are enough people who wish to understand the Indian mind, that we are not going to harm anyone, that we are peaceful people, we are not aggressive people. In this lies our strength and from here we will pick up. I believe that we will survive, I still believe we will survive. That is our dream.

APPENDIX

JUDGE DUNDY'S DECISION

(See Speeches #205 and #206)

While historically important and quite readable, Judge Elmer S. Dundy's 1879 decision has lain buried in old legal records, not readily available to the general public. For these reasons it is printed here in full as it appeared in *U.S. v. Crook* 5 Dillon, 453-69. Keep in mind that the American Indian was not granted citizenship until 1924.

(Editor)

UNITED STATES, *ex rel.* STANDING BEAR, *v.* GEORGE CROOK, a Brigadier-General of the Army of the United States.

1. An Indian is a *person* within the meaning of the *habeas corpus* act, and as such is entitled to sue out a writ of *habeas corpus* in the federal courts when it is shown that the petitioner is deprived of liberty under color of authority of the United States, or is in custody of an officer in violation of the constitution or a law of the United States, or in violation of a treaty made in pursuance thereof.

2. The right of expatriation is a natural, inherent, and inalienable right, and extends to the Indian as well as to the white race.

3. The commissioner of Indian affairs has ample authority for removing from an Indian reservation all persons found

189

thereon without authority of law, or whose presence may be detrimental to the peace and welfare of the Indians.

4. The military power of the government may be employed to effect such removal; but where the removal is affected, it is the duty of the troops to convey the persons so removed, by the most convenient and safe route, to the civil authorities of the judicial district in which the offence may be committed, to be proceeded against in due course of law. In time of peace, no authority, civil or military, exists for transporting Indians from one section of the country to another, without the consent of the Indians, nor to confine them to any particular reservation against their will; and where officers of the government attempt to do this, and arrest and hold Indians who are at peace with the government, for the purpose of removing them to and confining them on a reservation in the Indian Territory, they will be released on *habeas corpus.*

(*Before* DUNDY, J.)

Habeas Corpus.—Right of Indian to Writ.

The facts are fully stated in the opinion of the court.

A. J. Poppleton and *John L. Webster,* for the relators.

G. M. Lambertson, United States attorney, for the government.

DUNDY, J.—During the fifteen years in which I have been engaged in administering the laws of my country, I have never been called upon to hear or decide a case that appealed so strongly to my sympathy as the one now under consideration. On the one side, we have a few of the remnants of a once numerous and powerful, but now weak, insignificant, unlettered and generally despised race; on the other, we have the representative of one of the most powerful, most enlightened, and most christianized nations of modern times. On the one side, we have the representatives of this wasted race coming into this national tribunal of ours, asking for justice and liberty to enable them to adopt our boasted civilization, and to pursue the arts of peace, which have made us great and happy as a nation; on the other side, we have this magnificent, if not magnanimous, government, resisting this application with the determination of sending these people back to the country which is to them less desirable than perpetual imprisonment in their own native land. But I think it is creditable to the heart and mind of the brave and distinguished officer who is made respondent herein to say that he has no sort of sympathy in the business in which he is forced by his position to bear a part so conspicuous; and, so far as I am individually concerned, I think it not improper to say that, if the strongest possible sympathy could give the relators title to freedom, they would have been restored to liberty the moment the arguments in their behalf were closed. No examination or further thought would then have been necessary or expedient. But in a country where liberty is regulated by law, something more satisfactory and enduring than mere sympathy must furnish and constitute the rule and basis of judicial action. It follows that this case must be examined and decided on principles of law, and that unless the relators are entitled to their discharge under the constitution or laws of the United States, or some treaty made pursuant thereto, they must be remanded to the custody of the officer who caused their arrest, to be returned to the Indian Territory, which they left without the consent of the government.

On the 8th of April, 1879, the relators, Standing Bear and twenty-five others, during the session of the court held at that time at Lincoln, presented their petition, duly verified, praying for the allowance of a writ of *habeas corpus* and their final discharge from custody thereunder.

The petition alleges, in substance, that the relators are Indians who have formerly belonged to the Ponca tribe of Indians now located in the Indian Territory; that they had some time previously withdrawn from the tribe, and completely severed their tribal relations therewith, and had adopted the general habits of the whites, and were then endeavouring to maintain themselves by their exertions, and without aid or assistance from the general government; that whilst they were thus engaged, and without being guilty of violating any of the laws of the United States, they were arrested and restrained of their liberty by order of the respondent, George Crook.

The writ was issued and served on the respondent on the 8th day of April, and, the distance between the place where the writ was made returnable and the place where the relators were confined being more than twenty miles, ten days were alloted in which to make return.

On the 18th of April the writ was returned, and the authority for the arrest and detention is therein shown. The substance of the return to the writ, and the additional statement since filed, is that the relators are individual members of, and connected with, the Ponca tribe of Indians; that they had fled or escaped from a reservation situated some place within the limits of the Indian Territory—had departed therefrom without permission from the government; and, at the request of the secretary of the interior, the general of the army had issued an order which required the respondent to arrest and return the relators to their tribe in the Indian Territory, and that, pursuant to the said order, he had caused the relators to be arrested on the Omaha Indian reservation, and that they were in his custody for the purpose of being returned to the Indian Territory.

It is claimed upon the one side, and denied upon the other, that the relators had withdrawn and severed, for all time, their connection with the tribe to which they belonged; and upon this point alone was there any testimony produced by either party hereto. The other matters stated in the petition and the return to the writ are conceded to be true; so that the questions to be determined are purely questions of law.

On the 8th of March, 1859, a treaty was made by the United States with the Ponca tribe of Indians, by which a certain tract of country, north of the Niobrara river and west of the Missouri, was set apart for the permanent home of the said Indians, in which the government agreed to protect them during their good behavior. But just when, or how, or why, or under what circumstances, the Indians left their reservation in Dakota and went to the Indian Territory, does not appear.

The district attorney very earnestly questions the jurisdiction of the court to issue the writ, and to hear and determine the case made herein, and has supported his theory with an argument of great ingenuity and much ability. But, nevertheless, I am of the opinion that his premises are erroneous, and his conclusions, therefore, wrong and unjust. The great respect I entertain for that officer, and the very able manner in which his views were presented, make it necessary for me to give somewhat at length the reasons which lead me to this conclusion.

The district attorney discussed at length the reasons which led to the origin of the writ of *habeas corpus,* and the character of the proceedings and practice in connection therewith in the parent country. It was claimed that the laws of the realm limited the right to sue out this writ to the *free subjects* of the kingdom, and that none others came within the benefits of such beneficent laws; and, reasoning from analogy, it is claimed that none but American citizens are entitled to sue out this high prerogative writ in any of the federal courts. I have not examined the English laws regulating the suing out of the writ, nor have I thought it necessary so to do. Of this I will only observe that if the laws of England are as they are claimed to be, they will appear at a disadvantage when compared with our own. This only proves that the laws of a limited monarchy are sometimes less wise and humane than the laws of our own republic—that whilst the parliament of Great Britain was legislating in behalf of the favored few, the congress of the United States was legislating in behalf of all mankind who come within our jurisdiction.

Section 751 of the revised statutes declares that "the supreme court and the circuit and district courts shall have power to issue writs of *habeas corpus.*" Section 752 confers the power to issue writs on the judges of said courts, within their jurisdiction, and declares this to be "for the purpose of inquiry into the cause of restraint of liberty." Section 753 restricts the power, limits the jurisdiction, and defines the cases where the writ may properly issue. That may be done under this section where the prisoner "is in custody under or by color of authority of the United States, * * * or is in custody for an act done or omitted in pursuance of a law of the United States, * * * or in custody in violation of the constitution or of a law or treaty of the United States." Thus, it will be seen that when a *person* is in custody or deprived of his liberty under color of authority of the United States, or in violation of the constitution or laws or treaties of the United States, the federal judges have jurisdiction, and the writ can properly issue. I take it that the true construction to be placed upon this act is this, that in *all* cases where federal officers, civil or military, have the custody and control of a person claimed to be unlawfully restrained of liberty, they are *then* restrained of liberty under color of authority of the United States, and the federal courts can properly proceed to determine the question of unlawful restraint, because no other courts can properly do so. In the other instance, the federal courts and judges can properly issue the writ in *all* cases where the *person* is alleged to be in custody in violation of the constitution or a law or treaty of the United States. In such a case, it is wholly immaterial what *officer,* state or federal, has custody of the person seeking the relief. These relators may be entitled to the writ in either case. Under the first paragraph they certainly are—that is, if an Indian can be entitled to it at all—because they are in custody of a federal officer, under color of authority of the United States. And they may be entitled to the writ under the other paragraph, before recited, for the reason, as they allege, that they are restrained of liberty in violation of a provision of their treaty, before referred to. Now, it must be borne in mind that the *habeas corpus* act describes applicants for the writ as *"persons,"* or *"parties,"* who may be entitled thereto. It nowhere describes them as *citizens,* nor is citizenship in any way or place made a qualification for suing out the writ, and, in the absence of express provision or necessary implication which would require the interpretation contended for by the district attorney, I should not feel justified in giving the words *person* and *party* such a narrow construction. The most natural, and therefore most reasonable, way is to attach the same meaning to *words* and *phrases* when found in a statute that is attached to them when and where found in general use. If we do so in this instance, then the question cannot be open to serious doubt. Webster describes a person as "a living soul; a self-conscious being; a moral agent; especially a living human being; a man, woman, or child; an individual of the human race." This is comprehensive enough, it would seem, to include even an Indian. In defining certain generic terms, the 1st section of the revised statutes declares that the word *person* includes copartnerships and corporations. On the whole, it seems to me quite evident that the comprehensive language used in this section is intended to apply to all mankind—as well the relators as the more favored white race. This will be doing no violence to language, or to the spirit or letter of the law, nor to the intention, as it is believed, of the law-making power of the government. I must hold, then, that *Indians,* and consequently the relators, are *persons,* such as are described by and included within the laws before quoted. It is said, however, that this is the first instance on record in which an Indian has been permitted to sue out and maintain a writ of *habeas corpus* in a federal court, and *therefore* the court must be without jurisdiction in the premises. This is a *non sequitur.* I confess I do not know of another instance where this has been done, but I can also say that the occasion for it perhaps has never before been so great. It may be that the Indians think it wiser and better, in the end, to resort to this peaceful process than it would be to undertake the hopeless task of redressing their own alleged wrongs by force of arms. Returning reason, and the sad experience of others similarly situated, have taught them the folly and madness of the arbitrament of the sword. They can readily see that any serious resistance on their part would be the signal for their utter extirmination [sic]. Have they not, then, chosen the wiser part by resorting to the very tribunal erected by those they claim have wronged and oppressed them? This, however, is not the tribunal of their own choice, but it is the *only* one into which they can lawfully go for deliverance. It cannot, therefore, be fairly said that because no Indian ever before invoked the aid of this writ in a federal court, the rightful authority to issue it does not exist. Power and authority rightfully conferred do not necessarily cease to exist in consequence of long non-use. Though much time has elapsed, and many generations have passed away, since the passage of the original *habeas corpus* act, from which I have quoted, it will not do to say that these Indians cannot avail themselves of its beneficent provisions simply because none of their ancestors ever sought relief thereunder.

Every *person* who comes within our jurisdiction, whether he be European, Asiatic, African, or "native to the manor born," must obey the laws of the United States. Every one who violates them incurs the penalty provided thereby. When a *person* is charged, in a proper way, with the commission of a crime, we do not inquire upon the trial in what country the accused was born, nor to what sovereign or government allegiance is due, nor to what race he belongs. The questions of guilt and innocence only form the subjects of inquiry. An Indian, then, especially off from his reservation, is amenable to the criminal laws of the United States, the same as all other persons. They being subject to arrest for the violation of our criminal laws, and being *persons* such as the law contemplates and includes in the description of parties who may sue out the writ, it would indeed be a sad commentary of the justice and impartiality of our laws to hold that Indians, though natives of our own country, cannot test the validity of an alleged illegal imprisonment in this manner, as well as a subject of a foreign government who may happen to be sojourning in this country, but owing it no sort of allegiance. I cannot doubt that congress intended to give to *every person* who might be unlawfully restrained of liberty under color of authority of the United States, the right to the writ and a discharge thereon. I conclude, then, that, so far as the issuing of the writ is concerned, it was properly issued, and that the relators are within the jurisdiction conferred by the *habeas corpus* act.

A question of much greater importance remains for consideration, which, when determined, will be decisive of this whole controversy. This relates to the right of the government to arrest and hold the relators for a time, for the purpose of being returned to a point in the Indian Territory from which it is alleged the Indians escaped. I am not vain enough to think that I can do full justice to a question like the one under consideration. But, as the matter furnishes so much valuable material for discussion, and so much food for reflection, I shall try to present it as viewed from my own standpoint, without reference to consequences or criticisms, which, though not specially invited, will be sure to follow.

A review of the policy of the government adopted in its dealings with the friendly tribe of Poncas, to which the relators at one time belonged, seems not only appropriate, but almost indispensable to a correct understanding of this controversy. The Ponca Indians have been at peace with the government, and have remained the steadfast friends of the whites, for many years. They lived peaceably upon the land and in the country they claimed and called their own.

On the 12th of March, 1858, they made a treaty with the United States, by which they ceded all claims to lands, except the following tract: "Beginning at a point on the Niobrara river, and running due north so as to intersect the Ponca river twenty-five miles from its mouth; thence from said point of intersection up and along the Ponca river twenty miles; thence due south to the Niobrara river; and thence down and along said river to the place of beginning; which tract is hereby reserved for the future homes of said Indians." In consideration of this cession, the government agreed "to protect the Poncas in the possession of the tract of land reserved for their future homes, and their persons and property thereon, during good behavior on their part." Annuities were to be paid them for thirty years, houses were to be built, schools were to be established, and other things were to be done by the government, in consideration of said cession. (See 12 Stats. at Large, p. 997.)

197

On the 10th of March, 1865, another treaty was made, and a part of the other reservation was ceded to the government. Other lands, however, were, to some extent, substituted therefor, "by way of rewarding them for their constant fidelity to the government, and citizens thereof, and with a view of returning to the said tribe of Ponca Indians their old burying-grounds and cornfields." This treaty also provides for paying $15,080 for spoliations committed on the Indians. (See 14 Stats. at Large, p. 675.)

On the 29th day of April, 1868, the government made a treaty with the several bands of Sioux Indians, which treaty was ratified by the senate on the 16th of the following February, in and by which the reservations set apart for the Poncas under former treaties were completely absolved. (15 Stats. at Large, p. 635.) This was done without consultation with, or knowledge or consent on the part of, the Ponca tribe of Indians.

On the 15th of August, 1876, congress passed the general Indian appropriation bill, and in it we find a provision authorizing the secretary of the interior to use $25,000 for the removal of the Poncas to the Indian Territory, and providing them a home therein, with consent of the tribe. (19 Stats. at Large, p. 192.)

In the Indian appropriation bill passed by congress on the 17th day of May, 1878, we find a provision authorizing the secretary of the interior to expend the sum of $30,000 for the purpose of removing and locating the Ponca Indians on a new reservation, near the Kaw river.

No reference has been made to any other treaties or laws, under which the right to arrest and remove the Indians is claimed to exist.

The Poncas lived upon their reservation in southern Dakota, and cultivated a portion of the same, until two or three years ago, when they removed therefrom, but whether by force or otherwise does not appear. At all events, we find a portion of them, including the relators, located at some point in the Indian Territory. *There,* the testimony seems to show, is where the trouble commenced. Standing Bear, the principal witness, states that out of five hundred

198

and eighty-one Indians who went from the reservation in Dakota to the Indian Territory, one hundred and fifty-eight died within a year or so, and a great proportion of the others were sick and disabled, caused, in a great measure, no doubt, from change of climate; and to save himself and the survivors of his wasted family, and the feeble remnant of his little band of followers, he determined to leave the Indian Territory and return to his old home, where, to use his own language, "he might live and die in peace, and be buried with his father." He also states that he informed the agent of their final purpose to leave, never to return, and that he and his followers had finally, fully, and forever severed his and their connection with the Ponca tribe of Indians, and had resolved to disband as a tribe, or band, of Indians, and to cut loose from the government, go to work, become self-sustaining, and adopt the habits and customs of a higher civilization. To accomplish what would seem to be a desirable and laudable purpose, all who were able so to do went to work to earn a living. The Omaha Indians, who speak the same language, and with whom many of the Poncas have long continued to intermarry, gave them employment and ground to cultivate, so as to make them self-sustaining. And it was when at the Omaha reservation, and when *thus* employed, that they were arrested by order of the government, for the purpose of being taken back to the Indian Territory. They claim to be unable to see the justice, or reason, or wisdom, or *necessity*, of removing them by force from their own native plains and blood relations to a far-off country, in which they can see little but new-made graves opening for their reception. The land from which they fled in fear has no attractions for them. The love of home and native land was strong enough in the minds of these people to induce them to brave every peril to return and live and die where they had been reared. The bones of the dead son of Standing Bear were not to repose in the land they hoped to be leaving forever, but were carefully preserved and protected, and formed a part of what was to them a melancholy procession homeward. Such instances of parental affection, and such love of home and native land, may be *heathen* in origin, but it seems to me that they are not unlike *christian* in principle.

What is here stated in this connection is mainly for the purpose of showing that the relators did all they could to separate themselves from their tribe and to sever their tribal relations, for the purpose of becoming self-sustaining and living without support from the government. This being so, it presents the question as to whether or not an Indian can withdraw from his tribe, sever his tribal relation therewith, and terminate his allegiance thereto, for the purpose of making an independent living and adopting our own civilization.

If Indian tribes are to be regarded and treated as separate but dependent nations, there can be no serious difficulty about the question. If they are not to be regarded and treated as separate, dependent nations, then no allegiance is owing from an individual Indian to his tribe, and he could, therefore, withdraw therefrom at any time. The question of expatriation has engaged the attention of our government from the time of its very foundation. Many heated discussions have been carried on between our own and foreign governments on this great question, until diplomacy has triumphantly secured the right of every person found within our jurisdiction. This right has always been claimed and admitted by our government, and it is now no longer an open question. It can make but little difference, then, whether we accord to the Indian tribes a national character or not, as in either case I think the individual Indian possesses the clear and God-given right to withdraw from his tribe and forever live away from it, as though it had no further existence. If the right of expatriation was open to doubt in this country down to the year 1868, certainly since that time no sort of question as to the right can now exist. On the 27th of July of that year congress passed an act, now appearing as section 1999 of the revised statutes, which declares that: "Whereas, the right of expatriation is a natural inherent right of all people, indispensable to the enjoyment of the rights of life, liberty, and the pursuit of happiness; and, whereas, in the recognition of this principle the government has freely received emigrants from all nations, and invested them with the rights of citizenship. * * * Therefore, any declaration, instruction, opinion, order, or decision of any officer of the United States which denies, restricts, impairs, or questions the right of expatriation, is declared inconsistent with the fundamental principles of the republic."

This declaration must forever settle the question until it is reopened by other legislation upon the same subject. This is, however, only reaffirming in the most solemn and authoritative manner a principle well settled and understood in this country for many years past.

In most, if not all, instances in which treaties have been made with the several Indian tribes, where reservations have been set apart for their occupancy, the government has either reserved the right or bound itself to protect the Indians thereon. Many of the treaties expressly prohibit white persons being on the reservations unless specially authorized by the treaties or acts of congress for the purpose of carrying out treaty stipulations.

Laws passed for the government of the Indian country, and for the purpose of regulating trade and intercourse with the Indian tribes, confer upon certain officers of the government almost unlimited power over the persons who go upon the reservations without lawful authority. Section 2149 of the revised statutes authorizes and requires the commissioner of Indian affairs, with the approval of the secretary of the interior, to remove from any "tribal reservation" any person being thereon without authority of law, or whose presence within the limits of the reservation may, in the judgment of the commissioner, be detrimental to the peace and welfare of the Indians. The authority here conferred upon the commissioner fully justifies him in causing to be removed from Indian reservations *all* persons thereon in violation of law, or whose presence thereon may be detrimental to the peace and welfare of the Indians upon the reservations. This applies as well to an Indian as to a white person, and manifestly for the same reason, the object of the law being to prevent unwarranted interference between the Indians and the agent representing the government. Whether such an extensive discretionary power is wisely vested in the commissioner of Indian affairs or not, need not be questioned. It is enough to know that the power rightfully exists, and, where existing, the exercise of the power must be upheld. If, then, the commissioner has the right to cause the expulsion from the Omaha Indian reservation of all persons thereon who are there in violation of law, or whose presence may be detrimental to the peace and welfare of the Indians, then he must of necessity be authorized to use the necessary force to accomplish his purpose. Where, then, is he to look for this necessary force? The military arm of the government is the most natural and most potent force to be used on such occasions, and section 2150 of the revised statutes specially authorizes the use of the army for this service. The army, then, it seems, is the proper force to employ when intruders and trespassers who go upon the reservations are to be ejected therefrom.

The first subdivision of the revised statutes last referred to provides that "the military forces of the United States may be employed, in such manner and under such regulations as the president may direct, in the apprehension of every person who may be in the Indian country in violation of law, and in conveying him immediately from the Indian country, by the nearest convenient and safe route, to the civil authority of the territory or judical district in which such person shall be found, to be proceeded against in due course of laws." * * * This is the authority under which the military can be lawfully employed to remove intruders from an Indian reservation. What may be done by the troops in such cases is here fully and clearly stated; and it is *this* authority, it is believed, under which the respondent acted.

All Indian reservations held under treaty stipulations with the government must be deemed and taken to be a part of the *Indian country,* within the meaning of our laws on that subject. The relators were found upon the Omaha Indian reservation. That being part of the Indian country, and they not being a part of the Omaha tribe of Indians, they were there without lawful authority, and if the commissioner of Indian affairs deemed their presence detrimental to the peace and welfare of the Omaha Indians, he had lawful warrant to remove them from the reservation, and to employ the necessary military force to effect this object in safety.

General Crook had the rightful authority to remove the relators from the reservation, and must stand justified in removing them therefrom. But when the troops are thus employed they must exercise the authority in the *manner* provided by the section of the law just read. This law makes it the duty of the troops to convey the parties arrested, by the nearest convenient and safe route, *to the civil authority of the territory or judicial district in which such persons shall be found, to be proceeded against in due course of law*. The *duty* of the military authorities is here very clearly and sharply defined, and no one can be justified in departing therefrom, especially in time of peace. As General Crook had the right to arrest and remove the relators from the Omaha Indian reservation, it follows, from what has been stated, that the law required him to convey them to this city and turn them over to the marshal and United States attorney, to be proceeded against in due course of law. Then proceedings could be instituted against them in either the circuit or district court, and if the relators had incurred a penalty under the law, punishment would follow; otherwise, they would be discharged from custody. But this course was not pursued in this case; neither was it intended to observe the laws in that regard, for General Crook's orders, emanating from higher authority, expressly required him to apprehend the relators and remove them by force to the Indian Territory, from which it is alleged they escaped. But in what General Crook has done in the premises no fault can be imputed to him. He was simply obeying the orders of his superior officers, but the orders, as we think, lack the necessary authority of law, and are, therefore, not binding on the relators.

I have searched in vain for the semblance of any authority justifying the commissioner in attempting to remove by force any Indians, whether belonging to a tribe or not, to any place, or for any purpose than what has been stated. Certainly without some specific authority found in an act of congress, or in a treaty with the Ponca tribe of Indians, he could not lawfully force the relators back to the Indian Territory, to remain and die in that country, against their will. In the absence of all treaty stipulations or laws of the United States authorizing such removal, I must conclude that no such arbitrary authority exists. It is true, if the relators are to be regarded as a part of the great nation of Ponca Indians, the government might, in time of war, remove them to any place of safety so long as the war should last, but perhaps no longer, unless they were charged with the commission of some crime. This is a war power merely, and exists in time of war only. Every nation exercises the right to arrest and detain an alien enemy during the existence of a war, and all subjects or citizens of the hostile nations are subject to be dealt with under this rule.

But it is not claimed that the Ponca tribe of Indians are at war with the United States, so that this war power might be used against them; in fact, they are amongst the most peaceable and friendly of all the Indian tribes, and have at times received from the government unmistakable and substantial recognition of their long-continued friendship for the whites. In time of peace the war power remains in abeyance, and must be subservient to the civil authority of the government until something occurs to justify its exercise. No fact exists, and nothing has occurred, so far as the relators are concerned, to make it necessary or lawful to exercise such an authority over them. If they could be removed to the Indian Territory by force, and kept there in the same way, I can see no good reason why they might not be taken and kept by force in the penitentiary at Lincoln, or Leavenworth, or Jefferson City, or any other place which the commander of the forces might, in his judgment, see proper to designate. I cannot think that any such arbitrary authority exists in this country.

The reasoning advanced in support of my views, leads me to conclude:

1st. That an *Indian* is a PERSON within the meaning of the laws of the United States, and has, therefore, the right to sue out a writ of *habeas corpus* in a federal court, or before a federal judge, in all cases where he may be confined or in custody under color of authority of the United States, or where he is restrained of liberty in violation of the constitution or laws of the United States.

2d. That General George Crook, the respondent, being commander of the military department of the Platte, has the custody of the relators, under color of authority of the United States, and in violation of the laws thereof.

3d. That no rightful authority exists for removing by force any of the relators to the Indian Territory, as the respondent has been directed to do.

4th. That the Indians possess the inherent right of expatriation, as well as the more fortunate white race, and have the inalienable right to *"life, liberty, and the pursuit of happiness,"* so long as they obey the laws and do not trespass on forbidden ground. And,

5th. Being restrained of liberty under color of authority of the United States, and in violation of the laws thereof, the relators must be discharged from custody, and it is so ordered.

ORDERED ACCORDINGLY.

NOTES

1 Cecil Thompson, *The Dutch and English in America,* 19.
2 C. Bradbury, *Lives of Celebrated American Indians,* 179–80.
3 Francis Parkman, *The Pioneers of New France in the Old World,* 457–58.
4 Paul Radin, *The Story of the American Indian,* 21–22.
5 Herbert Milton Sylvester, *Indian Wars of New England,* vol. I, 386.
6 Roger Williams, *A Key into the Language of America,* 133. Williams' *Key* was written in the Narragansett language; 300 years later it was still used successfully among non-English-speaking Algonquian Indians in Labrador who had the same linguistic roots as Narragansett.
7 Donald M. McNicol, *The Amerindians,* 39. Black Hawk, the Sauk chief, after his capture in 1832, was sent down the Mississippi River to prison at St. Louis. Lt. Jefferson Davis was put in charge of the prisoner. In his autobiography, Black Hawk comments: "On our way down, we called at Galena, and remained a short time. The people crowded to the boat to see us; but the war chief [Davis] would not permit them to enter the apartment [on the steamboat] where we were—knowing, from what his own feelings would have been, if he had been placed in a similar situation, that we did not wish to have a gaping crowd around us." (Donald Jackson, ed., *Black Hawk: An Autobiography,* 163).

8   Francis Parkman, *The Jesuits of North America*, 384–85.

9   Emma Helen Blair, trans. and ed., *The Indian Tribes of the Upper Mississippi Valley . . .* [Nicolas Perrot's journal], vol. I, 207.

10 John Gilmary Shea, *Discovery and Exploration of the Mississippi Valley*, 23.

11 Annie Cole Cady, ed., *Worthington's History of the United States*, 131.

12 Samuel Smith, *The Dutch History of New Jersey*, 101–02.

13 James Truslow Adams, *The Epic of America*, 32.

14 Carl Carmer, ed., *Cavalcade of America*, 24.

15 Albert Cook Myers, *Narratives of Early Pennsylvania*, 234–35.

16 William W. Campbell, *The Life and Writings of De Witt Clinton*, 365–66, 368–69.

17 Milo M. Quaife, *Lake Michigan*, 72.

18 John Reinhold Foster, *Travels Through Louisiana*, 29.

19 Ibid., 58.

20 William N. Fenton, ed., *Parker on the Iroquois*, Book III, 30–31, 49.

21 Ibid., 38–39.

22 Ibid., 32.

23 Ibid., 58–60.

24 Albert Henry Smyth, ed., *The Writings of Benjamin Franklin*, vol. IV, 182.

25 Julian P. Boyd, ed., *Indian Treaties Printed by Benjamin Franklin, 1736–1762*, 7.

26 Ibid., 5–6, 26.

27 Ibid., 27–29.

28 Laurence J. Burpee, ed., *Journals and Letters of Pierre Gaultier de Varrennes*, 354–55.

29 *Minutes of the Provisional Council of Pennsylvania*, vol. IV, February 7, 1736 to October 15, 1745, 730.

30 Smyth, ed., *Writings of Franklin*, vol. X, 98–99. Benjamin Franklin's version of Canassatego's speech has become the traditionally accepted one. However, it is possible that Frankin embellished it slightly from Canassatego's original which may not have included a counter offer after all. Franklin referred to Canassatego's speech in a number of his writings through the years, but presumably the first time was in a

letter of May 9, 1753. The earlier *Minutes of the Provisional Council of Pennsylvania* for July 3–4, 1744, records the exchange of speeches. The first speech is by a Commissioner from Virginia on July 3:

> The way to have such a Friend is for you to send three or four of your Boys to Virginia, where we have a fine House for them to Live in, and a Man on purpose to teach the Children of you, our Friends, the Religion, Language, and Customs of the White People. To this Place we kindly invite you to send some of your Children, and we promise you they shall have the same care taken of them, and be Instructed in the same manner as our own Children, and be returned to you again when you please; and to confirm this we give you this String of Wampum. (vol. IV, 730)

The second speech is Canassatego's reply on July 4:

> You told us likewise you had a Great House Provided for the Education of Youth, and that there were several white People and Indian Children there to learn languages and to write and read, and invited us to send some of our Children among you, &.
>
> We must let you know we love our Children too well to send them so great a way, and the Indians are not inclined to give their Children learning. We allow it to be good, and we thank you for your Invitation; but our Customs differing from your's you will be so good as to excuse us. (vol. IV, 733)

31 Don Marshall Larrabee, ed., *A Reprint of the Journals of George Washington and His Guide, Christopher Gist*, 13–14.

32 "Journal of the Proceedings of the Congress Held at Albany, in 1754," Massachusetts Historical Society *Collections*, Third Series, vol. V, 1836, 41–42.

33 Sylvester, *Indian Wars*, vol. III, 454–55.

34 Alvin M. Josephy, Jr., et al., eds., *The American Heritage Book of Indians*, 200.

35 James H. Perkins and J. M. Peck, *Annals of the West*, 104.

36 Foster, *Travels Through Louisiana*, 170.

37   Reuben Gold Thwaites, ed., *Early Western Travels 1748–1846,* vol. I, 213–16.

38   Perkins and Peck, *Annals of the West,* 106.

39   Francis Parkman, *The Conspiracy of Pontiac,* 224.

40   Alexander Henry, *Travels and Adventures in Canada and the Indian Territories,* 209.

41   Parkman, *Pontiac,* 168–69.

42   Henry, *Travels and Adventures,* 122.

43   Rufus Blanchard, *Discovery and Conquests of the Northwest,* 132.

44   Parkman, *Pontiac,* 343.

45   Smyth, ed., *Writings of Franklin,* vol. I, 308–09.

46   Raymond McCoy, *The Massacre of Old Fort Mackinac,* 153–54.

47   Stella Pendleton Lyles, "Shawneetown," Illinois State Historical Society *Journal,* vol. XXII, 1929, 167.

48   Blanchard, *Discovery and Conquests,* 150.

49   John P. Brown, *Old Frontiers,* 9–10.

50   Samuel Hardin Stille, *Ohio Builds a Nation,* 17.

51   Glenn Tucker, *Tecumseh: Vision of Glory,* 26–27.

52   Thomas Jefferson, *Notes on the State of Virginia,* 66. For discussion of the Logan speech controversy, see Edward D. Seeber, "Critical Views on Logan's Speech," *Journal of American Folklore,* vol. LX, 1947, 130–46.

53   Blanchard, *Discovery and Conquests,* 164.

54   Stewart Edward White, *Daniel Boone, Wilderness Scout,* 174.

55   F. H. Huddleston, *Gentleman Johnny Burgoyne,* 153–54.

56   Archibald Henderson, "The Treaty of Long Island of Holston, July 1777," *North Carolina Historical Review,* vol. VIII, 1931, 66.

57   Albert Britt, *Great Indian Chiefs,* 79.

58   Joel Tyler Headley, *Washington and His Generals,* vol. II, 193–98.

59   Clark Wissler, *Indians of the United States,* 120.

60   William Cristie Macleod, *The American Indian Frontier,* 516–17.

61   Smyth, ed., *Writings of Franklin,* vol. IX, 625.

62   Perkins and Peck, *Annals of the West,* 355.

63   Humphrey Milford, *Chronicles of the Proprietors of America,* 161.

64 William M. Beauchamp, *The History of the New York Iroquois,* 137.

65 Andrew A. Lipscomb, ed., *The Writings of Thomas Jefferson,* vol. XVI, 378–81. See also John C. Fitzpatrick, ed., *The Writings of George Washington,* vol. XXXII, 327n.

66 Lipscomb, ed., *Writings of Jefferson,* vol. XVI, 383–84.

67 Ibid., 385–86.

68 Ibid., 386–87.

69 "Journal of a Treaty Held in 1793 . . . [Commissioner Benjamin Lincoln's journal]," Massachusetts Historical Society *Collections,* Third Series, vol. V, 1836, 164–66.

70 Brown, *Old Frontiers,* 411.

71 Blanchard, *Discovery and Conquests,* 219.

72 Perkins and Peck, *Annals of the West,* 351–52.

73 Ibid., 441–42.

74 Brown, *Old Frontiers,* 442–43.

75 Fenton, ed., *Parker on the Iroquois,* Book II, 27, 31, 32.

76 Campbell, *De Witt Clinton,* 237.

77 Donald D. Jackson, ed., *Letters of the Lewis and Clark Expedition,* 281–82.

78 Ibid., 284–85.

79 William L. Stone, *The Life of Joseph Brant,* vol. II, 481.

80 Henry Raymond Hamilton, *The Epic of Chicago,* 210.

81 Mabel Powers, *The Portage Trail,* 189. Subsequent research has shown this speech to be an impromptu talk given by Wa-o-wo-da-no-onk (Dr. Peter Wilson) in May 1847.

82 Milo M. Quaife, *Chicago and the Old Northwest, 1673–1835,* 189.

83 Thomas L. Blaine, *Indian Tribes of North America,* 79.

84 Samuel G. Drake, *The Book of the Indians of North America,* Book V, 121–22.

85 Alvin M. Josephy, Jr., *The Patriot Chiefs,* 159.

86 Edward Eggleston, *A First Book in American History,* 150.

87 Tucker, *Tecumseh,* 197.

88 J. Seymour Currey, *The Story of Old Fort Dearborn,* 87.

89 Ibid., 119.

90 Eggleston, *First Book in American History,* 151.

91   Jackson, ed., *Black Hawk,* 80.
92   Albert James Pickett, *History of Alabama,* 594, for first
     half of Red Eagle's speech, up to first ellipsis; John
     Henry Eaton, *The Life of Andrew Jackson,* 177–78,
     for second half of speech. See Marquis James, *The
     Life of Andrew Jackson: The Border Captain,* chp.
     X, notes 47–49, for helpful but not entirely satis-
     factory comments on various versions of Red Eagle's
     speech.
93   "Prairie du Chien Documents, 1814–15," Wisconsin
     State Historical Society *Collections,* vol. IX, 1909,
     278.
94   Addison Edwin Sheldon, *History and Stories of Ne-
     braska.* 46.
95   Alexander Ross, *Fur Hunters of the Far West,* 51.
96   Doane Robinson, *A History of the Dakota or Sioux
     Indians,* 100.
97   Ross, *Fur Hunters,* 171.
98   Robinson, *History of the Dakota or Sioux Indians,* 97.
99   Clara Ingram Judson, *The Mighty Soo,* 106–07.
100 C. Fayne Porter, *Our Indian Heritage,* 89. Many sim-
     ilar stories of young Indian men saving maidens from
     such deaths were told about various tribes, but most
     do not have the follow-up story this one has.
101 Ibid., 92-93.
102 Frank R. Grover, "Indian Treaties Affecting Lands in
     the Present State of Illinois." Illinois State Historical
     Society *Journal,* vol. VIII, 1915, 394–95.
103 D'Arcy McNickle, *They Came Here First,* 188.
104 James Buchanan, *Sketches of the History, Manners, and
     Customs of the North American Indians,* 38–42.
105 William Jennings Bryan and Francis W. Halsey, eds.,
     The World's Famous Orations, vol. VIII, 20.
106 Grover, "Indian Treaties," 400.
107 Radin, *Story of American Indian,* 367.
108 Quaife, *Chicago and the Old Northwest,* 319.
109 Herman J. Viola, "Thomas L. McKenney and the Ad-
     ministration of Indian Affairs 1824–1830," Ph.D.
     diss., Indiana University, 1970, 123.
110 Hamilton, *The Epic of Chicago,* 27.
111 *Niles' Weekly Register,* vol. XXXVI, no. 36, June 20,
     1829, 274.
112 Percival Graham Rennick, "The Peoria and Galena

Trail and Coach Road," *Illinois State Historical Society Journal,* vol. XXVII, 1935, 403–05.

113 William L. Stone, *The Life and Times of Sa-Go-Ya-Wat-Ha,* 272.

114 Cyrus Thomas, *The History of North America in Historic Times,* 109.

115 Washington Irving, *Astoria,* 146.

116 Archer Butler Hulbert, *Pilots of the Republic,* 303–04. For details of the fact and the fiction of this story see C. M. Drury, *Henry Harmon Spalding,* chp. 3, "The Nez Perce Delegation"; and Francis Haines, *The Nez Perces,* chp. 6, "The Macedonian Cry." Drury calls the speech "the work of an old man's [Spalding's] imagination." (88) Haines calls it "an outright fake" (58) and suggests that the delegation "were not divinely inspired toward Christianity, nor were they seeking for a higher moral standard. They wanted better 'medicine' to increase their prestige and power." (60) For George Catlin's account of the delegation and of his painting Rabbit Skin Leggings and No Horns on His Head, see *North American Indians,* vol. II, 124 (illustrations opposite page 124): "When I first heard the report of the object of this extraordinary mission across the mountains, I could scarcely believe it; but on conversing with General Clarke on a future occasion, I was fully convinced of the fact."

117 Washington Irving, *The Adventures of Captain Bonneville,* 93–94.

118 Hamilton, *The Epic of Chicago,* 204–09.

119 John H. Hauberg, "The Black Hawk War, 1831–1832," *Illinois State Historical Society Transactions,* vol. XXXIX, 1932, 119–20.

120 Thomas Ford, *A History of Illinois . . . to 1847,* 246.

121 John H. Hauberg, "The New Black Hawk State Park," *Illinois State Historical Society Journal,* vol. XX, 1927, 278–79.

122 Irving, *Adventures of Bonneville,* 88.

123 John Treat Irving, *Indian Sketches,* vol. II, 280.

124 Ibid., 281.

125 Irving, *Adventures of Bonneville,* 135–36.

126 Arrell Morgan Gibson, *The Kickapoos,* 112.

127 John H. Hauberg, "Black Hawk's Mississippi," *Illinois*

State Historical Society *Journal,* vol. XXII, 1929, 158.

128 Ibid.

129 Alexander R. Fulton, *The Red Men of Iowa,* 238.

130 George Catlin, letter from St. Louis, 1835, in Thomas Donaldson, "The George Catlin Indian Gallery," Smithsonian Institution *Annual Report 1885,* pt. V, 505, for first paragraph of Catlin quote; George Catlin, *Last Rambles Amongst the Indians of the Rocky Mountains and the Andes,* 354–55, for last paragraph, which is adapted from Catlin's long twelve-sentence "I-love-a-people" credo which he printed in response to charges of being an Indian lover.

> It has been sneeringly said that I have "spoken too well of the Indians," (better to speak too well of them than not to speak well enough)—"that I have flattered them"—(better to *flatter* them than to *caricature* them; there have been enough to do this). . . .
> I have had some unfriendly denunciations by the press, and by those critics I have been reproachfully designated the *"Indian-loving Catlin."* What of this? What have I to answer? Have I any apology to make for loving the Indians? The Indians have always loved me, and why should I not love the Indians? (355, 354 Catlin's italics)

131 Irving, *Adventures of Bonneville,* 289-90.

132 Josephy et al., *Book of Indians,* 228.

133 Annie H. Abel, ed., *Chardon's Journal at Fort Clark,* 124.

134 Blaine, *Indian Tribes of North America,* 79.

135 John Tebbel, *The Compact History of the Indian Wars,* 135.

136 Hamilton, *The Epic of Chicago,* 278–79.

137 Father Pierre Jean de Smet, *Letters and Sketches,* 25.

138 Charles Larpenteur, *Forty Years a Fur Trader,* 153–54.

139 Carleton Beals, *American Earth,* 41.

140 Larpenteur, *Forty Years a Fur Trader,* 244.

141 John Russell Bartlett, *Personal Narrative of Explorations and Incidents in Texas, New Mexico . . . ,* 219.

142 S. M. Barrett, ed., *Geronimo's Story of His Life,* 31.

143 I lost my reference for Chequito's speech and in sub-

sequently tracking down the source, I located what must be its original appearance: in the journal of Horace Capron (Merritt Starr, "General Horace Capron, 1804–1885," Illinois State Historical Society *Journal,* vol. XVII, 1925, 271–72). Here one discovers that only the last two sentences of Speech #143 are put forth by Capron as direct quotes from Chequito. The remainder of the speech is a close paraphrase of Capron's original paraphrase of Chequito's remarks to the General in the latter's tent. I used the speech anyway, for two reasons: In the first place, the paraphrase is very faithful to Capron's original; in the second place, it serves to illustrate how some Indian speeches have developed or changed through time and various transmissions.

144 U.S. Congress, 36th, 1st ses., *House of Repr. Exec. Doc. No. 56,* vol. XI, pt. 1, 74.

145 Ibid., 115.

146 Stanley Vestal, *New Sources of Indian History 1850–1891,* 124.

147 Archie Binns, *Northwest Gateway,* 100–04.

148 Flora Warren Seymour, *The Story of the Red Man,* 259–60.

149 Hazard Stevens, *Life of Isaac Ingalls Stevens,* vol. II, 47.

150 "Taoyateduta is Not a Coward," *Minnesota History,* vol. XXXVIII, 1962, 115.

151 J. H. Johnson, *Indian Wars in Minnesota,* 169.

152 Charles A. Eastman, *Old Indian Days,* 15.

153 Ibid., 137.

154 Philippe Regis de Trobriand, *Army Life in Dakota,* 160.

155 Larpenteur, *Forty Years a Fur Trader,* 359.

156 Trobriand, *Army Life in Dakota,* 81–82.

157 Ibid., 241–42.

158 Stanley Vestal, *Warpath and Council Fire,* 124–26.

159 James Mooney, "Calendar History of the Kiowa Indians," U.S. Bureau of American Ethnology, *17th Annual Report,* 1895–96, pt. 1, 207–08.

160 Trobriand, *Army Life in Dakota,* 187–88.

161 Elliott Arnold, *Blood Brother,* 322.

162 U.S. Secretary of the Interior, *Annual Report 1868,* 503–04.

163 U.S. Congress, 49th, 1st ses., *House of Repr. Exec. Doc. No. 263*, 15.

164 Stanley Vestal, *Sitting Bull: Champion of the Sioux*, 107–08. See also Gilbert J. Garraghan, "Father de Smet's Sioux Peace Mission of 1868 and the Journal of Charles Galpin," *Mid-America: An Historical Review*, vol. XIII, New Series, vol. II, 1930, 161. Father Garraghan's printing of Si ting Bull's speech, "accurately typed from the original Ms." (147), actually is in Galpin's journal a paraphrase, third-person account by Galpin, de Smet's interpreter—e.g., "He loved to look upon the groves of Oak and felt a reverence for them." Presumably Vestal himself turned this Sitting Bull speech into a first-person version, for although Vestal (324) suggests that he used the original Galpin manuscript (at St. Louis University) for his *Sitting Bull* book, there is no reason to assume that Fa her Garraghan's *Mid-America* version of Galpin's journal differs from the manuscript version.

165 Martin F. Schmitt and Dee Brown, *The Fighting Indians of the West*, 43.

166 James S. Brisbin, ed., *Belden, The White Chief*, 432.

167 Hazard Stevens, "The Ascent of Mount Takhoma," *The Atlantic Monthly*, November 1876, 36–37.

168 *New York Times*, June 17, 1870, 1.

169 Ibid., 2.

170 Flora Warren Seymour, *Indian Agents of the Old Frontier*, 64.

171 Chief Joseph, "An Indian's Views of Indian Affairs," *North American Review*, vol. CXXVIII, 1879, 419.

172 Helen Hunt Jackson, *A Century of Dishonor*, 124.

173 Mooney, "Calendar History," pt. 1, 329.

174 A. N. Ellis, "Recollections of an Interview with Cochise," Kansas State Historical Society *Collections*, vol. XIII, 1913–14, 391–92. This account by Dr. Ellis of the Cochise speech is the one traditionally quoted from, but there is another account, presumably of the same occasion, by Henry Stuart Turrill, who said of Cochise's speech: "I wish it were within my power to give as I heard it this finest bit of Indian oratory that I ever listened to. He commenced in meager, somewhat guttural Apache, but as he warmed to his subject he slid into the more

graceful Spanish, of which he was a master, and with the expressive 'sign talk' he made an address that affected me as but one other orator ever has, and that was Wendell Phillips in one of his early abolition speeches." Turrill's version:

This for a very long time has been the home of my people. . . . We came to these mountains about us; no one lived here, and so we took them for our home and country. Here we grew from the first feeble band to be a great people and covered the whole country as the clouds cover the mountains. Many people came to our country. First the Spanish, with their horses and their iron shirts, their long knives and guns, great wonders to my simple people. We fought some, but they never tried to drive us from our homes in these mountains. After many years the Spanish soldiers were driven away and the Mexican ruled the land. With these, little wars came, but we were now a strong people, and we did not fear them. At last in my youth came the white man, under your people. . . . I have fought long and as best I could against you. I have destroyed many of your people, but where I have destroyed one white man many have come in his place where an Indian has been killed, there has been none to come in his place, so that the great people that welcomed you with acts of kindness to this land are now but a feeble band that fly before your soldiers as the deer before the hunter, and must all perish if this war continues. I have come to you, not from any love for you or for your great father in Washington, or from any regard for his or your wishes, but as a conquered chief, to try to save alive the few people that still remain to me. I am the last of my family, a family that for very many years have been the leaders of this people, and on me depends their future, whether they shall utterly vanish from the land or that a small remnant remain for a few years to see the sun rise over these mountains, their home. I here pledge my word, a word that has never been broken, that if your great father will set aside a part of my own country, where I and my little

217

band can live, we will remain at peace with your people forever. . . . I have spoken. ("A Vanished Race of Aboriginal Founders," The New York Society of the Order of the Founders and Patriots of America *Publication no. 18,* 1907, 19–20. Made available through the courtesy of Eve Ball, Ruidoso, New Mexico.)

175 Marshall Sprague, *Massacre,* 96–97.
176 Brisbin, ed., *Belden,* 435.
177 Porter, *Our Indian Heritage,* 134–35.
178 Hamlin Garland, *The Book of the American Indian,* 92.
179 Helen Cody Wetmore, *Last of the Great Scouts,* 253.
180 *Missoula* (Montana) *Missoulian,* April 26, 1876.
181 U.S. Commissioner of Indian Affairs, *Annual Report 1875,* 188.
182 Ibid., 189–90.
183 Josephy et al., *Book of Indians,* 347.
184 Vestal, *Sitting Bull,* 170–72. For pictographs with text, drawn and written by White Bull himself, depicting various stages and versions of this fight, see Stanley Vestal, "The Man Who Killed Custer," *American Heritage,* vol. VIII, no. 2, February 1957; and James H. Howard, trans. and ed., *The Warrior Who Killed Custer: The Personal Narrative of Chief Joseph White Bull.*
185 U.S. Congress, 44th, 2nd ses., *Senate Exec. Doc. No. 9,* 38.
186 Ibid., 38–39.
187 Ibid., 40.
188 Ibid., 41–43.
189 Ibid., 69.
190 Homer W. Wheeler, *Buffalo Days,* 253.
191 U.S. Secretary of War, *Annual Report 1877,* 593–94.
192 Chief Joseph, "An Indian's Views," 425.
193 John Gibbon, "The Battle of Big Hole," *Harper's Weekly,* December 28, 1895, 1235.
194 Wissler, *Indians,* 191.
195 Chief Joseph, "An Indian's Views," 429.
196 Ibid., 432–33.
197 Wheeler, *Buffalo Days,* 199–200.
198 William G. Hardy, *From Sea Unto Shining Sea, 1850–1910,* 294.

199   George Bird Grinnell, *The Fighting Cheyennes*, 386–88.

200   Wissler, *Indians*, 227.

201   J. T. Naylor, *Frontier and Indian Life, 1866–1889*, 239.

202   U.S. Congress, 46th, 3rd ses., *Senate Exec. Doc. No. 30*, 2, 14–15.

203   Ibid., 15.

204   Thomas Henry Tibbles, *Ponca Chiefs*, 199–200.

205   U.S. Congress, 46th, 3rd ses., *Senate Exec. Doc. No. 14*, 8, 13.

206   Garland, *American Indian*, 254.

207   Robert H. Davis, *Canada Cavalcade*, 118.

208   Schmitt and Brown, *Fighting Indians*, 93–94.

209   Marvin and Dorothy Rosenberg, "The Only Indian Left," *American Heritage*, June 1966, 19.

210   From the corners one itself.

211   Garland, *American Indian*, 254.

212   Oliver La Farge, *A Pictorial History of the American Indian*, 191.

213   James Mooney, "The Ghost Dance Religion and the Sioux Outbreak of 1890," U.S. Bureau of American Ethnology, *14th Annual Report*, 1892–93, pt. 2, 178.

214   Ibid., 1072.

215   Garland, *American Indian*, 58.

216   Ibid., 63.

217   Clark Wissler, *Indian Cavalcade*, 171.

218   Ibid., 178.

219   The reference for this speech has been lost.

220   Francis La Flesche, "The Osage Tribe: Rite of the Wa-xo-be," U.S. Bureau of American Ethnology, *45th Annual Report*, 1927–28, 530, 534.

221   Joseph B. Thompson, "Minutes of a Conference Held at Fort Sill, Oklahoma, August 22, 1909," ms. of the secretary at the conference. Made available through the courtesy of Eve Ball, Ruidoso, New Mexico.

222   U.S. Congress, 62nd, 3rd ses., Senate, *Congressional Record*, 1913, 49, pt. 4, 3908–09.

223   John G. Neihardt, *Black Elk Speaks*, 219–20.

224   U.S. Congress, 64th, 1st ses., Senate, *Congressional Record*, May 12, 1916, 7843–45.

225   Wa-Sha-Quon-Asin, *Tales of an Empty Cabin*, 91–95.

226 Francis A. Garrecht, "An Indian Chief," *The Washington Historical Quarterly*, vol. XIX, July 1928, 170.

227 Rubert Costo, ed., *Textbooks and the American Indian*, 2–3.

228 Carl Carmer, *Listen for a Lonesome Drum*, xvi.

229 Correspondence from Henry Standing Bear to Korczak Ziolkowski. Made available through the courtesy of Mr. and Mrs. Ziolkowski, Black Hills, South Dakota.

230 Ellsworth Jaeger, *Woodsmoke: The Book of Outdoor Lore*, 66.

231 Alfred W. Gilpin, Association on American Indian Affairs, mimeographed report. Made available through the courtesy of Roger Welsch, Lincoln, Nebraska.

232 American Indian Chicago Conference, *Declaration of Indian Purpose*, 19–20.

233 *Reno Nevada State Journal*, March 28, 1964.

234 Ibid., April 27, 1964.

235 U.S. Congress, 90th, 1st ses., Senate, Committee on Labor and Public Welfare, Special Subcommittee on Indian Education, *Hearings*, December 14 and 15, 1967, pt. 1, 182.

236 Ibid., 183–84.

237 Ibid., 86.

238 Ibid., 79–81.

239 Ibid., 47–48.

240 Ibid., 221–22.

241 Ben Black Elk, "How It Feels to be an Indian in the White Man's World," *Red Cloud Country*, vol. 5, no. 2, April-June 1968, 1–3.

242 Christopher Davis, *North American Indian*, 108, 105. In the late 1960s, Thames Television of England produced a documentary on the North American Indian. "Now that the Buffalo's Gone." Many of the interviews gathered by Thames Television were used in Davis' book.

243 Ibid., 105–08.

244 Peter Arnett and Horst Faas, "In Search of America," *Chicago Sun-Times*, April 18, 1971, Section 2, 16.

245 Davis, *North American Indian*, 139.

246 Ibid., 15–18.

247 Ibid., 96, 139.

248 *New York Times*, January 17, 1971.

249 Davis, *North American Indian*, 139.

250   Vine Deloria, Jr., *Custer Died for Your Sins*, 250–51, 257.
251   Davis, *North American Indian*, 139.

The first quotation on page xxi is from *American State Papers: Indian Affairs*, vol. I, 53–54; the second is from Viola, "Thomas L. McKenney," 176 (spelling modernized).

BIBLIOGRAPHY

BOOKS

Abel, Annie H., ed. *Chardon's Journal at Fort Clark*. Pierre: Department of History, State of South Dakota, 1932.

Adams, James Truslow, *The Epic of America*. Boston: Little, Brown & Co., 1928.

American Indian Chicago Conference. *Declaration of Indian Purpose*. Chicago: AICC, University of Chicago, 1961; Washington: Center for the Study of Man, Smithsonian Institution.

Arnold, Elliott, *Blood Brother*. New York: Duell Sloan & Pearce, 1947.

Astrov, Margot, ed., *The Winged Serpent: An Anthology of American Indian Prose and Poetry*. New York: John Day Co., 1946.

Barrett, Steven M., ed. *Geronimo's Story of His Life*. New York: Duffield & Co., 1907.

Bartlett, John Russell. *Personal Narratives of Explorations and Incidents in Texas, New Mexico . . . 1853*. New York: D. Appleton & Co., 1854.

Beals, Carleton. *American Earth*. Philadelphia: J. B. Lippincott Co., 1938.

Beauchamp, William M. *The History of the New York Iroquois*. New York: Charles Scribner's, 1913.

Binns, Archie. *Northwest Gateway: The Story of the Port of Seattle*. New York: Doubleday & Co., 1941.

Blaine, Thomas L. *Indian Tribes of North America*. Philadelphia: D. Rice & Co., 1870.

Blair, Emma Helen, trans. and ed. *The Indian Tribes of the Upper Mississippi Valley and Region of the Great Lakes*

223

as described by Nicolas Perrot. . . . Cleveland: Arthur Clark, 1911.

Blanchard, Rufus. *Discovery and Conquests of the Northwest.* Chicago: Thomas Cushing & Co., 1880.

Boyd, Julian P., ed. *Indian Treaties Printed by Benjamin Franklin, 1736–1762.* Philadelphia: Historical Society of Pennsylvania, 1938.

Bradbury, C. *Lives of Celebrated American Indians.* Boston: Soden & Co., 1843.

Brisben, James S., ed. *Belden, The White Chief.* Cincinnati and New York: C. F. Vent Co., 1882.

Britt, Albert. *Great Indian Chiefs.* New York: McGraw-Hill Book Co., 1938.

Brown, Dee. *Bury My Heart at Wounded Knee: An Indian History of the American West.* New York: Holt, Rinehart & Winston, 1970.

Brown, John P. *Old Frontiers.* Kingsport: Southern Publishers, 1938.

Bryan, William Jennings and Francis W. Halsey, eds. *The World's Famous Orations.* New York: Funk & Wagnalls Co., 1906.

Buchanan, James. *Sketches of the History, Manners and Customs of the North American Indians.* New York: W. Borradaile, 1824.

Burpee, Laurence J., ed. *Journals and Letters of Pierre Gaultier de Varrennes.* Toronto: The Champlain Society, 1927.

Cady, Annie Cole, ed. *Worthington's History of the United States.* New York: R. Worthington Co., 1890.

Campbell, William W. *The Life and Writings of De Witt Clinton.* New York: Baker & Scribner, 1849.

Carmer, Carl, ed. *Cavalcade of America.* New York: Lothrop, Lee & Shepard Co., Inc., 1956.

————. *Listen for a Lonesome Drum.* New York: Farrar, Rinehart Inc., 1936.

Catlin, George. *Last Rambles Amongst the Indians of the Rocky Mountains and the Andes.* London: Sampson Low, Son and Marston, 1868.

————. *North American Indians.* Philadelphia: Leary, Stuart & Co., 1913.

Costo, Rupert, ed. *Textbooks and the American Indian.* San Francisco: American Indian Historical Society, 1970.

Currey, J. Seymour. *The Story of Old Fort Dearborn.* Chicago: A. C. McClurg Co., 1912.

Davis, Christopher. *North American Indian*. Feltham, Middlesex, England: Hamlyn House, 1969.

Davis, Robert H. *Canada Cavalcade*. New York: D. Appleton & Co., 1938.

Deloria, Vine, Jr. *Custer Died for Your Sins*. New York: Avon Books, 1970.

Drake, Samuel G. *The Book of the Indians of North America*. Boston: Josiah Drake at Antiquarian Bookstore, 1883.

Drury, C. M. *Henry Harmon Spalding*. Caldwell: Caxton Printers, 1936.

Eastman, Charles A. *Old Indian Days*. New York: The McClure Co., 1907.

Eaton, John Henry. *The Life of Andrew Jackson*. Philadelphia: S. F. Bradford, 1824.

Eggleston, Edward. *A First Book in American History*. New York: D. Appleton & Co., 1889.

Fenton, William N., ed. *Parker on the Iroquois*. Syracuse: Syracuse University Press, 1968.

Forbes, Jack D., ed. *Nevada Indians Speak*. Reno: University of Nevada Press, 1967.

Ford, Thomas, *A History of Illinois . . . to 1847*. Chicago: R. R. Donnelley & Sons Co., 1945.

Foster, John Reinhold. *Travels Through Louisiana*. London: T. D. Davies, 1771.

Fulton, Alexander R. *The Red Men of Iowa*. Des Moines: Mills & Co., 1882.

Garland, Hamlin. *The Book of the American Indian*. New York: Harper Bros., 1923.

Gibson, Arrell Morgan. *The Kickapoos: Lords of the Middle Border*. Norman: University of Oklahoma Press, 1963.

Grinnell, George Bird. *The Fighting Cheyennes*. New York: Charles Scribner's Sons, 1915.

Haines, Francis. *The Nez Percés: Tribesmen of the Columbia Plateau*. Norman: University of Oklahoma, 1955.

Hamilton, Charles, ed. *Cry of the Thunderbird: The American Indian's Own Story*. New York: Macmillan Co., 1951.

Hamilton, Henry Raymond. *The Epic of Chicago*. Chicago: Willet, Clark & Co., 1932.

Hardy, William G. *From Sea Unto Shining Sea, 1850–1910* (Canadian History Series, vol. IV). New York: Doubleday & Co., 1960.

Headley, Joel Tyler. *Washington and his Generals*. New York: Charles Scribner, 1859.

Henry, Alexander. *Travels and Adventures in Canada and*

the Indian Territories. Chicago: R. R. Donnelley & Sons Co., 1921.

Huddleston, F. H. *Gentleman Johnny Burgoyne*. Indianapolis: The Bobbs-Merrill Co., 1927.

Hulbert, Archer Butler. *Pilots of the Republic*. Chicago: A. C. McClurg Co., 1906.

Irving, John Treat. *Indian Sketches*. Philadelphia: Carey, Lee and Blanchard, 1835.

Irving, Washington. *The Adventures of Captain Bonneville*. New York: R. Worthington Co., 1884.

————. *Astoria*. New York: R. Worthington Co., 1884.

Jackson, Donald, ed. *Black Hawk: An Autobiography*. Urbana: University of Illinois Press, 1955.

————. *Letters of the Lewis and Clark Expedition with Related Documents 1783–1854*. Urbana: University of Illinois Press, 1962.

Jackson, Helen Hunt, *A Century of Dishonor*. New York: Harper & Bros., 1881.

Jaeger, Ellsworth. *Woodsmoke: The Book of Outdoor Lore*. New York: Macmillan Co., 1953.

James, Marquis. *The Life of Andrew Jackson*. New York: Garden City Publishing Co., 1940.

Jefferson, Thomas. *Notes on the State of Virginia*. Boston: Lilly & Wait, 1832.

Johnson, J. H. *Indian Wars in Minnesota*. Minneapolis: (privately printed) 1901.

Jones, Louis Thomas. *Aboriginal American Oratory: The Tradition of Eloquence Among the Indians of the United States*. Los Angeles: Southwest Museum, 1965.

Josephy, Alvin M., Jr., et al., eds. *The American Heritage Book of Indians*. New York: The American Heritage Press, 1961.

————. *The Patriot Chiefs*. New York: The Viking Press, 1961.

Judson, Clara Ingram. *The Mighty Soo*. Chicago: Follett Publishing Co., 1955.

La Farge, Oliver. *A Pictorial History of the American Indian*. New York: Crown Publishing Co., Inc., 1957.

Larrabee, Don Marshall, ed. *A Reprint of the Journals of George Washington and His Guide, Christopher Gist*. (privately printed) 1950.

Larpenteur, Charles. *Forty Years a Fur Trader*. Chicago: R. R. Donnelley & Sons Co., 1941.

Lipscomb, Andrew A., ed. *The Writings of Thomas Jefferson*.

Washington: The Thomas Jefferson Memorial Association of the United States, 1905.

McCoy, Raymond. *The Massacre of Old Fort Mackinac.* Bay City, Michigan: (privately printed) 1950.

Macleod, William Cristie. *The American Indian Frontier.* New York: Alfred A. Knopf, 1928.

McNickle, D'Arcy. *They Came Here First.* Philadelphia: J. B. Lippincott Co., 1949.

McNicol, Donald M. *The Amerindians,* New York: Frederick A. Stokes Co., 1937.

Milford, Humphrey. *Chronicles of the Proprietors of America.* London: The Oxford Press, 1898.

Minutes of the Provisional Council of Pennsylvania. Volume IV, February 7, 1736 to October 15, 1754. Harrisburg: Theodore Finn, 1851.

Myers, Albert Cook. *Narratives of Early Pennsylvania . . . 1630–1708.* New York: Charles Scribner's Sons, 1912.

Naylor. J. T. *Frontier and Indian Life, 1866–1889.* Bismarck: (privately printed) 1892.

Neihardt, John G. *Black Elk Speaks.* New York: Wiliam Morrow & Co., 1932.

Parkman, Francis. *The Conspiracy of Pontiac.* New York: Collier Books, 1962.

———. *The Jesuits of North America.* Boston: Little, Brown & Co., 1935.

———. *The Pioneers of New France in the Old World.* Boston: Little, Brown & Co., 1930.

Perkins, James H. and J. M. Peck. *Annals of the West.* St. Louis: Albach Publishers, 1851.

Pickett, Albert James. *History of Alabama.* Birmingham: The Webb Book Co., 1900, reprint of 1851 edition.

Porter, C. Fayne, *Our Indian Heritage.* Philadelphia: Chilton Books, 1964.

Powers, Mabel. *The Portage Trail.* East Aurora, New York: The Roycroft Shops, 1924.

Quaife, Milo M. *Chicago and the Old Northwest, 1673–1835.* Chicago: The University of Chicago Press, 1913.

———. *Lake Michigan.* Indianapolis: The Bobbs-Merrill Co., 1944.

Radin, Paul. *The Story of the American Indian.* London: John Murray; New York: Liveright Publishing Corp., 1944.

Robinson, Doane. *A History of the Dakota or Sioux Indians.* Minneapolis: Ross and Haines, Inc., 1956. Reprint of

South Dakota State Historical Society *Collections*, vol. II, 1904, pt. 2.

Ross, Alexander. *Fur Hunters of the Far West.* Chicago: R. R. Donnelley & Sons Co., 1945.

Schmitt, Martin F. and Dee Brown. *The Fighting Indians of the West.* New York: Charles Scribner's Sons, 1948.

Seymour, Flora Warren. *Indian Agents of the Old Frontier.* New York: D. Appleton-Century Co., 1941.

——. *The Story of the Red Man.* New York: Longmans, Green & Co., 1925.

Shea, John Gilmary. *Discovery and Exploration of the Mississippi Valley.* New York: J. S. Redfield, 1852.

Sheldon, Addison Erwin. *History and Stories of Nebraska.* Lincoln: The University Publishing Co., 1919.

Smet, Pierre Jean de. *Letters and Sketches, with a Narrative of a Year's Residence Among the Indian Tribes of the Rocky Mountains.* Philadelphia: M. Fithian, 1843.

Smith, Samuel. *The Dutch History of New Jersey.* New York: Hurst & Co., 1886.

Smyth, Albert Henry, ed. *The Writings of Benjamin Franklin.* New York: Macmillan Co., 1905–07.

Sprague, Marshall. *Massacre.* Boston: Little, Brown & Co., 1957.

Stevens, Hazard. *Life of Isaac Ingalls Stevens.* New York: Houghton Mifflin Co., 1904.

Stille, Samuel Hardin. *Ohio Builds a Nation.* New York: Arlendale Book House, 1939.

Stone, William L. *The Life and Times of Sa-Go-Ya-Wat-Ha.* Albany: J. Munsell, 1886.

——. *The Life of Joseph Brant.* Albany: J. Munsell, 1864.

Sylvester, Herbert Milton. *Indian Wars of New England.* Cleveland: Arthur Clark, 1910.

Tebble, John. *The Compact History of the Indian Wars.* New York: Hawthorne Books, 1966.

Thomas, Cyrus. *The History of North America in Historic Times.* London: George Barrie & Sons, 1903.

Thompson, Cecil. *The Dutch and English in America.* Boston: Fields, Osgood & Co., 1870.

Thwaites, Reuben Gold, ed. *Early Western Travels 1748–1846.* Volume I. Cleveland: Arthur Clark, 1904.

Tibbles, Thomas Henry. *Ponca Chiefs.* New York: Zyliff Co., 1905.

Trobriand, Philippe Regis de. *Army Life in Dakota.* Chicago: R. R. Donnelley & Sons Co., 1941.

Tucker, Glenn. *Tecumseh: Vision of Glory*. Indianapolis: The Bobbs-Merrill Co., 1956.

Vestal, Stanley. *New Sources of Indian History 1850—1891*. Norman: University of Oklahoma Press, 1934.

————. *Sitting Bull: Champion of the Sioux*. New York: Houghton Mifflin Co., 1932.

————. *Warpath and Council Fire: The Plains Indians' Struggle for Survival in War and Diplomacy, 1851–1891*. New York: Random House, 1948.

Wa-Sha-Quon-Asin. *Tales of an Empty Cabin*. New York: Dodd, Mead & Co., 1936.

Wetmore, Helen Cody. *The Last of the Great Scouts*. New York: Grosset & Dunlap Co., 1899.

Wheeler, Homer W. *Buffalo Days*. Indianapolis: The Bobbs-Merrill Co., 1905.

White, Stewart Edward. *Daniel Boone, Wilderness Scout*. New York: Doubleday & Co., 1929.

Williams, Roger. *A Key into the Language of America: or, An help to the Language of the Natives in that part of America, called New-England*. London: Gregory Dexter 1643, reprinted as 5th edition, Providence: The Rhode Island and Providence Plantations Tercentenary Committee Inc., 1936.

Wissler, Clark. *Indian Cavalcade*. New York: Sheridan House, 1938.

————. *Indians of the United States: Four Centuries of Their History and Culture*. New York: Doubleday, Doran & Co., 1940.

DISSERTATIONS, MANUSCRIPTS, NEWSPAPERS, PERIODICALS

Arnett, Peter and Horst Faas. "In Search of America." *Chicago Sun-Times,* April 18, 1971.

Balgooyen, Theodore John. 'The Public Speaking of the Typical North American Plains Indians of the Nineteenth Century." Ph.D. dissertation. Stanford University, 1957.

Black Elk, Ben. "How It Feels to be an Indian in the White Man's World." *Red Cloud Country* (Pine Ridge, South Dakota: Red Cloud Indian School, Inc.), April-June 1968.

Chief Joseph. "An Indian's View of Indian Affairs." *North American Review,* vol. CXXVIII, 1879.

Ellis, A. N. "Recollections of an Interview with Cochise." Kansas State Historical Society *Collections,* vol. XIII, 1913–14.

Garraghan, Gilbert J. "Father de Smet's Sioux Peace Mission of 1868 and the Journal of Charles Galpin." *Mid-America: An Historical Review*, vol. XIII, New Series, vol. II, 1930.

Garrecht, Francis A. "An Indian Chief." *The Washington Historical Quarterly*, vol. XIX, July 1928.

Gibbon, John. "The Battle of Big Hole." *Harper's Weekly*, December 28, 1895.

Gilpin, Alfred W. Speech mimeographed by Association on American Indian Affairs, 1954.

Grover, Frank R. "Indian Treaties Affecting Lands in the Present State of Illinois." Illinois State Historical Society *Journal*, vol. VIII, 1915.

Hauberg, John H. "Black Hawk's Mississippi." Illinois State Historical Society *Journal*, vol. XXII, 1929.

————. "The Black Hawk War, 1831–1832." Illinois State Historical Society *Transactions*, vol. XXXIX, 1932.

————. "The New Black Hawk State Park." Illinois State Historical Society *Journal*, vol. XX, 1927.

Henderson, Archibald. "The Treaty of Long Island of Holston, July 1777." *North Carolina Historical Review*, vol. VIII, 1931.

"Journal of the Proceedings of the Congress Held at Albany, in 1754." Massachusetts Historical Society *Collections*, Third Series, vol. V, 1836.

[Lincoln, Benjamin.] "Journal of a Treaty Held in 1793. . . ." Massachusetts Historical Society *Collections*, Third Series, vol. V, 1836.

[Little Crow.] "Taoyateduta is Not a Coward." *Minnesota History*, vol. XXXVIII, 1962.

Lyles, Stella Pendleton. "Shawneetown." Illinois State Historical Society *Journal*, vol. XXII, 1929.

Missoula (Montana) *Missoulian*, April 26, 1876.

New York Times, June 17, 1870 and January 17, 1971.

"Prairie du Chien Documents, 1814–15." Wisconsin State Historical Society *Collections*, vol. IX, 1909.

Rennick, Percival Graham. "The Peoria and Galena Trail and Coach Road." Illinois State Historical Society *Journal*, vol. XXVII, 1935.

Reno Nevada State Journal, March 28 and April 27, 1964.

Rosenberg, Marvin and Dorothy. "The Only Indian Left." *American Heritage*, June 1966.

Seeber, Edward D. "Critical Views on Logan's Speech." *Journal of American Folklore*, vol. LX, 1947.

Starr, Merritt. "General Horace Capron, 1804–1885." *Illinois State Historical Society Journal,* vol. XVIII, 1925.

Stevens, Hazard. "The Ascent of Mount Takhoma." *The Atlantic Monthly,* November 1876.

Thompson, Joseph B. "Minutes of a Conference Held at Fort Sill, Oklahoma, August 22, 1909." Ms., Eve Ball Collection, Ruidoso, New Mexico.

Turrill, Henry Stuart. "A Vanished Race of Aboriginal Founders." The New York Society of the Order of the Founders and Patriots of America *Publication no. 18,* 1907. Eve Ball Collection, Ruidoso, New Mexico.

Viola, Herman J. "Thomas L. McKenney and the Administration of Indian Affairs 1824–1830." Ph.D. dissertation. Indiana University, 1970.

GOVERNMENT PUBLICATIONS

Donaldson, Thomas. "The George Catlin Indian Gallery." Smithsonian Institution, *Annual Report 1885,* pt. V. Washington: G.P.O., 1886.

La Flesche, Francis. "The Osage Tribe: Rite of the Wa-xo-be." U.S. Bureau of American Ethnology, *45th Annual Report,* 1927–28. Washington: G.P.O., 1930.

Mooney, James. "Calendar History of the Kiowa Indians." U.S. Bureau of American Ethnology, *17th Annual Report,* 1895–96. Washington: G.P.O., 1898.

————. "The Ghost Dance Religion and the Sioux Outbreak of 1890." U.S. Bureau of American Ethnology, *14th Annual Report,* 1892–93, pt. 2. Washington: G.P.O., 1896.

U.S. Commissioner of Indian Affairs, *Annual Report 1875.*

U.S. Congress, 36th, 1st ses. *House of Repr. Exec. Doc. No. 56,* vol. XI, pt. 1 (Pacific Railroad Surveys series, vol. XII, Book I); Isaac I. Stevens, "Narrative and Final Report of Explorations for a Route for a Pacific Railroad . . . from St. Paul to Puget Sound." Washington: Thomas H. Ford, 1860.

U.S. Congress, 44th, 2nd ses. *Senate Exec. Doc. No. 9.*

U.S. Congress, 46th, 3rd ses. *Senate Exec. Doc. No. 14.*

U.S. Congress, 46th, 3rd ses. *Senate Exec. Doc. No. 30.*

U.S. Congress, 49th, 1st ses. *House of Repr. Exec. Doc. No. 263.*

U.S. Congress, 62nd, 3rd ses. Senate, *Congressional Record,* 1913, 49, pt. 4.

U.S. Congress, 64th, 1st ses. Senate, *Congressional Record,* May 12, 1916.

U.S. Congress, 90th, 1st ses. Senate, Committee on Labor and Public Welfare, Special Subcommittee on Indian Education, *Hearings,* December 14 and 15, 1967, pt. 1.

U.S. Secretary of the Interior, *Annual Report 1868.*

U.S. Secretary of War, *Annual Report 1877.*

ACKNOWLEDGMENTS

Where fair use did not apply or the material was not in public domain, permission was obtained from publishers for the right to reprint here. With seven exceptions the publishers' names and the copyright dates noted in the Bibliography reflect the acknowledgement information requested. The variations are as follows: Davis' *North American Indian* is published by The Hamlyn Publishing Group, Ltd. Rights for Davis' *Canada Cavalcade* are now handled by Hawthorne Books, Inc. The copyright date and original publisher for Deloria's *Custer Died for Your Sins* is The Macmillan Co., 1969. Rights for Garland's *The Book of the American Indian* are controlled and were granted by his daughters, Mrs. Constance Garland Doyle and Mrs. Isabel Garland Lord. Similarly, Neihardt's *Black Elk Speaks* by the author and by his daughter, Mrs. Hilda Neihardt Petri. Also, Vestal's *Warpath and Council Fire* by the author. Vestal's *Sitting Bull* is now published by the University of Oklahoma Press. Grateful acknowledgement is made for all the permissions granted.

Appreciation is also extended to the many persons who helped through the mails in tracking down information: Marie Ellis at the College of William and Mary library, Roger Welsch at Nebraska Wesleyan University, Theodore J. Balgooyen at San Jose State College and Herman J. Viola at the National Archives, both of whom loaned personal copies of their dissertations, Eve Ball, Alvin M.

Josephy, Jr., Virgil J. Vogel, and many others. I also want to thank the cooperative personnel at the four institutions where I did the bulk of my research: Barrington (Illinois) Public Library, Chicago Public Library, Newberry Library, and Northwestern University Library.

INDEX

Persons, organizations, wars, battles, towns and places are indexed. Names of speakers/writers quoted are in bold face. Numerals indicate page numbers, not speech numbers.

237

240

How to do <u>almost</u> everything

What are the latest time and money-saving shortcuts for painting, papering, and varnishing floors, walls, ceilings, furniture? (See pages 102-111 of HOW TO DO *Almost* EVERYTHING.) What are the mini-recipes and the new ways to make food—from appetizers through desserts—exciting and delicious? (See pages 165-283.) How-to-do-it ideas like these have made Bert Bacharach, father of the celebrated composer (Burt), one of the most popular columnists in America.

This remarkable new book, HOW TO DO *Almost* EVERYTHING, is a fact-filled collection of Bert Bacharach's practical aids, containing thousands of tips and hints—for keeping house, gardening, cooking, driving, working, traveling, caring for children. It will answer hundreds of your questions, briefly and lucidly.

How to do <u>almost</u> everything

Is chock-full of useful information—information on almost everything you can think of, arranged by subject in short, easy-to-read tidbits, with an alphabetical index to help you find your way around —and written with the famed Bacharach touch.

SEND FOR YOUR FREE EXAMINATION COPY TODAY

We invite you to mail the coupon below. A copy of HOW TO DO *Almost* EVERYTHING will be sent to you at once. If at the end of ten days you do not feel that this book is one you will treasure, you may return it and owe nothing. Otherwise, we will bill you $6.95, plus postage and handling. At all bookstores, or write to Simon and Schuster, Dept. S-52, 630 Fifth Ave., New York, N.Y. 10020.

How to stay healthy all the time.

> "I can recommend this book for authoritative answers to questions that continually come up about health and how to live."—Harry J. Johnson, M.D., Chairman, Medical Board Director, Life Extension Institute.

Wouldn't it be wonderful if your whole family could stay healthy all the time?

It may now be possible, thanks to PREVENTIVE MEDICINE. This is the modern approach to health care. Its goal is to prevent illness before it even has a chance to strike!

A new book called THE FAMILY BOOK OF PREVENTIVE MEDICINE shows how you can take advantage of this preventive approach, and make it an everyday reality for yourself and your family. More than 700 pages long—and written in clear, simple language.

TELLS YOU ALL ABOUT THE LATEST MEDICAL ADVANCES

For example, the new knowledge of risk factors in disease is a vital tool of preventive medicine. With it, your doctor might pinpoint you as, say, a high heart attack risk *long before your heart actually gives you any trouble*. He could then prescribe certain changes in your diet and habits—perhaps very minor ones—that could remove the danger entirely. This would be preventive medicine at its ideal best! But even if a disease has already taken root, new diagnostic techniques can reveal its presence earlier than ever before. And, as a rule, the sooner a disease is discovered, the more easily it is cured.

SEND NO MONEY—10 DAYS' FREE EXAMINATION

Mail the coupon below, and THE FAMILY BOOK OF PREVENTIVE MEDICINE will be sent to you for free examination. Then, if you are not convinced that it can help you protect the health of your entire family, return it within 10 days and owe nothing. Otherwise, we will bill you for $12.95 plus mailing costs. At all bookstores, or write to Simon and Schuster, Dept. S-53, 630 Fifth Ave., New York, N.Y. 10020.

SIMON AND SCHUSTER, Dept. S-53
630 Fifth Ave., New York, N.Y. 10020
Please send me on approval a copy of THE FAMILY BOOK OF PREVENTIVE MEDICINE. If not convinced that this book belongs permanently in my home, I may return it within 10 days and owe nothing. Otherwise, you will bill me for $12.95, plus mailing costs.

Name..

Address...

City...State..............Zip..........

☐ SAVE. Enclose $12.95 now, and publisher pays mailing costs. Same 10-day return privilege with full refund guaranteed. (New York residents please add applicable sales tax.)

P 65/2

I HAVE SPOKEN is a collection of the oratory of the American Indian from the 17th century to the present day. With integrity, with statesmanship, with poetic imagery and caustic wit, Indian chiefs and orators describe their relations with the white man. It is a story of proffered friendship, of broken promises, of hopes that ended in disillusionment—and of a vision of life so strong that it has survived defeat.

In a land that the white man has raped and violated, these voices from the Indian heritage of America speak to us with haunting relevance.

"In a work of magnificent research that could only have been a labor of love, Virginia Armstrong has achieved a unique 'history' of the American Indian . . . multi-voiced, strong-flowing and in many passages movingly eloquent." —*Publishers' Weekly*

"The words of the victims who perished under the great American steamroller of Manifest Destiny and westward expansion. . . Those aroused by *Bury My Heart at Wounded Knee* will find further documentation of systematic destruction here."
—*Kirkus Reviews*

PUBLISHED BY POCKET BOOKS PRINTED IN U.S.A.